*LEGAL AND ECONOMIC
REGULATION IN
MARKETING*

LEGAL AND ECONOMIC REGULATION IN MARKETING

A Practitioner's Guide

RAY O. WERNER

Q

QUORUM BOOKS

New York • Westport, Connecticut • London

Library of Congress Cataloging-in-Publication Data

Werner, Ray O.
    Legal and economic regulation in marketing : a practitioner's
guide / Ray O. Werner.
        p.   cm.
    Bibliography: p.
    Includes index.
    ISBN 0-89930-287-4 (lib. bdg. : alk. paper)
    1. Marketing—Law and legislation—United States.   I. Title.
KF1609.W47   1989
343.73′084—dc19
[347.30384]   88-39909

British Library Cataloguing in Publication Data is available.

Library of Congress Catalog Card Number: 88–39909
ISBN: 0-89930-287-4

First published in 1989 by Quorum Books

Greenwood Press, Inc.
88 Post Road West, Westport, Connecticut 06881

Printed in the United States of America

∞

The paper used in this book complies with the
Permanent Paper Standard issued by the National
Information Standards Organization (Z39.48-1984).

10 9 8 7 6 5 4 3 2 1

To my gentle muse who, in reply to my once-wearying question, "Why should I bother to finish this book?" gave the only reply that could have moved me on: "Because I want you to." For that response, I offer my deepest appreciation. Thank you, my dear friend, for caring enough about me to make this book a reality.

Contents

Preface

Law is an all-encompassing instrument of social control. Law is an institution, a process, a propositions governing action. It is one of the most dynamic and pervasive influences on American life. No less, therefore, law dominates American marketing. A marketing practitioner, ignorant of law and regulations, is a buffoon clowning on the business stage.

The current conception of marketing in the United States is very broad. It includes the traditional functions associated with promotion and distribution of products, but marketing practitioners have effectively broadened the concept of marketing to encompass more than it traditionally included. Properly broadened to cover what marketing means, marketing is, to choose G. David Hughes's definition: "those activities that relate an organization *successfully* to its *environment*. The main *activities* are the identification of unmet needs, the development of products and services to meet these needs, pricing, the distribution of goods to the marketplace, and the communication of the ability of the products and services to meet these needs."[1]

Although marketing is conceived as a "total system," the consideration given to the pervasive legal environment of marketing is too often neglected by marketing practitioners. First, this study will provide a framework for interpreting how laws condition and control the environment in which practitioners carry out contemporary marketing functions. Second, it will provide direction for a generalized understanding of the laws and regulations that constitute the marketing framework. Third, we will analyze how current legal controls influence marketing decisions. Finally, we will attempt to indicate probable future courses the legal and regulatory controls of marketing will take.

The general process of creating and moving desired goods and services from those who possess them to those who desire them was never unrestricted. Even under primitive barter systems, tribal taboos conditioned exchange. As transactions became increasingly complex, social control of marketing, narrowly conceived, increased. Craft guild regulations provide ample evidence of this growing control. When society codified its demands and expectations, nominal legal control of the marketing environment appeared.

Speculation and research about the speed with which legal controls developed are interesting and important. Brief historical departures from the developing trend are also interesting, particularly in any era in which "deregulation" is a buzzword. These digressions lie outside the scope of this study. What concerns us here is first, the contemporary legal regulations affecting marketing and second, the direction of change that seems to be developing.

The interested marketing practitioner should know exactly how this study approaches the marketing aspects of legal control. Logically, marketing practitioners must devote attention to the statutes that constrain marketing before undertaking further analysis of marketing regulation. Law, however, is much more than statutes. Law includes the interpretations the judicial system has embodied in its precedents and in its dicta. Marketing practitioners must also analyze rules and regulations of administrative agencies of executive departments of governments. Some administrative regulations make their impact on the general business practices of the entire economy. Some of them impact on the practices of entire industries. Some apply narrowly to the specific practices of specific firms. However, marketing law includes all these authorized directives issued either by business or governmental executives. Practitioners and students of marketing will discover that the regulations controlling marketing are broad, changing, and, to their dismay and peril, ambiguous. They will also discover that those regulations frequently conflict.

Yet the growing complexity of the modern economy leads to two important conclusions to those interested in the daily practice of marketing. Regulation's narrowing of the realm of private and autonomous decision making by marketers is startlingly apparent. Marketing practitioners must be aware of the constant challenges to the legitimacy of private marketing actions lest they fail in their responsibility to society. Marketing practitioners must also be aware that this growing challenge is of concern to other persons and social groups. The challenge is an issue of national and, increasingly, international importance. However, society may not recognize the importance of the challenge. Marketers may fail to make regulation an important national issue. If marketers fail in this duty, then all society will lose.

An almost countless number of persons have supported me over many years of study that have led to this book. My sons, Craig, Blake, Brian, their wives Leslee, Ellen, and Wendy, as well as Barbara Talmadge and Chris Griffiths persisted in their belief in the work and encouraged me to complete it. The Colorado College Chapman Foundation in Economics provided financial support for my research and writing. Countless others including students to whom I have devoted a lifetime of care and concern—I could not begin to name them all—have challenged, tested, and improved my ideas about the relation of business and government. Many writers before me have absolved these "countless others," named and unnamed, from any responsibility for errors the authors have made. I will not do this. If there are flaws because one or more of the "others" convinced me of a mistaken view I might not otherwise have taken, they share my guilt. If readers find useful insights and knowledge here, those "others" share my triumphs. To all of them, however, I give my full love and gratitude.

NOTE

1. G. David Hughes, *Marketing Management: A Planning Approach* (Reading, MA.: Addison-Wesley, 1978), p. 3 (emphasis in original).

LEGAL AND ECONOMIC REGULATION IN MARKETING

1

Introduction

The marketing practitioner who wishes to understand how the legal environment conditions and controls marketing requires a framework of analysis. A mere recital of legislative provisions and administrative regulations does not indicate the impact of the law. What the marketing practitioner needs is a framework for understanding that encompasses the basic areas of economic activity of marketing.

Hughes's definition of marketing supports the inference that laws and regulations influence three segments of marketing: the organization of the marketing institution, the operations of the marketing institution, and the procedural constraints on the marketing institution. Often a given regulation may contain provisions that influence more than one of these segments. Students of marketing may facilitate analysis if they ask the right question, which is simply, what are the specific and independent consequences of this specific law or regulation? The analyst may thus gain a clear perception of the specific regulatory policy or practice.

In a private enterprise economy, marketers would choose the business form that most effectively maximizes attainment of their perceived goals.[1] For most businesses, the goal they would prefer is the maximization of long-run profits. However, for public institutions such as hospitals, maximization of something other than profit presents the same problem it presents for profit-seeking firms. In every case, the enterprise must construct an appropriate organization (or business system) to achieve the ends of the enterprise.

In a general sense, the governing political jurisdiction determines the legal form the enterprise may adopt. The several states usually regulate incorporation although in some fields such as banking, state and federal regulations govern. Both local and state governments may regulate sole proprietorships and partnerships. The development of professional corporations in the fields in which partnerships formerly flourished has altered the organization of partnerships. Either states of the federal government may authorize cooperatives. Such diversity only provides evidence that the form adopted by any given business organization depends fundamentally on constitutions, statutes, ordinances, and custom.

Organization of the marketing structure to distribute goods and services may take a number of forms subject to regulatory control. A business form providing for direct distribution by the ultimate seller to the consumer is the simplest organizational structure. Either a producer that sells its own product or a producer that distributes its product through another firm may adopt this form. Beyond the broad legal provisions governing the formation of the business unit, these legal constraints are of little added consequence.

Legal control of marketing expands when the complexity of the distributional process increases. When businesses add layers to the distributional mechanism, those businesses usually face new legal restraints. When a producer chooses to market through wholesale channels, multiplying governmental limitations on the autonomy of all of the businesses are probable. When a marketer chooses to distribute its product both directly through its own marketing organizations and through independent wholesale outlets, legal control grows.

Exclusive dealerships and exclusive territories are closely related issues. The marketing organization's natural inclination may be to assert that questions about exclusivity ought to be independent of legal regulation. Nevertheless, governmental regulation of exclusive dealing arrangements has been and continues to be extensive. Not only do court precedents direct the marketing organization into specific forms, but administrative agencies maintain constant surveillance over them. Finally, society through government regulates marketing through franchise programs extensively. No matter what channels of distribution marketers adopt or what variants they create, the legal environment is an irresistible conditioning force.

Governmental controls on the expansion of the marketing organization are even more powerful than controls on its form or method of distribution. Governments limit the ways by which firms may raise capital for internal expansion. The Securities and Exchange Commission makes, interprets and enforces regulations governing how firms may raise capital through the sale of stock. Political jurisdictions adopt laws limiting the interest financial institutions may charge sole proprietorships when they raise capital by borrowing. Political jurisdictions limit sharply the expansion of a business through the acquisition either of another product or another firm.

Merger regulations, often changing with changes in the political climate, impose requirements that regulate both product and geographical expansion of firms. Government subjects both horizontal and non-horizontal mergers alike to regulatory control.[2] If a firm wishes to expand by creating or participating in a joint venture, government imposes legal restrictions. Regulatory controls extend even to the question of whether a given marketing organization may expand by saving a "failing company." The conclusion for marketing practitioners is obvious. A marketing organization cannot relate its organization to its mission successfully without meeting the overwhelming force of the "legal environment."

Procedural constraints, too often ignored by marketers, also exert an expanding major conditioning power on marketing. These constraints are more pervasive than many marketers appear to realize. Marketers become acutely aware of their pervasiveness when they contemplate or actually undertake legal action. The code of civil procedure imposes the first of the procedural constraints. In some rare instances, the formal requirements of criminal procedure limit marketers' freedom to act.

Marketers find their autonomy reduced when they must accept court-created definitions of "business or property." They meet restrictions when courts or administrative agencies decide how those agencies will protect property. Courts, legislatures, and administrative agencies determine who may or may not be subject to legal control. Class action suits brought by litigants on their own behalf and persons similarly situated also define the reach of legal regulation. Regulations of governmental agencies imposing reporting and notification procedures on business influence how marketers conduct their business. Rules governing remedies for violation of legal restrictions exert a market impact on marketing decisions. The reach of the regulatory mechanism, both legal and administrative, is broad and its consequences for marketing are far reaching.

What follows first is an analysis of the major regulatory techniques governments use. Then the analysis extends to the resulting laws, precedents, and trade regulations as they control the major areas of concern of marketing practitioners. What will emerge is an assessment of how the legal environment limits autonomy of marketing institutions in their organization and operation.

NOTES

1. The contemporary debate about what a firm maximizes either through its management or a Galbraithian "technostructure" is irrelevant here. George Stig-

ler argued persuasively that the issue is beside the point for contemporary marketers. For an old but still outstanding elaboration of the question, see Stigler, *The Theory of Price* (New York: Macmillan, 1946), p. 13.

2. The Merger Guidelines of the Department of Justice have vacillated in the terminology applied to mergers. The Department has alternatively used "non-horizontal" and "vertical" to characterize mergers that clearly are not horizontal. See, for example, U.S. Department of Justice and Federal Trade Commission, *Merger Guidelines—1982* (Chicago: Commerce Clearing House, 1982), pp. 39–51.

2

The Goals of Marketing Regulation

Our concern throughout the analysis that follows will be what marketing regulation is attempting to do and how well it does in reaching its goals. This is necessary to survey the specific regulatory techniques that will be explained and evaluated later.

Goals of marketing regulation may be producer-oriented goals or they may be consumer-oriented goals. As one might expect, these goals sometimes overlap, but it is possible to study each goal separately. However, the adoption of either goal leads to different criteria for assessing marketing regulation.

Traditionally, businessmen, politicians, and economists alike have paid lip service to the view that marketing regulations should be and are consumer oriented. This widespread acceptance of consumer sovereignty flows from the view that the end of all economic activity should be to enhance the welfare of the consumer. Adam Smith, the first systematic economist expressed that view well: "Consumption is the sole end and purpose of all production; and the interest of the producer ought to be attended to, only so far as it may be necessary for promoting that of the consumer. The maxim is so perfectly self-evident, that it would be absurd to attempt to prove it."[1]

Although it seems unusual, to some degree, the goal of producer sovereignty also exists. Producer sovereignty does not receive support as vigorous as does consumer sovereignty. High-sounding verbiage about the desirability of high employment and the full utilization of resources usually camouflages the approval of producer sovereignty. Producer sovereignty and consumer sovereignty rest on the view that the activity of creating utility is, in itself, a desirable end of human activity. Both are deeply rooted in tradition. Biblical injunctions about the merit of the full application of talents and effort as a goal of the religious man embracing the Protestant Ethic, illustrate the deep-rooted nature of the praiseworthiness of effort.[2] Thorstein Veblen's praise of the "instinct of workmanship" and Benjamin Franklin's admiration of effort revealed in the admonitions of *Poor Richard's Almanac*, reinforce that view.

A conflict between the goals of producer sovereignty and consumer sovereignty may arise. Sometimes full utilization of productive resources may be achieved only at higher prices for the consumer. The desire to achieve full utilization of domestic labor and other resources may lead to demands to exclude foreign-made products and services which, if admitted into the domestic market, would destroy the productive activity of a domestic producer. Such exclusion would also lead to a reduction in the variety of goods available to the consumer. Resolution of the potential conflicts may give rise to regulatory indecision and inconsistencies.

COMPETITION AS A REGULATORY GOAL

Despite the potential conflict of producer and consumer sovereignty, in a general sense competition affords an economic resolution of it. Marketing regulations are, again in a general sense, devoted to assuring a maximum degree of competition.

Yet if marketing regulation attempts simply to implement the theoretical economic model of pure competition, the regulations will not succeed in carrying out an effective regulatory policy. Pure economic theory presupposes the existence of a product or service that is completely homogenous as the buyer perceives it. Pure competition requires the existence of so many buyers and so many sellers of the commodity or service that no one buyer or seller, by that buyer or seller's own action, is able to affect price. It requires the existence of perfect information on the part of both buyers and sellers and their willingness to act on that information. Finally, it requires the complete absence of either private or governmental collusion in the free working of the market.

Given the requisites of perfect competition, market price falls to its natural level, which corresponds to a maximum level of output, which, in turn, reflects the level of earnings of any resource in the most lucrative alternative. The search of the economically motivated producer will lead to improvements in product quality and variety in an attempt to secure, at least for a limited period of time, earnings above the natural level. This can be done only if the marketing effort is successfully directed to determining the unmet needs of the consumer. So a wonderful world emerges from the operation of a theoretically perfect competitive economy.

The perfectly competitive scenario bears little resemblance to the contemporary economic world. It may never have borne even a resemblance to a historical world. First, consumers do not regard products as homogenous in a way that any unit of one product may be substituted for a unit of another product with complete indifference. In no field is this seem more clearly than in the consumer's attitudes toward aspirin. Aspirin is chemically and physically standardized to achieve legal compliance with the *United States Pharmacopeia*. Yet buyers of aspirin perceive differences that may not be based in fact that, nevertheless, exert tremendous economic effects. Moreover, the entire advertising industry exists to differentiate homogeneous products in the minds of the buyers and, to the extent advertisers succeed—and impressions suggest the extent is remarkable—perfect competition is rendered nonexistent.

Second, sellers of a product frequently are so few that their increases and decreases in the quantity of the product exert no influence on price. This reflects the growth of large productive units responding not only to the advances of productive technology but also to market limitations in which the number of buyers will not support large numbers of producers. When a single supplier controls a significant portion of output, the supplier will control to some degree the price of the product.

More frequently many buyers of a product are found, but this is not always the case. Some products, such as Rolls-Royces, and some services will, either because of the extraordinarily high price tag or unappreciative consumer tastes (100-year-old duck eggs are a case in point), encounter a limited number of buyers. Those buyers will, because of their small number, acquire the ability to exert, by withholding or expanding purchases, a perceptible influence on price. Yet in a mass consumption economy such as that of the United States today, a significant number of buyers is not often encountered in an actual market situation.

Consumers often do not have full knowledge of the attributes of products and services, nor do consumers worry very much about the lack of such knowledge. Possibly even the producers do not have full knowledge about their products and services for it is not unusual for product effects to manifest themselves years after their production and use. The case of the drug thalidomide is indicative of limited producer knowledge. What may be more important is that consumers do not seek perfect knowledge because the search itself is time-consuming, and therefore, economically costly. The result of imperfect knowledge is that consumers frequently buy the product that is perceived to be most satisfying to them but which, if more information were known, would not be so perceived. At least one authority on the personal computer industry has suggested that IBM computer hardware and software may be second

rate and that this is known to sophisticated customers, yet these customers still buy IBM computer products. If this situation prevails, the
seller of the product may receive a price above the competitive level and
the consumer may purchase a product that is not of the highest quality
in a chemical and physical sense.

Finally, the absence of private collusion or governmental interference
with the competitive market mechanism is not realized in practice.
Again, as Adam Smith observed: "People of the same trade seldom meet
together, even for merriment and diversion, but the conversation ends
in a conspiracy against the public, or in some contrivance to raise
prices."[3]

Private attempts to avoid being placed at the mercy of the market
forces are perfectly understandable and occur no matter what the law
may say about them. Attempts to secure legislative sanction of joint
economic arrangements are common. Moreover, industries and fields
of production exist in which the government does not look with favor
on leaving the market mechanism unrestrained. Agriculture is an illustrative industry in which, more nearly than any other sector of the
economy, competition is approximated. In that field the government
intervenes actively so that the normal competitive results of economic
forces are not experienced. Nor should buyer collusion in forming buying cooperatives be minimized. These forces coalesce so that the full
effect of competition will not be felt. In short, perfect competition, despite its supposed advantages, is not the environment in which marketing regulation takes place.

WORKABLE COMPETITION AS A REGULATORY STANDARD

Since the model of perfect competition is not applicable as a policy
goal in marketing regulation, workable competition is the goal that has
replaced it. Yet it seems that no regulatory agency, despite embracing
the goal, has ever defined it. Contours of the model can be discerned
only by deducing them from economists' views and the pragmatic application of law and administrative decrees by legislatures, administrative agencies, and the courts.

Many empirical economic studies of competition have discussed competition as an objective of government policy. General agreement exists
that workable competition requires, as Corwin Edwards observed, "access by buyers and sellers to a substantial number of alternatives and
in their ability to reject those which are relatively unsatisfactory."[4] To
achieve this goal of a substantial number of realistic alternatives, Edwards outlined the requisites. First, the number of traders must be great
enough that, although any single trader may not lack any influence on

market conditions, potential buyers must be able to find acceptable alternatives. The buyer must not, however, be unable to secure the commodity or a reasonably close substitute at all. Second, no trader must be able to act, either because of its size or its coercive power, so that rivals are unable to take over a substantial portion of the trade. Third, traders must respond to economic incentives of profit and loss levels rather than to non-economic incentives such as the pursuit of political power. Fourth, rivals must not enter into agreements in determining issues of economic policy. Fifth, market entry must not be blocked by any force other than the mere existence in the market of earlier entrants. Sixth, access to the market may be impaired by distance or ignorance but not by obstacles participants in the market have consciously imposed. Seventh, neither governmental policy nor commercial collusion may afford preferential market status to any market participant.

These requisites of workable competition allow for the existence of differentiated products marketers recognize to constitute reasonably close alternatives. A buyer deprived of Tide detergent may turn to Bold to accomplish the goal of cleaning clothes. Consumers who find Colgate toothpaste undesirable may easily substitute Crest and still clean their teeth. Absolute price uniformity may not exist, but as substitutes appear great variation of prices indicative of monopoly power—the power to control price or exclude competitors—will not long continue if it ever does, in fact, exist. The seller's ability to find alternative buyers, which usually exists, is also a prerequisite for workable competition. An example of the contrasting case is one in which the government, by law, decrees itself the only legal buyer, as was the case with uranium.

As a policy guide, workable competition lacks precision. How large a number of alternatives must exist to be "appreciable" is not subject to precise quantification. The point at which a price is so high that it cannot be "satisfactorily" rejected is debatable. When mere ignorance or distance are impairments to market access is not subject to precise measurement. Whenever the rigor of the pure economic model of competition is surrendered and the nonrigorous and imprecise guide of workable competition is substituted, controversy over the meaning of the subjective and qualifying adjectives used to describe what is "workable" becomes unavoidable.

Yet it is because the concept of "workable competition," which is at the heart of the regulation of marketing, is quantitatively imprecise that the concept of workable competition cannot be dismissed. Marketing regulation does require a goal. Once an imprecise goal is accepted, resolution of the imprecision becomes the crucial problem. The variety of opinions that are possible in resolution of the issue explains much of the controversy that surrounds specific regulatory cases. Final resolution comes in the crucible of the courtroom, the legislative chamber, or the administrative hearing room. Moreover, if the resolution is imprecise, changes may develop in subsequent controversies. In short, it is in the rough-and-tumble milieu of government policy making that the ever-changing, inexact outline of the legal environment of marketing emerges.

CRITERIA FOR ASSESSING MARKETING REGULATION

If workable competition is to be effectuated by marketing regulation, the next step involves ascertaining how the regulations operate to accomplish their goal. Using a three-point method of analysis of the specific regulations is the most effective way to do this. All marketing regulations are directed at the structure, conduct, or performance of the marketing organization. Interrelationships exist among the categories, but a marketer may analyze them separately. We will first examine them separately here.

If structure is considered the relevant criteria in assessing the marketing organization, the marketer need ask only one question: Is the structure of this business organization a desirable one? A simple answer may follow: A single firm, though it operates as a benign monopoly selling its product at fair and reasonable prices, progressive in both product development and production, and responsible to the consumer's manifested needs, is to be prevented. Bigness, either absolutely or relatively, and no matter what its outcomes, is equated with badness. All questions of consumer sovereignty are dismissed summarily. Strict structuralists will not question the marketing effectiveness or other business practices that may benefit consumers. Emphasis on the per se desirability of a business structure is a product of the concept of producer sovereignty in which issues of business form are given complete precedence over economic results.

Few observers would accept such a brittle formulation of the structuralist's position. Observers would insist that structural adherents are interested in the effects that flow from structure. Yet economic outcomes remain irrelevant considerations if the policy goal is the establishment of a "good" marketing structure. Structural adherents argue that undesirable political, social, and moral outcomes result from business structures they consider malignant. They deny, in effect, that large and dominating organizations may operate in the social interest. Their implicit remedy, sometimes made explicit in specific regulatory situations, are policies to reduce the size of the large business organizations. Some analysts of business structure may suggest that organizations might, per se, be too small and that consolidation ought to be considered. But structuralists seldom make this argument in public presentations.

Discussion of the pure structuralist's position makes it appear shallow. Indeed it is; yet there are adherents to it. More judicious defenders of elements of structuralism infer a relationship between structure and economic results; they assume that whenever a structure is, by their standards, questionable, the economic results are, for that reason, objectionable. Nobel Laureate Economist George Stigler has argued that if he is shown an undesirable business structure, he can presume undesirable consequences to follow. Stigler's position, however, is not a pure one, and, as we will see shortly, it is a more readily defensive one than that of the pure structuralist.

The conduct-oriented analyst does not find either large or small business establishments persuasive in framing regulatory policy. Such an analyst holds that only if practices—such as overt price-fixing, collusion, discriminatory prices, or the use of tying contracts—are inherently undesirable should regulatory policy bar them. No automatic connection between the practices and the prices, the quality of product, or progressiveness of the firm and the industry is made. Instead the judgment is exclusively in terms of the behavior that "ought" to be tolerated. As in the case of the pure structuralists, conduct-oriented partisans infer results from the practices that they condemn. Some partisans may conclude that bad conduct leads to bad results, but the pure conduct-oriented regulatory policy simply determines some practices are, per se, deserving of prohibition.

The third criterion by which regulatory action may be evaluated is performance. In its pure form this criterion holds that the structure of a firm or an industry is irrelevant in deciding whether or how to regulate it. This criterion holds that the practices—that is, the conduct—should not determine whether or how business should be regulated. Performance-oriented analysts contend that those who regulate should first determine what ends they wish to attain and then ask if the business organization is attaining them. If the performance-oriented regulator desires low prices consistent with high quality and a great variety of products, then, if products are low and products exist in such a number and of such quality that the buyers are offered effective choices, they accept the outcome as proof that the business is economically efficient and that regulation is not required.

Performance-oriented economists, usually also guided by consumer sovereignty as the end of economic activity, frequently look for no more than low prices, high quality of products, and a great variety of them. This is not an inherent limitation on the scope of inquiry of the performance-oriented regulator. Some such regulators seek more than maximum real income for the consumer. Some ask that the firms and the industry—or one or the other—be progressive so that appropriate advances occur in research and development and related innovation. Others argue that regulation should attempt to assure full employment of the factors of production, especially labor. At this point the proponents become producer-sovereignty advocates—it matters not to them if the consumers suffer a reduction in the choice of products or higher prices than would otherwise prevail. Finally, some performance-oriented regulators wish to regulate the economy to achieve equity in the distribution of real income and in providing returns for productive effort.[5]

Marketers will see very quickly that as the number of performance standards increases, the possibility of conflict among them also increases. This is particularly true if regulators are expected to attain consumer-sovereign and producer-sovereign goals simultaneously. Illustratively if regulators are expected to maximize the variety of products, imports should be stimulated yet imports may reduce the number of jobs available to domestic workers. Equity as a consideration becomes an even more complicating factor since either domestically produced or imported new products may destroy incomes of skilled workers—for example, machine-crafted furniture from abroad replacing hand-crafted furniture made by skilled artisans in the domestic economy—and thereby increase inequity in income distribution. Despite these complications, the marketer can draw three conclusions: (1) adherents to conflicting performance standards do exist in significant numbers; (2) as conflicting standards are embraced, the pattern of regulation that will emerge becomes increasingly unpredictable; and (3) almost no regulator nor student of regulation embraces any one of the three regulatory criteria in an absolutely pure form.

CONFLICT OF PER SE RULES AND RULES OF REASON

Which regulatory criterion regulators adopt is a critical determinant of the nature of the regulatory rules that result. Structural adherents, finding the evil in the conformation of an industry, usually argue that buyer or seller concentration or product differentiation is so great that ready substitutability of products cannot take place and that regulations prohibiting or limiting a given structure are required. No rebuttal that the concentration or the differentiation led to low-priced high-quality goods or that innovation and product improvement occurred is acceptable. The firm is held to be guilty of a regulatory excess upon presentation of adequate evidence that the structure is suspect. Remedy must be fast and effective and the offending structural elements altered in some way that is frequently undefined and difficult of realization. Per se regulations, meaning simply that no economic justification is allowed to offset any established offense, find the offense in the character of the offense. Violators of per se rules are allowed to make no refutation of the offense once the required facts are demonstrated to the satisfaction of the regulator.

Rules of reason provide that once certain operative facts, which might constitute a per se offense, are established to the satisfaction of the regulator and then the alleged defender may balance the alleged harm with alleged benefits. In effect, the defender may negate the charge of offending behavior by showing that desirable offsetting results flow from the behavior. Circumstances that may be advanced to counterbalance alleged economic evils may be explicitly made by the regulator or may be accepted on the basis of the regulator's determination of whether, in the specific case, a reasonable and prudent arbiter would call the counterbalancing effects reasonable. Performance-oriented analysts, especially those who also accept consumer sovereignty as a goal, are more likely to advocate a rules-of-reason approach than are structuralists.

Conduct-oriented regulators can easily combine the acceptance of per se rules with rules of reason. Thus collusion of some sellers of a product to drive another price-cutting seller from business by agreeing with the supplier that the price-cutter will not receive shipments of the product may be considered an abuse of power and hence a per se offense. Conversely, a conduct-oriented analyst may find that contracts to buy a firm's entire product needs from a single supplier is perfectly reasonable if the agreement is of short duration, but those contracts become illegal if they are of long duration such as twenty years.

From this discussion of per se rules and rules of reason, the marketer may deduce quickly the preference of structuralists for per se rules and the preference of performance analysts for rules of reason. This pattern is discernible. Yet, as we shall see, what has emerged is a combination of both types of rules, which creates another problem for the marketer.

Rules of the "thou shalt not" per se type lead to relative certainty for the businessman as to when the law has been violated. To know that the undertaking of a specific act, no matter how benign the intent or the result, is not acceptable makes business planning less difficult than it might be otherwise. The appropriate action is to shun the offensive act. Rules of the "maybe thou may" type (rules of reason) provide the businessman with flexibility. Yet to know that some act or practice might be found to contribute to consumer welfare or some other desirable social goal gives the marketer no assurance that it will be accepted. In the final analysis, the determination of reasonableness depends upon the person or group that makes the determination. The old cliché that "reasonable men differ" is appropriate. Business practices that regulators may accept cannot be known in advance when rules of reason prevail.

Yet if businesses lose certainty in the face of rules of reason, they gain flexibility. Business practices are not automatically rejected under rules of reason. Marketers and other business managers may adopt new techniques, new organizational structures, and new procedures in an attempt to meet the unmet needs of their clientele. Progressive businessmen find the conflict between desire for certainty and the desire for flexibility difficult to resolve. Programs believed to be unacceptable are never undertaken and losses that might otherwise occur are easily avoided. Businesses may avoid programs they believe have a high probability of meeting consumer goals and potential profits may be lost. So the conflict between uncertainty and flexibility pervades business's stance on what kind of regulations it prefers. The conflict, however, should not be underestimated as a pervasive influence on the creation and modification of the legal environment of marketing.

The Extent of Workable Competition

If the approach to an analytical framework for studying the legal environment of marketing is useful in achieving workable competition, marketers need some knowledge of the extent of workable competition. If workable competition exists, the probability of regulatory intervention is reduced though it is not eliminated. To the extent the goal of regulating the legal environment is to attain workable competition, knowledge of the amount of workable competition that exists is important.

Extensive studies of the extent of workable competition and deviations from it have been undertaken in the past. Unfortunately marketers cannot compare them easily since researchers have used different definitions and criteria for determining workability of competition.[6] If William Shepherd's frequently cited analysis is accepted, the marketer will conclude that from 1958 to 1980 the segment of the United States economy that was workably competitive rose from just over 56 percent to nearly 77 percent. In some sectors—construction, wholesale and retail trade, finance, insurance, and real estate—the percentages of workably effective competition approximates 95 percent. Only in the fields of transportation and public utilities—to a large degree publicly regulated monopolies—is the percentage under 50 (39.1 percent). So, in the face of three explanatory changes presented by Shepherd—rising import competition, antitrust enforcement, and deregulation (although Shepherd did not include other possible explanatory variables because of the lack of adequate data for measurement)—the extent of workable competition has increased. Marketers, however, should not overlook that two explanations accepted by Shepherd for the increase of workable competition—antitrust and deregulation—involve conscious manipulation of the legal environment within which the marketing institution functions. If, therefore, the economy is growing more competitive in a "workable" sense, then the probability of expanding regulatory control of business may be reduced. But finally the long battle between consumer sovereignty and producer sovereignty and the outcomes that producer-sovereignty adherents seek may, nevertheless, lead to new regulations although they may be of a social rather than an economic nature.

SUMMARY

So we see that a growing area of workable competition toward which the regulation of the legal environment is directed has developed in the United States. Even though workable competition is at best only imperfectly quantifiable and so remains a vague goal of regulation, that form of competition seems to dominate the economy. This is logical since, given the dynamism of the business environment, workable competition is a more practicable working model than the precise, though unrealizable, model of perfect competition.

Analysis of regulatory orientation in the United States indicates that pure, but seldom purely used, analytical categories exist. To achieve workable competition, regulators may emphasize the structure of firms and industries, on their conduct, or on their performance. A performance orientation, coupled with an emphasis on the concept of consumer sovereignty in contrast to the less frequently adopted producer-sovereignty concept, leads to rules of reason. This pattern contrasts with the alternative structuralist criterion, which may be guided by noneconomic considerations. Whatever combination of goals and rationales policy makers adopt, a conflict between business's search for *both* certainty and flexibility emerges. Consistency in resolution of the conflict, as we will see, does not result, nor should it be expected to result.

NOTES

1. Adam Smith, *An Inquiry into the Nature and Causes of the Wealth of Nations* (New York: Modern Library, 1937), p. 625. Smith's view of consumer sovereignty is based on the argument that if it is unhampered by regulatory actions, business will respond by marketing the products that consumers desire. Those products, it is contended, will be priced at the lowest level consistent with competitive costs, will be of the highest possible quality, and will be provided in a satisfying and expanding variety. These goals, marketers declare, are also the goals of an efficient and effective marketing organization. Former Judge Robert Bork, whose failure to secure appointment to the United States Supreme Court was a recent major judicial cause, represents a current legal scholar championing the Smithian view.

2. Matt. 25:14–30.

3. Smith, *The Wealth of Nations*, p. 128.

4. Corwin Edwards, *Maintaining Competition* (New York: McGraw-Hill, 1949). The discussion that follows is based on Edwards's analysis.

5. For a comprehensive discussion of market performance as a regulatory criterion, see Richard Caves, *American Industry: Structure, Conduct, Performance*, 5th ed. (Englewood Cliffs, N.J.: Prentice-Hall, 1982), pp. 66–83. Caves also discusses market conduct at pp. 48–65. Robert Bork, in *The Antitrust Paradox* (New York: Basic Books, 1978), analyzes and defends the free-market efficiency criterion strongly. William Shepherd in *Public Policies toward Business*, 7th ed.

(Homewood, IL: R. Irwin, 1985), p. 125, characterizes Borks's defense as "an extreme version."

6. Older studies are examined in the study upon which this discussion relies. William G. Shepherd, "Causes of Increased Competition in the U.S. Economy, 1939–1980," *The Review of Economics and Statistics* (November 1982): 613–626. Shepherd, in *Public Policies toward Business*, p. 69, utilizes his statistics to confirm the continuation of the same statistical pattern of workable competition.

3

Federal Laws Regulating the Marketing Organization

There is extensive legislation regulating the environment of marketing. The more significant enactments are federal laws, although marketers operating in individual states must be aware that extensive state laws also regulate their marketing activities. They must also be aware of the constant expansion of the coverage of the statutes as well as judicial and administrative interpretations and modifications that occur. What will concern us here is the pattern of the federal laws and the historical background from which regulation of the marketing environment developed.*

HISTORICAL BACKGROUND OF FEDERAL
REGULATION OF THE MARKETING ENVIRONMENT

The accretion of regulatory statutes is the gradual response of government to the evolution of a complex economy. Inevitably the evolution rested upon a foundation of contract law suited to an undeveloped economy in which exchanges were limited and in which barter may have been characteristic. In the more ancient of such economies, craft guilds imposed restrictions on their members, and apprenticeship regulations

---

*An Appendix includes the most important excerpts from the important federal statutes that comprise the statutory legal environment of marketing. There are other acts, not included, that impinge on what marketers can do. The various tariff acts with provisions governing procedures to prevent dumping and hence unfair competition are illustrative. Marketers who are interested in the most important state laws governing their marketing activities in specific states should consult Commerce Clearing House, *Trade Regulation Reports* (Chicago: Commerce Clearing House) of the current date.

controlled the competition in the crafts. Such an environment, however, did not lead to widespread public concern about marketing organizations or their operations nor did it lead to extensive statutory enactments.

In the United States, the Industrial Revolution and its expanding scope pushed us to our first important enactment. Precise dating of the Revolution is not necessary; we need only recognize the growth in the size of the business unit as technology developed and expanded. The growth of the business unit led to political concern about its potential power and an era named by Matthew Josephson as the age of the "robber barons."[1] That expansion led to public outcries against large enterprises. This era, which Josephson dates from 1861–1901, was accompanied by the development of progressive and populist political movements contending that the small, independent businessmen and farmers, whom they conceived as the centerpiece of an idyllic Jefferson world, were seriously endangered. Qualifications of this truncated historical view may be made, but had the growth of industrial organizations—and hence marketing organizations—not occurred, the legal environment might have remained simple. The Sherman Antitrust Act of 1890, the first major federal regulatory enactment, might never have been passed.

The initial response to the abuses, real or imagined, of industrialism was followed by a second wave of regulation prior to and during America's participation in World War I. Two major pieces of legislation, the Clayton Act and the Federal Trade Commission Act, were passed in 1914 in response to the perceived need to maintain a workable competitive environment in the face of perceived questionable business practices.

The third major wave of legislation modifying and conditioning the legal environment of marketing developed as a result of the economic dislocations of the Great Depression of 1932–1939. The movement toward intervention in the private autonomy of business has been well documented. The number of federal laws, as will be seen, proliferated with the Robinson-Patman Act of 1936. Though not a powerful enactment then, and perhaps not even now, it is the most notable of the regulatory laws impacting directly on marketing.[2]

The 1950 Celler-Kefauver Amendment to the Clayton Act ushered in in the mid–1960s a fourth wave of legislation that may still be washing over us. Laws were enacted to increase the responsiveness of marketers to the wants of the consumer and vociferous public interest groups as perceived by legislators of a liberal inclination. Laws regulating advertising, labeling, and product promotion as well as laws regulating product quality were extensive. Again, as we shall see, these laws, usually implemented by administrative agencies, were expanded by what now seem to have been liberal interpretations of the judiciary.

Court Interpretations of Regulatory Statutes

Surveying the major provisions of the statutes governing the marketing environment is a necessary prerequisite to understanding the constraints that marketers experience. In itself, this recital is neither an exciting nor a revealing activity. Metaphorically, the language of the acts is the skeleton of the environmental framework; the court interpretations and the administrative regulations are the flesh. What will follow is the fleshing out of the legal environment in such a way that the marketer will understand the limitations that are imposed on the marketing institution.

Earlier marketers were cautioned that court interpretations present difficulties in determining exactly what the body of marketing law is. Different canons of interpretation were noted, and marketers were cautioned that, once courts adopt a given canon, marketers still have no assurance that a later court will adopt the same canon as an earlier court. The possibility of explicit reversal of a given judicial interpretation is always present and sometimes manifests itself. A court may articulate a principle in one case which, though seemingly analogous to another, may be differentiated by a later court that finds some small real or imagined difference. Administrative agencies such as the Federal Trade Commission also display the same precariousness of interpretation.

Yet we may caution about the precariousness of regulation in a dynamic world without leading the marketer to ignore general guidelines that we seem to discern, no matter how dimly. Marketers, in short, need to know the generalizations that can be developed from the rules, regulations, and decisions that seem to be the current governing ones. In the following sections, we will attempt to determine what the most important federal laws and regulations provide and how they have been interpreted. We will then infer what they indicate for marketing organization, operation, and procedures.

The Constraints on the Marketing Organization

Although economic theory has speculated about the normal pattern of business growth under dynamic conditions, we will assume that if marketers were all-powerful they would meet consumers' needs to maximize long-run profits. Whether or not slothful habits and the search for the easy life would lead business firms with significant market power to lose innovativeness and reduce the variety of products available to consumers (poor performance in terms of our earlier analysis) is an interesting topic for debate that need not concern us now. Realistically, public policy does not long tolerate omnipotence and so businesses may not create whatever marketing organization they choose.

In determining what the marketing organization may do, the first restraint on it is in terms of size. Monopolies—clear deviations from the goal of workable competition previously argued to be that of the United States—may be granted by law, but they do not predominate. Legal monopolies are generally confined to public utilities providing light, heat, and power and in some lesser areas in which local grants of exclusive franchises (taxicab service or garbage collection) are found. Even here, regulation is particularly hostile to "legal" monopolies using their power to expand into competitive markets even though the monopoly allowed by law is diminutive.[3] Monopolies are also found in situations in which a limited local market will not support several firms or in which a product innovator is entering a market with a wholly new product meeting unique consumer needs. These monopolies—as even Polaroid and Xerox demonstrate—will eventually succumb to developing competition. Public policy does not gladly suffer monopolies, so the first legal constraint is on the size of the marketing organization.

The second major restraint on the organization of the marketing institution is on the process of growth. Some methods of growth involve nothing more complicated than acquiring another firm producing a product the marketing institution believes would enable it to better meet the perceived unmet needs of the consumer. However, not all techniques of growth are accorded equal public approval. Some methods, believed not to reflect superior business skill, may be subject to regulation. Current concern—though eras of past concern can be detected about the legitimacy of mergers and joint ventures as a means of expanding the marketing organization—are illustrative of this aspect of restraints on the growth of the marketing organization.

The third major restraint on the organization of the marketing institution is on the expansion of the marketing organization through means other than the internal growth of the firm. At issue are the adoption of marketing techniques that lead to an expansion of market share for a product through the use of other independent producers. Franchising is an obvious technique for accomplishing this end. It would be absurd to consider the adoption of such a technique as one that does not modify the marketing organization, yet the business that adopts franchising clearly will not have grown to monopoly proportions nor has it engaged in a merger.

The fourth major restraint on the marketing organization is on the scope of the organization. In this case monopoly is not at issue, growth by asset or stock acquisition is not involved, and franchising is not involved. Yet the marketing institution may wish to control the market areas in which it produces. It may wish, simply put, to restrict the distributional rights of marketing firms in the channels of distribution. At stake will be territorial restrictions the firm imposes to enable the firm to meet perceived consumer needs in the most effective manner. Public policy may see fit to outline the extent and methods by which the scope of the marketing organization may be developed and enhanced. As we will see later, each of these four aspects of the marketing organization are subject to legal control of the marketing environment.

The Major Statutes

Sherman Antitrust Act of 1890 The first major federal law regulating the form and size of the marketing organization was the Sherman Antitrust Act of 1890.[4] The major principle of the Act that governs organization is the prohibition contained in Section 2 against monopolization, conspiracies to monopolize, or attempts to monopolize. As originally adopted, the Act provided that a person found guilty of violating the section was guilty of a misdemeanor with a possible fine not exceeding $5,000 and imprisonment not to exceed one year. In 1955 the maximum fine was raised to $50,000. In 1974, violation of the Act was changed from a misdemeanor to a felony and the maximum fine for a corporation was raised to one million dollars and for an individual, one hundred thousand dollars. The maximum term of imprisonment of a convicted violator of the Act was increased to three years.

Clearly the authors of the Sherman Act were not so naïve as to believe that only when a single seller controlled 100 percent of the production, however defined, of a good or service would the Act become operative. What concerned them, as we have noted earlier, was the trust* movement, which was seen as constituting a serious threat to both consumer welfare and political democracy. The authors of the Act feared the amassing of business units in such a way that, to use Dominick T. Armentano's vague definition, consistent with the development of the concept the consolidated unit has the "power to arbitrarily restrict attractive opportunities and market adjustments to other market participants."[5] Exactly how this power is manifested—withholding new products from the market, profits that exceed a "normal" level, excessive prices—has varied in specific cases. Yet the authors of the Sherman Act were aware that the acquisition of enough power to free its possessor from the constraints

---

*A trust is a business arrangement in which businesses in the same field of production place stock under the control of a common "trustee" (usually a major producer) who then is expected to operate the combined firms in the interest of all trust participants. The firm holding the stock in trust trys to eliminate destructive competition, control output, or regulate price to achieve gains that might not be attained if each firm engaged in business rivalry with other members of the trust. Even though society frowns on business trusts today, individuals still use trusts extensively to achieve personal goals.

of rivals was desired by many independent entrepreneurs. Consequently, the authors of the act attempted to prevent the acquisition of enough power to threaten competitive rivalry.

The first major interpretation of the Sherman Act by the United States Supreme Court was the *E. C. Knight* case[6] decided in 1895. The attack by the federal government on the so-called "sugar trust" occurred when the American Sugar Refining Company, the leading firm in acquiring the last three independent sugar refiners, secured control of 95 percent of the refined sugar market. Yet the Court did not find this power, which it admitted did tend to be a monopoly, violative of the Sherman Act. The Court argued that a manufacturing monopoly such as American Sugar Refining had acquired affected interstate commerce, a Constitutional prerequisite for federal regulation, only indirectly. In its resolution of the case, the Court declared: "There was nothing in the [government's] proofs to indicate any intention to put a restraint upon trade or commerce, and the fact, as we have seen, that trade or commerce might be indirectly affected, was not enough to entitle complainants to a decree." Furthermore, the Court did not want to place manufacturing under exclusive federal jurisdiction as would have occurred if the case had been decided in favor of the government's challenge to the trust. Had the Court decided the case for the government, the effect would have been to preempt state regulatory jurisdiction in favor of what was almost nonexistent federal regulation. Nevertheless, by 1988 the Supreme Court and lesser jurisdictions have repudiated the holding in the *Knight* case in its entirety.

It was not until 1904 that the prosecution of monopoly under the Sherman Act again called forth Supreme Court analysis. In the *Northern Securities* case the Northern Securities Company, a holding company of two interstate railways, Northern Pacific and Great Northern, was held to be a trust in restraint of commerce.[7] While unique aspects of the case arising from the clear interstate character of national railways and the acquisition of stock distinguish this case from the *E. C. Knight* case, the statement of Justice Harlan in the majority opinion was indicative of the direction in which interpretation of Section 2 seemed to be moving. Declared Justice Harlan: "The mere existence of such a combination and the power acquired by the holding company as its trustee, constitute a menace to, and a restraint upon, that freedom of commerce which Congress intended to recognize and protect, and which the public is entitled to have protected." The significance of this statement is found in Harlan's argument that *mere existence* of the trust was sufficient to bring it under the proscription of the Act; clearly the Court refused to accept, under a rule of reason, benign results that might follow from the acquisition. However, the decision was marred by extensive dissents that were argued with unusual sharpness; the clear delineation of the coverage of the Sherman Act was yet to be made.

In 1911, the Supreme Court decided a famous and important interpretation of the Sherman Act in the *Standard Oil of New Jersey* case.[8] Reinforcing that decision was the *American Tobacco* case decided on the same day as the *Standard Oil* case.[9] The Court, in laying its analytical groundwork in the *Standard Oil* case, began by examining English and American common law prior to the passage of the Sherman Act. The Court concluded:

it becomes obvious that the criteria to be resorted to in any given case for the purpose of ascertaining whether violations of the section have been committed, is the *rule of reason* guided by the established law and by the plain duty to enforce the prohibitions of the act, and thus the public policy which its restrictions were obviously enacted to subserve. [emphasis added]

Having eliminated a per se rule of monopolization in both the *Standard Oil* and the *American Tobacco* cases, the Court had only to ask if the restraints found in the cases constituted reasonable behavior. In both cases the Court found the monopolizing activity to be unreasonable.[10] The significance of the decisions is not found in the guilty verdicts but in the adoption of the rule of reason and the Court's apparent abandonment of its holding in the *E. C. Knight* case.

In 1920, the Supreme Court again confronted the issue of what constituted a monopoly sufficient to violate Section 2 of the Sherman Act. In the *United States Steel Corporation* case the Court encountered a firm producing approximately one-half the output of the industry.[11] Acquisitions had occurred in the industry and the government argued that the motivation of United States Steel was to secure domination of the industry through its sheer size. In arguing its case the government contended, "a combination may be illegal because of its purpose; it may be illegal because it acquires a dominating power, not as a result of normal growth and development, but as a result of a combination of competitors." The counsel for United States Steel contended that United States Steel's mere size was no offense and that the parallel pricing that other companies adopted in following United States Steel was only a reflection of a desire to maximize returns—a perfectly legitimate activity. In a famous summary to the case, the Court by a four-to-three vote with two justices not participating, declared:

The Corporation is undoubtedly of impressive size and it takes an effort of resolution not to be affected by it or to exaggerate its influence. But we must adhere to the law and the law does not make mere size an offense or the existence of unexerted power an offense. It [the Sherman Act], we must repeat, requires overt acts and trusts to its prohibition of them and its power to repress or punish them. It does not compel competition nor require all that is possible.

With that declaration, perhaps augmented by a favorable political climate, the structural approach of the per se rule was squashed, not to reappear until 1945 in the *Alcoa* case.[12]

Although the Alcoa decision did not explicitly reverse the earlier rule of reason holdings, the effect was the adoption, by a tortuous reasoning process, of a per se rule governing violations of Section 2 of the Sherman Act. The holding in the Alcoa case persists to the present day, although, as we shall see, the Court has made significant extensions and modifications of the holding.

The Aluminum Company of America (Alcoa) was charged by the government with monopolizing the market for virgin aluminum ingot. By the government's statistics, which the court accepted, Alcoa's control of the market as the government defined it, was in excess of 90 percent. Alcoa contended that the relevant market should be defined to include secondary recycled aluminum and that the portion of ingot aluminum processed by Alcoa itself should be excluded. Had both modifications been accepted, Alcoa's market share would have been decreased to 33 percent; if only secondary aluminum had been excluded, the percentage would have been approximately 64 percent. Judge Leonard Hand, speaking for the Court, observed: "The percentage we have already mentioned—over ninety—results only if we include all Alcoa's production and exclude secondary. That percentage is enough to constitute a monopoly; it is doubtful whether sixty or sixty-four percent would be enough; and certainly thirty-three percent is not."

The crucial consideration was clearly what constituted the relevant market. Economists may utilize the concept of cross-elasticity of demand to ascertain the relevant market and the courts may bow in its direction, but in a typical case evidence is lacking to quantify the cross-elasticity of demand.[13] What is necessary, then, is to determine on the best other evidence what constitutes the relevant market.

The search of a court—and the marketer concerned with problems of monopolization—if for all those firms whose production has such an immediate and substantial effect on prices and production of the firms in question that the actions of one group cannot be explained without direct reference to the actions of the other. One who attempts to define a relevant market must include in the market all firms whose products are, in fact, good and directly available substitutes for one another in sales to some significant group of buyers and exclude all others.[14] In its analysis, the court first concluded that Alcoa's own fabrication of the ingots it produced reduced market demand and hence affected price. Second, the court concluded that Alcoa's foresight caused it to control the supply of secondary aluminum through its initial (though distantly removed) production of virgin ingot. These conclusions led the Court to hold that the relevant market was the virgin ingot aluminum market. The court, therefore, found that because Alcoa's share of the market thus defined was so large, monopolization of the market by Alcoa did result.

The Court recognized that, even if monopolization by Alcoa did exist, monopoly might have "been thrust upon" Alcoa. However, the court did not find that Alcoa had "unwittingly" found itself to be a monopolist. The court went back thirty years in the history of Alcoa and found examples of misconduct by Alcoa in attaining monopoly power. The court did not find the size of the market so limited that only one producer would have been economically sustained by it. Nor did the court find Alcoa "the survivor out of a group of active competitors, merely by virtue of . . . superior skill, foresight, and industry." Alcoa did not fall "within the exception established in favor of those who do not seek, but cannot avoid, the control of a market." Finally, Alcoa's progressiveness in "embracing each new opportunity as it opened, and facing every newcomer with new capacity already geared into a great organization, having the advantage of experience, trade connections and the elite of personnel" were held not to be honest industrial maneuvers. The court found them to be "exclusionary" and hence unacceptable behavior of a monopolist. Finally, in summary, the Court contended that specific intent required to find Alcoa guilty of criminal monopolizing of the aluminum market was confirmed by the government's demonstration "that many transactions, neutral on their face, were not in fact necessary to the development of Alcoa's business, and had not motive except to exclude others and perpetuate its hold upon the ingot market." In a final damning thrust establishing self-conviction for intent, the Court asserted solemnly, "no monopolist monopolizes unconscious of what he is doing."

Clearly performance was not an acceptable test of Alcoa's marketing organization. Alcoa's overall profits of approximately 10 percent, though Alcoa's profits on virgin ingot aluminum were substantially higher, over the half century of its existence were not found exorbitant. A "fair profit" (the level of which the Court conveniently did not address) might, the Court averred without proof, have been made at lower prices. The Court did not deny that Alcoa had been progressive; in fact as we have noted, it conceded and stressed Alcoa's progressiveness as one of the techniques Alcoa adopted to meet consumer demand. The Court even admitted that Alcoa had undertaken to develop new uses for its products. Yet neither reasonableness of its organization nor favorable economic performance would save Alcoa.

In the last analysis, Alcoa was found guilty, not on economic grounds of questionable conduct or poor economic performance, but upon structural considerations of a sociopolitical nature. The Court revealed this position most clearly in its analysis of Section 2 of the Sherman Act when it argued:

The Sherman Act has wider purposes. Indeed, even though we disregarded all but economic considerations, it would by no means follow that such concentration of producing power is to be desired, when it has not been used extortionately. Many people believe that possession of unchallenged economic power deadens initiative, discourages thrift and depresses energy; that immunity from competition is a narcotic, and rivalry is a stimulant, to industrial progress; that the spur of constant stress is necessary to counteract an inevitable disposition to let well enough alone. Such people believe that competitors, versed in the craft as no consumer can be, will be quick to detect opportunities for saving and new shifts in production and be eager to profit by them . . . .True, it might have been thought adequate to condemn only those monopolies which could not show that they had exercised the highest possible ingenuity, had adopted every possible economy, had anticipated every conceivable improvement, stimulated every possible demand. No doubt, that would be one way of dealing with the matter, although it would imply constant scrutiny and constant supervision, such as courts are unable to provide. Be that as it may, that was not the way that Congress chose; it did not condone "good trusts" and condemn "bad" ones; it forbade all. Moreover, in so doing, it was not necessarily actuated by economic motives alone. *It is possible, because of its indirect social or moral effect, to prefer a system of small producers, each dependent for his success upon his own skill and character, to one in which the great mass of those engaged must accept the direction of a few. These considerations, which we have suggested only as possible purposes of the Act, we think the decisions prove to have been in fact its purposes.* [emphasis added]

From this lengthy though devastatingly clear statement, the court concluded that "great industrial consolidations are *inherently undesirable,* regardless of their economic results" (emphasis added).

Alcoa has been examined here in great detail because it is a still valid precedent upon which the Supreme Court and the lower courts rely in interpreting the Sherman Act. In addition, the marketer will find in Alcoa, a number of important conclusions that influence and perhaps even govern if a marketer holds a dominant market share that someone might challenge under the Sherman Act.

First, the marketer may conclude that economic concepts of what constitutes a relevant market may be considered only superficially. As a result, a narrow definition of the market may impale a marketing organization upon a monopolistic sword. Second, monopoly in a relevant market may be found simply in the percentage of production a business organization controls. Third, both economic performance and conduct may be considered irrelevant in determining the legitimacy of a monopoly once either a public or a private party alleges that a business is a monopoly. Superior skill, foresight and industry may, in undefined circumstances, insulate a monopolistic organization from prosecution. Fourth, requisite specific intent to monopolize may be inferred from the mere existence of monopoly power. First and last, economic structure may be condemned on the ground of the inherent undesirability of large accretions of economic power. Marketers may infer from these five points that performance in fulfilling the goals of a marketing organization with which we began, does not insulate an organization from attack for monopolizing in violation of Section 2 of the Sherman Act.

In 1956, the Supreme Court, acting in its own right, again faced the question of monopolization under Section 2 of the Sherman Act. In an action against the du Pont Company generally known as "The Cellophane Case" the basic question of monopolization was resolved by an analysis of the relevant market.[15] Du Pont was accused of monopolizing 75 percent of the cellophane sold in the United States. Justice Reed, speaking for a one-vote majority of the Supreme Court, agreed with the government that a 75 percent control (now down from the 90 percent control utilized in Alcoa) of a relevant market would constitute monopoly power. However, the Court did not accept the government's definition of the product market; it found the relevant market to be "flexible packaging material" sales rather than cellophane sales.

The Court argued that "determination of the competitive market for commodities depends on how different from one another are the offered commodities in character for use, how far buyers will go to substitute one for another." Applying this view, the Court found that buyers would respond readily to small increases in the price of cellophane and would substitute such products as glassine or pliofilm for it. When all the products the Court found substitutable in some uses for cellophane were included, du Pont's share of the relevant market dropped to approximately 20 percent. Reinforcing the implicit conclusion that in the flexible packaging market, du Pont did not earn monopoly profits was the Court's assessment of the evidence that it held showed that du Pont's profits "did not demonstrate the existence of a monopoly."[16]

While the cellophane case did not reverse nor modify the Alcoa decision significantly, marketers should be aware of the conclusions inherent in the du Pont case. First, the case emphasizes the importance of the definition of the product market and the need, if challenged for monopolizing activity, to broaden it to avoid prosecution. Broadening the product market definition in effect, induces the marketer to emphasize the demand elements of the market (the buyer's actual business behavior in the substitution of products) in contrast to the supply elements of the market (the share of the total output produced) emphasized in Alcoa. Effective workable competition, in contrast to economic conceptualization, becomes the touchstone of success.

Sandwiched between Alcoa and the Cellophane Case was the *United Shoe Machinery* case.[17] The government charged United Shoe Machinery with monopolization in violation of Section 2 because of barriers to competition United Shoe had erected by its leasing practices for its shoe machinery. The Court did not find United Shoe's activities, it economies of scale, and its original creation through a combination of constituent companies were objectionable.[18] Following earlier precedents that market control "is inherently evil and constitutes a violation of Section 2 unless economically inevitable or specifically authorized and regulated by law," the Court held that in "having willed the means, United Shoe Machinery has willed the end." Hence the Court found that illegal monopolization had occurred. At issue was the remedy that might be imposed for a violation of Section 2 of the Sherman Act.

The government had proposed that United Shoe Machinery, although unified in its operations into a single organic system, be divided into "three equal and viable parts." The Court, emphasizing "practical problems" and "supporting economic data," held the government's proposed remedy was "Draconian." Instead the Court provided that United Shoe's leasing practices be modified to weaken its market power and introduce competition into the shoe machinery market. The Court's remedy required United Shoe Machinery to divest the production of supplies that complemented shoe machinery from United Shoe's production of machinery. In 1968 when the District Court reviewed the effectiveness of its order in restoring competition to the industry, it held that further relief to restore workable competition to the industry was required. For the marketer, however, the message of the United Shoe Machinery case is clear: in remedying monopolization when it is found to exist, the judicial system is free to prescribe whatever relief, including the divestiture of specific product lines, courts find necessary to attain or maintain the goal or workable competition.

The *Grinnell Corporation* case decided by the Supreme Court in 1966 gave further indication of how far Section 2 might be expanded in attacking size great enough to be considered a monopoly.[19] Grinnell, through a series of acquisitions, had achieved domination in the production of plumbing supplies and fire sprinkler systems. Grinnell's acquired companies controlled a significant share of fire protection and burglary protection systems supported by "accredited central service" stations.[20] Of all the accredited central services in the United States, the government contended that Grinnell controlled 87 percent. If the nation was the proper geographic market and if accredited central service protection was the relevant product market, under the principles governing monopolization the Court had enunciated, Grinnell was a monopolist. In what seemingly has become the traditional definition of monopolization, the Court defined its criteria: "The offenses of monopoly under

Section 2 of the Sherman Act has two elements: (1) the possession of monopoly power in the relevant market and (2) the willful acquisition or maintenance of that power as distinguished from growth or development as a consequence of a superior product, business acumen, or historical accident."

Since the evidence was that it was in control of the several products that motivated Grinnell in its acquisition, the question became, in the Court's formulation, "what is the relevant market?" In the Court's reasoning and in its answer to its question, marketers find the importance of *Grinnell* in fashioning the organizational constraints of marketing's legal environment. Grinnell raised the obvious objection to the government's conception of the product market—surely fire protection services and burglar alarms are so dissimilar that a buyer would not readily and willingly substitute one for the other. Moreover, Grinnell contended, accredited service stations might well face substitutes in night watchmen with guard dogs if the lower cost of such substitutes offset the lower insurance rates that resulted from use of accredited central service stations. In each case, realistic definition of the relevant market would reveal more workable competition than the government's alleged 87 percent control would indicate. Grinnell also objected to the formulation of the nation as the geographic market since each individual accredited service station was limited to a twenty-five-mile operating radius. In short, Grinnell argued that the government had defined the relevant product market too narrowly and that realistic competition was greater than the government indicated; Grinnell argued that the relevant geographic market had been too broadly defined and that at least in several significant local areas the relevant degree of competition was also greater than the government indicated.

The Court enunciated, though it did not explicitly recognize, a new concept in market delineation. The Court lumped together a variety of services under the concept of a "cluster of services" even though the services in the cluster were not interchangeable. It accomplished this with the unargued and unexplained declaration: "We see no barrier to combining in a single market a number of different products or services where that combination reflects commercial realities." The Court's elaboration extended only to the holding that providers of one accredited central service find that their offering of complementary services is economically desirable.

So the cluster of services concept of market definition was born without conceptual delineation beyond providing for judicial ascertainment of what a court believes constitutes "commercial realities."[21] Marketers will see immediately the mischief that inheres in this vague concept. Marketers of laundry products may find it desirable to provide complementary products of detergents, bleaches, and softeners for effective marketing strategies. Those same marketers would be horrified to find such products lumped together in a "home laundry products" market cluster. Such a combination of products may be unlikely in the government's attack on monopoly but the *Grinnell* case provides no clear marketing guidelines as to the cluster of services concept.[22]

The other major marketing conclusion that marketers may draw from the *Grinnell* case emerges from the Court's treatment of Grinnell's contention that the provision of accredited central station services was local, not national. Because the Court found Grinnell presided over and controlled the combination of products, the Court held that a national market designation was appropriate. Its reasoning was brief: "the relevant market for determining whether [Grinnell has] monopoly power is . . . the broader national market that reflects the reality of the way in which they built and conduct their business." What this signals to the marketer is that once marketing has proceeded beyond the local level and is supported by a national organization and operation, the existence of local competition will not prevent the aggregation of business activities to achieve a national market share. The aggregation of activities may lead, as it did in this Grinnell case, to a finding that an organized monopoly in violation of Section 2 exists.

We are brought, then, after this journey through the ambiguities of the analysis of monopolizing organization and its status under Section 2 of the Sherman Act to an ugly, though accurate, conclusion: the exercise is fraught with ambiguity and imprecision. Marketers will find little solace in the conclusion. What they must know and remember clearly is that, in a world in which turnover of lower court justices is high and in which, over time, even the Supreme Court's composition alters, Section 2 is basically a structural provision.[23] All these cautions do not mean that conclusions are impossible.

Marketers must recognize that the preliminary step to finding that monopolization has occurred is the definition of the relevant market—both in its product and in its geographical dimensions. The du Pont case seems an irregularity in which emphasis was placed on market assessment of substitutability. The latitude accorded the government in defining the market is shown in the more recent *Grinnell* decision, in which the undefined and ambiguous concept of cluster of services was introduced. Until the courts or the legislatures make a definitive specification of the outer boundaries of that concept, marketers, charged with monopolization, can only hope that their analyses of the commercial realities will prevail. Once a court discovers monopoly power, specific intent must be shown; but, given the Court's propensity for inference, the Court can deduce intent easily from the mere possession of market power. Finally, remedies the judiciary deems sufficient to cure monopolization can be fashioned to restructure either or both the industry or the firm in a way the judges concerned find congenial. At the root of all this concern with the way in which business organizes to meet the consumer's needs is a historically derived dogma that large economic structures are dangerous and only by preventing them can appropriate socio-political—not economic—goals be realized.

Marketing Organization and Mergers   While legal constraints on the size of marketing organizations are imposed by Section 7 of the Sherman Antitrust Act as it has been interpreted by the courts, it is Section 7 of the Clayton Act and Section 5 of the Federal Trade Commission Act that constrain growth by methods other than internal expansion.[24] Section 7 of the Clayton Act as adopted in 1914 is more limited than Section 7 as it was amended in 1950 by the Celler-Kefauver Act. The original section generally prohibited stock acquisitions by any corporation "where the effect of such acquisition *may be* to *substantially* lessen competition . . . or to restrain such commerce *in any section or community*, or *tend* to create a monopoly of *any line of commerce*" (emphasis added). Later, court interpretations authorized the Federal Trade Commission to reach offenses falling under Section 7 by applying Section 5 of the Federal Trade Commission Act's provision against "unfair methods of competition in commerce."

Mergers are of various types and some debate exists about the proper names to be applied to each of them.[25] A merger generally is indicative of the union of formerly independent business entities into a new independent entity. Acquisitions, amalgamation, and consolidations all represent mergers. Mergers are commonly called *horizontal* when firms that are competitors are united; as *vertical* when firms whose relation is that of buyer and seller are united; and as *conglomerate* in all other cases of the combination of firms, for example, when a steamship line acquires a spaghetti factory. Mergers are sometimes distinguished as *product extension* when a firm in one line of commerce, for example, wine making, extends its activity into a different but usually marginally related line of commerce, for example, beer making, or when a firm in one section of the nation, for example, California, unites with a firm producing the same product in a separate section of the country for example, the Northeast. The process of definition, as we will see later, raises problems under the antimerger prohibitions of federal legislation.

Although Section 7 was adopted in 1914, it was not until 1949 that the government instituted major actions under the original Section 7.[26] There are three reasons for this long lag between the adoption of the Clayton Act and major governmental prosecutions under it. First, the Act contained a major loophole in that while it applied to mergers achieved by stock acquisitions, it did not prohibit mergers achieved through the acquistion of assets. As marketers would expect, mergers by asset acquisitions grew sharply. Second, consolidations accomplished by the creation and expansion through trusts, as we have seen in the Standard Oil, sugar trust, and tobacco trust cases, were attacked under the Sherman Act. The narrow view of commerce in the sugar trust case and the enunciation of the rule of reason in evaluating militated against extensive attacks on mergers particularly nonhorizontal ones. Third, the period from 1900 to the Great Depression of 1932–1939 was not characteristically one of great antibusiness vigor. In the du Pont antimerger case, which reached the Supreme Court in 1957, du Pont was charged with having used its ownership of 23 percent of the stock of General Motors to "pry open" the General Motor's market for automobile finishes and fabrics manufactured by du Pont.[27] Allegedly, the result was that a substantial part of General Motor's purchases of finishes and fabrics was foreclosed to manufacturers competing with du Pont. This merger, clearly vertical in nature, was held to be prohibited under Section 7.

The Court noted that the "necessary predicate" for finding a violation of Section 7 by du Pont was the determination of the relevant market. The Court adopted a narrow view of the product market holding it to be the area of "effective competition" and was therefore a "line of commerce" within the meaning of the Clayton Act. Du Pont's contention that finishes and fabric sales to industrial users in general constituted the product market was rejected. In addition, the Court held that vertical mergers—not simply horizontal mergers as du Pont had contended—clearly fell within the reach of the Act. Even stock acquisitions held merely for investment, it was decided, may be violative of the Act at any time the stockholding is used or attempted to be used to bring about a substantial lessening of competition.

Marketers need to give special attention to the italicized section of the Act, which notes that the prohibited effect of an acquistion occurs when undesirable consequences *may* occur. This language gives rise to the incipiency doctrine, which holds that anticompetitive consequences need not be demonstrated by the government; the government need show only a "reasonable probability" of anticompetitive consequences. In the du Pont case, therefore, the government was not required to show that competition had been injured; the government needed to demonstrate only that such occurrence would be anticipated. In this case, the definition of "any section of the country" was not in dispute. Du Pont, the government, and the Court accepted the geographic market as national. Finally the Court adduced proof of substantiality from the share of General Motor's fabrics and finishes supplied by du Pont. When the Court concluded its analysis, it found du Pont clearly guilty.[28]

After the decision in du Pont, decided after the Act was amended in 1950 but rendered under the provision of the unamended 1914 Act, the amended Section 7 of the Clayton Act became the law under which merger activity was restrained. The amendment, adopted in 1950 and popularly known as the Cellar-Kefauver Act, extended the coverage of Section 7 by providing that asset acquisitions as well as stock acquisitions were prohibited on the same grounds that stock acquisitions had been condemned in the original Section 7. The amendment also clarified the language of the Act to bring vertical and conglomerate mergers as well as joint ventures under the Act.[29]

The *Brown Shoe* case, brought in 1955 and decided by the Supreme Court in 1962, first provided the Court's interpretation of the amended Act in a case that combined both vertical and horizontal merger considerations.[30] Brown Shoe, which manufactured men's, women's, and children's shoes, attempted to acquire Kinney, which manufactured shoes and also owned and operated retail outlets for shoes. The government, in its attack on the supplier-customer aspects of the merger, argued there were several appropriate lines of commerce and subdivided shoes into the men's, women's, and children's categories. To Brown's attempt to differentiate shoe markets on the basis of price/quality differences so that Brown's and Kinney's shoes actually fell into different markets, the Court was unsympathetic. Admitting that price/quality differences "where they exist" might be important in merger analysis, the Court resorted to the traditional logician's ploy of contending that since differences between $8.99 and $9.00 shoes were "unrealistic," no perceived degrees of differences justified distinguishing shoes on the basis of differences of kinds of shoes. Finding attempts to distinguish the relevant market to be "impractical" and "unwarranted," the Court included the shoes of Kinney and of Brown in the same product market.

The issue of the appropriate geographic market was somewhat muddled. Initially the Court held the relevant geographic market to be "the entire nation." Yet the Court, in undertaking its analysis of the horizontal aspects of the merger, discovered that utilizing the national market for analyzing the retail shoe merger would not have produced conclusive evidence that the merger might foreclose significant markets to other retail shoe sellers. Therefore, the government with the Court concurring, adopted the concept of relevant submarkets, which, it held, were comprised of "every city with a population exceeding 10,000 and its immediate contiguous territory in which both Brown and Kinney sold shoes at retail through stores they either owned or controlled."[31] Since within the product lines defined the foreclosure according to government's own statistics was significant, and since the shoes were lumped into the classes that the government defined, the Court found the "probable effect" of Brown's acquisition of Kinney might be to substantially lessen competition. The Court held further that Brown's merger through the acquisition of Kinney's assets at the level of competitive reselling would violate Section 7. The vertical merger was also disallowed although on a national basis the foreclosure to other marketers had to be very small.[32] Marketers were put on notice that the Court was willing to adopt persuasive definitions of both relevant geographic and product markets and to accept what appear to be gerrymandered statistics to limit the expansion of the marketing institution in facilitating autonomous decisions as the most effective marketing methods to meet consumers' perceived needs.

The Court's bent for accepting antibusiness market definitions also appeared in 1964 in the *Continental Can* case[33] and in the *Alcoa* case[34] decided in the same year. Continental Can Company, in 1955 the second largest producer of metal containers, acquired the assets of Hazel-Atlas Glass Company, which, with 9.6 percent of the shipments of glass containers, was the third largest producer of glass containers in the nation. Although this acquisition was clearly a product extension merger for Continental, the government challenged the merger as being illegal under Section 7 of the Clayton Act. The government argued and the Court agreed that the relevant market was the "glass and metal container market" in which the merged firms would have more than a 25 percent share. The rationale for the product market definition was that although glass containers and metal containers were unique in some uses, the realities of interindustry competition required the Court to accept the government's definition of the "line of commerce."

In *Alcoa*, the Court found that although copper conductor cable produced by Rome Cable Company, which had been acquired by Alcoa and which produced approximately 28 percent of the aluminum conductor cable, were in different submarkets, the merger was illegal on other grounds. The Court found that although Rome's production in the aluminum conductor cable market was only 1.3 percent, Rome was an aggressive firm with a great potential as an expanding competitor, and that since the nine largest firms controlled over 95 percent of that market, the merger was illegal. A vigorous dissent in *Alcoa* did little. The Court's majority maintained its view that even though business might operate in submarkets that were essentially separate, the business still could not merge marketing and production operations.

This interpretation of the antimerger provisions of the Clayton Act expanded in the Court's decision in 1965 in the *Consolidated Foods* case.[35] At issue was a conglomerate merger. Consolidated Foods owned both food processing plants and wholesale and retail food stores. Gentry manufactured dehydrated onion and garlic. The evil that flowed from Consolidated's acquisition of Gentry was alleged to be Consolidated's ability to engage in reciprocal buying from those that used Gentry's garlic and onion, thereby causing sellers to buy, to some degree unwillingly, from Gentry. Such reciprocity, the Court declared, was "one of the congeries of anticompetitive practices at which the antitrust laws are aimed." The possibilities of coercion were held to be implicit in an acquisition such as that of Gentry by Consolidated. The intrusion of this "irrelevant and alien factor" was sufficient to give rise to the Court's finding of the probability of a lessening of competition at which Section 7 is directed.

One additional consideration of the *Consolidated Foods* case beyond the inference that reciprocity inheres in conglomerate acquisitions was Consolidated's attempt to rebut the inference by demonstrating that post-acquisition evidence indicated that Gentry's market position had weakened, not strengthened, and therefore substantial lessening of competition had not occurred. Although the Court did not find the company's argument persuasive in factual terms, the Court's doctrinal pronouncement is important for marketers. The Court granted that the court of appeals erred in "considering" postacquisition evidence. The Court would allow postacquisition evidence to demonstrate that harm to competition occurred. It would give only a little weight if it shows harm has not yet occurred. However, the Court's argument nullified even the small concession it seemed to make. By emphasizing the need to establish a "probability" at the time of acquisition only, the Court reinforced its position, declaring:

[no] group acquiring a company with reciprocal buying opportunities is entitled to a "free trial" period. To give it such would be to distort the scheme of Section 7. The "mere *possibility*" of the prohibited restraint is not enough. Probability of the proscribed evil is required . . . .If the postacquisition evidence were given conclusive weight or allowed to override all probabilities, then acquisitions would go forward willy-nilly, the parties biding their time until reciprocity was allowed fully to bloom. It is, of course, true that postacquisition conduct may amount to a violation of Section 7 even though there is no evidence to establish probability [at the very beginning].

So market failure is clearly not a sufficient group upon which marketers may base an argument to absolve a merger from the penalties that flow from violation of the restrictions on mergers.

Nor did the *Consolidated Foods* case end the Supreme Court's interpretation of the antimerger law. In 1966 the Court decided the case of *Von's Grocery*.[36] Von's, a grocery chain in Los Angeles, acquired thirty-four Shopping Bag retail groceries in Los Angeles. In 1960, the year the United States brought suit against the merger, the combined sales of the two chains was 7.5 percent of the total Los Angeles grocery market. Both chains had been growing since 1948. Single-store ownership in the Los Angeles market had declined, and chain store ownership generally had grown. In a concurring opinion Justice White noted that the market share of the top four, the top eight, and the top twelve had grown since 1948. The Court held these facts "alone" enough to cause them to find the merger in violation of Section 7.

Although the decision was clear and divestiture of Shopping Bag stores by Von's was required, much of the lesson marketers must learn from this case is found in the biting dissent of Justices Harlan and Stewart.[37] Noting that Von's stores and Shopping Bag stores were for the most part in different sections of Los Angeles, the dissenters suggested that the relevant market had not been distinguished clearly. The merger was at least three-fourths a geographic market extension merger. "Transcending social and technological changes" were cited by Justices Harlan and Stewart to explain the development of a supermarket industry of rapid entry and turnover; the majority's opinion was castigated as "hardly more than a requiem for the so-called 'Mom and Pop' grocery stores . . . that are now obsolete in many parts of the country. No action by this Court can resurrect the old single-line Los Angeles food stores that have been run over by the automobile or obliterated by the freeway." Hence the minority emphasized the extent to which economic considerations of exit and entry of competitors, technological changes in the industry, or market realities could be disregarded when the Court wished to nullify a merger it found uncongenial. In a bitter conclusion, Justices Harlan and Stewart pierced the Court's exposed nerve: "in litigation under Section 7, the Government always wins."

The government found a new way to limit marketing mergers in the ensuing major case of the *Federal Trade Commission v. Procter & Gamble* in 1967. Procter & Gamble acquired the assets of the Clorox Chemical Company, the leading manufacturer of household liquid bleach with slightly less than one-half of the national liquid bleach sales. Procter did not produce liquid bleach but produced primarily soaps, detergents, and cleansers with its detergent sales at approximately 54 percent of the national market. The acquisition, which appeared to be a natural product extension merger, or alternatively simply a conglomerate merger, was challenged by the Federal Trade Commission as a violation of Section 7 of the Clayton Act.

Clearly a conglomerate merger does not increase concentration among the leading sellers of the acquired product line. Procter's acquisition of Clorox did not, in and of itself, increase either Clorox's share of the household bleach market nor did it alter the share of the market the top four producers held. The merger simply altered the ownership of the share of the market and enabled Procter to move quickly into a field of production allied to its other product lines. Logic dictates that, other considerations aside, a conglomerate, by the act of merging, never increases the market concentration among competitors.

The government's attack on mergers such as the Procter–Clorox merger had, therefore, to be premised on other actual or potential abuses of the merger. The government found two. First, the government contended that the acquisition by Procter removed it from "potential competition" in the industry. The government had determined that the liquid bleach market was "a natural avenue of diversification" of Procter, which more than overcame the earlier Procter decision against independently entering the bleach market in favor of the acquisition of Clorox. Barriers to entry by Procter, either in the form of technical productive considerations or marketing considerations, were held to be "not significant." Moreover, as long as Procter perched on the edge of the market, concentration in the bleach industry was found to persist because of Procter's chilling effect on other potential entrants. As to potential entrants, the Court declared: "the number of potential entrants was not so large that the elimination of one would be insignificant." So, both because Procter was viewed as a potential entrant and because that potential was found to maintain concentration by discouraging other potential entrants, the Court found the merger unacceptable.

However, the Court used a second arrow from its bow in striking down the merger. The government proposed and the court accepted what has come to be called the "deep pocket" (or alternatively, the "long purse") theory. Simply put, this theory holds that a major acquirer, such as Procter in this case, has resources so substantial as to command advertising and other marketing advantages (cross-couponing, free samples) that it would usurp the normal and legitimate market shares of smaller firms. Moreover, these advantages would also have the effect of raising entry barriers to other potential entrants. Then the Court, relying on its noneconomic rationale of *Brown Shoe*, concluded: "Possible economies cannot be used as a defense to illegality. Congress was aware that some mergers which lessen competition may also result in economies but it struck the balance in favor of protecting competition."

Thus the Procter-Clorox merger resulted in two additional reasons to be adduced to prevent marketing mergers. First, if potential competition, either of the acquiring firm or other firms overhanging the market is reduced or inhibited, then a merger may be proscribed. Second, if an acquiring firm possesses economic power so great that its marketing advantages might increase marketing concentration, the merger may be proscribed.[38]

The concept of potential competition, once noted earlier, naturally posed problems of interpretation: when is an acquiring firm a potential competitor? Not only has the Federal Trade Commission wrestled with this question in determining whether to challenge a merger as violative of Section 7, the Supreme Court also found the question a difficult one to answer. Its most nearly definitive statement was made in 1973 in the *Falstaff Brewing* case.[39]

In 1965, Falstaff, then a regional brewer not selling in the national beer market, decided that effective competition necessitated its selling in the entire national market. To achieve this end, Falstaff acquired the

Narragansett brewery, the largest seller of beer in the New England market in which concentration had increased since 1960. Prior to the consummation of the merger, the government challenged the acquisition on two grounds: first, because Falstaff was conceived as a potential entrant into the Northeastern beer market and second, because Falstaff's acquisition lessened the competition that might have resulted had Falstaff entered the market by acquisition and expansion of a smaller firm.[40]

The Supreme Court concluded that testimony of Falstaff's officers that Falstaff had no intention of entering the New England market except through acquisition and that therefore it was not a potential competitor had been weighted too heavily when the District Court had considered the case. Moreover, the Court held, that entry aside, it was necessary to consider "whether Falstaff was a potential competitor in the sense that it was so positioned on the edge of the market that it exerted beneficial influence on competitive conditions in that market." The case was remanded to the District Court "to make proper assessment of Falstaff as a potential competitor" recognizing that the consideration of Falstaff as a potential competitor must take cognizance of objective as well as subjective evidence.

In a separate concurring opinion, Justice Marshall discussed the "modes of potential competition," which for analytical purposes have been widely followed. First, Justice Marshall discussed "the dominant entrant" in which an acquiring firm with such "overpowering resources" that an acquisition by it "might drive other marginal companies out of business, thus creating an oligopoly, or it might raise entry barriers to such an extent that potential new entrants would be discouraged from entering the market." Second, Justice Marshall analyzed the "perceived potential entrant," which he considered to be a firm "on the fringe of the market" viewed as one ready to enter if entry barriers were lowered and hence deter anticompetitive conduct within the market. Withdrawal of such an overhanging firm by allowing an acquisition would potentially reduce competition. The third category of potential competitor examined by Justice Marshall was the "actual potential entrant." Marshall recognized that the perception of a potential entrant is difficult to establish. Yet, in Marshall's language, "where a powerful firm is engaging in a related line of commerce at the fringe of the relevant market, where it has a strong incentive to enter the market de novo, and where it has the financial capabilities to do so, we have not hesitated to ascribe to it the role of an actual potential entrant" with which a merger will be prohibited under Section 7. Marshall then, noting that the evidence presented by a potential acquirer will undoubtedly indicate accurately that entry by acquisition will be more profitable than de novo entry, dismisses this potential. The inferentially lower costs and prices to the consumer that would result from the entry by a potential entrant remain unmentioned and seem, in the Court's analysis, to be irrelevant.

When the District Court examined the question of whether or not Falstaff was a dominant entrant, a perceived entrant, or an actual potential entrant, it concluded in 1974, that Falstaff was neither a "potential competitor waiting in the wings, exerting a beneficial influence on existing competition in the New England market" nor would "the acquisition of Narragansett lead to a substantial lessening of competition in said market." The court reached this conclusion after studying the merger negotiations, the production capabilities of the breweries concerned, the distribution systems, the financing considerations, the possibility of a toehold acquisition, and the statements of Falstaff's management and other officials. Falstaff's acquisition of Narragansett was approved.

Private Action to Block Mergers   Marketers may wonder if, under the antitrust statutes and court interpretations of them, they may undertake successful action to block mergers they consider potentially injurious to them. The current answer seems to be they may not.

The Supreme Court, in *Cargill, Inc. and Excel Corp. v. Monfort of Colorado, Inc.,*[41] refused to grant an injunction staying a merger of competing firms. The Court denied Monfort's attempt to secure an injunction under Section 16 of the Clayton Act since the Court held that economic injury not caused by predatory pricing or other actions specifically prohibited by the antitrust laws could not be the basis for private action to block a merger. In the *Cargill* case, the Justice Department sought to broaden the view the Court adopted. The Department asked that the Court adopt a per se rule denying completely the right of a business to challenge mergers on the basis of predatory pricing theories. Speaking for the Court, Justice Brennan granted that predatory pricing actions that justify staying merger activity occur "only infrequently." However, he added, "there is ample evidence suggesting that the practice does occur." Moreover, as the Court of Appeals for the Fifth Circuit declared, in applying the *Cargill* guidelines in the *Phototron* case,[42] if a merger is consummated and results in illegal injury to a competitor, relief in the form of treble damages provides a viable alternative to the blocking of the merger.

Marketers may find solace in the fact that the government did not always win. Yet structuring of the marketing institution by way of mergers must be guided by what continue to be, despite the ultimate Falstaff outcome and the unavailability of a private antimerger remedy, structural considerations narrowly interpreted to assure the continued existence of competitors if not, as a consequence, competition.

The Institution of Antimerger Action   The indication that toehold acquisitions may go unchallenged when the acquired firm possesses no more than a 10 percent market share emphasizes that some guidelines must exist as to when the government might invoke Section 7. Emphasis should be that in general private persons may not initiate antimerger suits; initiation generally depends upon government action. However, mergers may violate Sections 1 and 2 of the Sherman Act and, if the government proves injury has occurred, a private suit for damages may be filed by the injured party using the decision the government has secured as prima facie evidence that the defendants did violate the Sherman Act. Then the party injured by the illegal merger may file and secure treble damages for the amount of its injury. Our concern here, however, is about government-initiated action.

Recognition that the Supreme Court cases examined here were all initiated prior to 1982 is important. Prior to that time the decisions of the Department of Justice and the Federal Trade Commission (both of whom are authorized to bring cases under Section 7), to initiate antimerger suits were based on enforcement criteria provided in the internal policies of those agencies. Then came the publication of the 1968 *Merger Guidelines*. The enforcement actions and Supreme Court decisions until 1982 reflect prior criteria; in 1982 new guidelines superseding the earlier 1968 guidelines were adopted.

Some indication of the changes in antimerger regulation may be found in the contrast of the merger guidelines of 1968 and 1982 and the modifications and interpretations that government agencies and the courts have made since 1982. The 1968 guidelines, unique in their attempt to codify antimerger criteria, were restrictive in their approach to defining both the product and the geographic markets, the necessary predicate to action under Section 7. The 1968 "line of commerce" (the law's language for product market) definition provided:

The sales of any product or service which is distinguishable as matter of commercial practice from other products or services will ordinarily constitute a relevant product market, even though, from the standpoint of most purchasers, other products may be reasonably, but not perfectly, interchangeable in terms of price, quality and use. On the other hand, the sales of two distinct products to a particular group of purchasers can also be appropriately grouped into a single market where the two products are reasonably interchangeable for that group in terms of price, quality, and use. In this latter case, however, it may be necessary also to include in that market the sales of one or more other products which are equally interchangeable with the two products in terms of price, quality, and use from the standpoint of that group of purchasers to whom the two products are interchangeable.

What is clearly implicit in this definition is the classical economic view of product homogeneity and perfect competition. Perfect interchangeability is the touchstone and, therefore, the concept of workable competition in which "substantial competitive influences" are not adequate to put two differentiated products with a reasonably high cross elasticity of demand in the same product market is adopted.

In a like definitional process, the 1968 guidelines defined the geographic market ("section of the country" in terms of the law) very narrowly. Indications of this definitional propensity is found in the language of the guidelines, which said:

Because data limitations or other intrinsic difficulties will often make precise delineation of geographic markets impossible, there may often be two or more groupings of sales which may reasonably be treated as constituting a relevant geographic market. In such circumstances, the Department of Justice believes it to be ordinarily most consistent with the purpose of Section 7 to challenge any merger which appears to be illegal in any reasonable geographic market, even though in another reasonable market it would not appear to be illegal.

The bias toward action is clearly implicit in this definition, which also makes it clear that if in a national or regional market evidence of illegality may seem to be present, no attention need be given to evidence of the impact of international production and sale on the market share of the producers singled out for antimerger action.

The application of these definitions called upon the Department of Justice or the Federal Trade Commission to ascertain the degree of increased market concentration that would result from any contemplated merger. This was done, as we have seen in examining Supreme Court decisions, by determining the four-firm concentration ratio (the percentage of the relevant indicia—usually the dollar value of sales although shipments or leases, or in banking, total deposits) controlled by the four largest firms in the "line of commerce." Then the percentage share controlled by the acquiring and the acquired firms was determined and the effect on the resulting four-firm ratio approximated. In highly concentrated markets (those in which the four largest firms controlled 75 percent or more of the sales), "ordinarily" horizontal mergers would be challenged if the acquiring firm with 4 percent or more of the market acquired a firm with another 4 percent or more of the market. Similarly an acquiring firm in a highly concentrated market would be challenged if it attempted acquisition of a firm with 2 percent or more of the industry sales; a merger by a firm with 15 percent or more would be challenged if the acquired firm had one or more percent of the industry sales. In "markets less highly concentrated," in which the top four firms had less than 75 percent of industry sales, challenges would occur at higher levels. Illustratively, an acquiring firm with 15 percent of the industry sales could not acquire, without challenge, a firm with three or more percent of industry sales.[43]

The 1968 guidelines were more vague on vertical mergers than on horizontal mergers but guidelines were provided in percentage terms. Thus a vertical merger that might be challenged for lessening either existing or potential competition in the supplying firm's market "ordinarily" would be challenged if the supplying firm accounted for 10 percent or more of the sales in its market and the purchasing firm accounted for approximately 6 percent of the purchases in the market "unless it clearly appears that there are no significant barriers to entry into the business of the purchasing firm or firms." Other special conditions led the Department to invoke other standards including the application of nonmarket-share standards in cases in which vertical mergers "would probably raise barriers to entry to impose a competitive disadvantage on unintegrated or partly integrated firms and . . . it does not clearly appear that the particular acquisition will result in significant economies of production or distribution unrelated to advertising or other promotional economies." Moreover, if the economies of production or distribution were realizable by internal expansion, the merger might still be challenged. The conclusion, buttressed by the *Brown Shoe* case, is that under the 1968 guidelines vertical mergers, as horizontal mergers, could not have been expected to fare well.

Conglomerate mergers, under the 1968 guidelines, were structural and involved percentage criteria. Specifically the conglomerate merger guidelines were directed against mergers that inhibited entry by the "most likely" entrants into a market or which created a "danger of reciprocal buying." "Most likely" entrants were those judged by evaluating:

the firm's capability of entering on a competitively significant scale relative to the capability of other firms (i.e., the technological and financial resources available to it) and to the firm's economic incentive to enter (evidenced by, for example, the general attractiveness of the market in terms of risk and profit; or any special relationship of the firm to the market; or the firm's manifested interest in entry; or the natural expansion pattern of the firm; or the like).

Then the Department would "ordinarily" challenge a merger between a likely entrant and:

(i) any firm with approximately 25% or more of the market;
(ii) one of the two largest firms in a market in which the shares of the two largest firms amount to approximately 50% or more;
(iii) one of the four largest firms in a market in which the shares of the eight largest firms amount to approximately 75% or more, provided the merging firm's share of the market amounts to approximately 10% or more; or
(iv) one of the eight largest firms in a market in which the shares of these firms amount to approximately 75% or more provided either (A) the merging firm's

share of the market is not insubstantial and there are no more than one or two likely entrants into the market or (B) the merging firm is a rapidly growing firm.

Other conglomerate mergers which entrenched market power were also subject to special evaluation and possible prosecution for violation of Section 7. Finally, the Department recognized that the conglomerate merger involved "novel problems that have not yet been subjected to as extensive or sustained analysis as those presented by horizontal or vertical mergers" and consequently, where adjudged appropriate, case-by-case analysis would be undertaken to determine if a challenge of such a merger was in order.

Review of the 1968 guidelines, then, leads to these general conclusions: (1) interpretation was very stringent in that definitions of markets and products were narrow and prosecution was not only facilitated but was encouraged; (2) percentage guidelines were set at very low levels and did not admit of economic performance, in contrast to structural characteristics, to legitimize mergers that the Department of Justice or the Federal Trade Commission might otherwise hold to be suspect; (3) in application, as the still-unreversed or unmodified Supreme Court precedents attest, the ability of marketers to create marketing organizations through mergers—no matter how desirable the results might be in meeting the perceived consumer's needs—is subject to very limited autonomy.

The 1982 merger guidelines, in their introduction by United States Attorney General William French Smith, signaled new and less restrictive criteria for the institution of antimerger actions. Smith declared: "Some mergers pose serious competitive problems, but most do not. The purpose of the Guidelines is to tell the public how the Antitrust Division draws that line." The Federal Trade Commission, joining in a lukewarm endorsement of the Department of Justice guidelines, did lay the 1968 guidelines to rest with the statement: "The two agencies have concluded that continued reliance on the Department of Justice's Merger Guidelines, promulgated in 1968, is no longer appropriate." The more lenient nature of the new guidelines may not, however, be revealed in judicial interpretations; instead it is signaled by the institution of fewer antimerger suits.

The new guidelines confront the issue of market definition immediately. In technical economic terms the definition of a market provides:

a group of products and an associated geographic area such that (in the absence of new entry) a hypothetical, unregulated firm that made all the sales of these products in that area could increase its profits through a small but significant and non-transitory increase in price (above prevailing or likely future levels).

Application of this definition is then based upon the Department's hypothesizing "a price increase of five percent and [asking] how many buyers would be likely to shift to the other products within one year." Obviously, in the Department's conceptualization, significant shifts indicate buyers' perceptions that the products are good substitutes and, if workable competition is accepted as the policy goal, indicative that such competition exists. Four factors are weighed in ascertaining the existence of product substitutability: (1) buyers' perceptions, particularly if past shifting of purchases support the inference of product substitutability; (2) "similarities or differences between the products in customary usage, design, physical composition and other technical characteristics"; (3) correspondence or lack of correspondence in price movements through time; and (4) seller's perceptions, particularly as revealed in past business decisions. This fourth factor implies that cross-elasticity of supply is being added to cross-elasticity of demand as a determinant. Cross-elasticity of supply asks: if prices are increased by a given percentage, what percentage increase in the quantity of the product by other firms will occur in a reasonable period of time? If the percentage is large, the ability of the price-increasing firm to control prices and profits by limiting competition is significantly reduced. In such circumstances, the product market is broad enough that a merger occurring in it may be relatively unimportant.

In delimiting the geographic market, the guidelines adopt a very broad approach. They do not, as did the 1968 guidelines, presumptively accept the least favorable definition for business possible. The general position of the guidelines is simple: "Depending on the nature of the product, the geographic market may be as small as a part of the city or as large as the entire world." Their test is again the ability of a firm to raise its price in an area without experiencing the entry of products that would make such an increase transitory. Shipment patterns are considered outside the initially delimited market, analyzed. In assessing foreign competition in the domestic market, special consideration is given to the vagaries of international marketing such as those occurring in exchange rates, quotas, tariffs, and political conditions.

After the product and geographic markets are determined, some measure of market concentration is required. No longer is the four-firm control of the relative measure (sales, shipments, employment) of the 1968 *Guidelines* used. In its place the Department embraced the Herfindahl-Hirschman Index (HHI) long advocated by economists as a more reliable measure of concentration than the four-firm ratio.[44] Eleanor M. Fox, in a detailed analysis of the 1982 merger guidelines, explained the HHI succinctly: "The HHI is calculated by listing the market shares of all firms in the market, squaring the share of each firm, and summing the squares."[45] The upper limit of the HHI, the market share of a perfect monopolist, thus becomes 10,000 (100% squared), while the lower limit approximates zero in an industry with so many firms that each firm's share of sales (or other measure) approaches an infinitesimally small amount. In a like manner, if four firms in an industry have shares of 30 percent, 30 percent, 20 percent, and 20 percent, squaring each value and summing them gives an HHI of 1,600. Four firms, each with 25 percent of the market, would have an HHI of 2,500. Four firms with shares of 50 percent, 25 percent, 15 percent, and 10 percent would have an HHI of 3,450. An industry with ten firms, each with 10 percent of the market, would have an HHI of 1,000. The generalization that follows is this: identical four-firm concentration ratios (in each illustration, the four firms control 100 percent of the output, yet as the pattern of control becomes increasingly asymmetrical is revealed an increasingly dominant leading firm), the HHI rises. Thus, by a built-in tendency to give increasing weight to industry dominance by the leading firm, the potential power of the dominant firm to effect anticompetitive practices is emphasized.

Once measures of market concentration are determined, division of concentration into categories for enforcement action follows. The Department guidelines characterize industries with an HHI of 1,000 or less as "unconcentrated"; industries with an HHI between 1,000 and 1,800 are characterized as "moderately concentrated." Horizontal mergers in the unconcentrated markets ordinarily are not challenged by the government. In moderately concentrated industries, horizontal mergers that produce an increase in HHI of less than 100 points ordinarily are not challenged. In highly concentrated markets, those with an HHI in excess of 1,800, an increase of less than 50 points in the HHI is unlikely to evoke a challenge. When a merger exceeds these general standards, a decision to challenge will take cognizance of the postmerger concentration, the actual increase in concentration, and a variety of conditioning factors outlined in the guidelines. A "leading firm proviso" also conditions the application of the HHI guidelines: "the Department is likely to challenge the merger of any firm with a market share of at least 1 percent with the leading firm in the market provided that the leading firm has a market share that is at least 35 percent and is approximately twice as large as that of the second largest firm in the market."

Marketers who are interested in the application of the HHI must recognize that the availability of statistics of relevant market shares for *all* firms may be difficult for the government or a firm contemplating a merger to obtain. Moreover, a number of small firms in an otherwise concentrated industry will complicate the problem of the lack of adequate statistical data. This problem is dismissed by the guidelines: "Although it is desirable to include all firms in the calculation, lack of information about small fringe firms is not critical because such firms do not affect the HHI significantly." What this implies is that the HHIs, whether based on dollar sales, physical unit sales, physical capacity, or physical reserve, will to a degree, and as were the 1968 four-firm concentration ratios, be an approximation.

Nonhorizontal mergers, including what the 1968 mergers identified as vertical mergers and conglomerate mergers, are treated in a way that, as with horizontal mergers, is less restrictive of the freedom of marketers to act autonomously. The Department of Justice stated its position simply: "The guidelines make clear that although non-horizontal mergers are less likely to harm competition, they are not always innocuous." Under the 1982 guidelines, nonhorizontal mergers may be challenged if "specific potential entrants into the market" are eliminated, if the merger creates barriers to entry into the market, if "collusion through vertical mergers which integrate the firms to include the retail level" is facilitated, or if a "disruptive buyer" is eliminated by a vertical merger. In addition, nonhorizontal mergers to evade existing rate regulation may be challenged. In terms of a merger that might involve potential competition, the Department will evaluate perceived potential competition and actual potential competition on a single structural standard similar to that employed in horizontal mergers. Thus, a potential competition merger is unlikely to be challenged "unless overall concentration of the acquired firm's market is above 1800 HHI." A lower HHI concentration ratio may call forth a challenge if unique entry advantages of an acquiring firm not also possessed by three or more other firms exist. Even so, if the acquiring firm's own documents on "the minimum efficient scale in the industry" indicate that actual entry appears "particularly strong," a vertical acquisition may be challenged.

The 1982 merger guidelines also address the issue of defenses the Department of Justice or Federal Trade Commission may consider as responses to challenges to mergers. The guidelines are explicit: "Except in extraordinary cases, the Department will not consider a claim of specific efficiencies as a mitigating factor for a merger that would otherwise be challenged." The general principle is elaborated by the guidelines:

At a minimum, the Department will require clear and convincing evidence that the merger will produce substantial cost savings resulting from the realization of scale economies, integration of production facilities, or multi-plant operations which are already enjoyed by one or more firms in the industry and that equivalent results could not be achieved within a comparable period of time through internal expansion or through a merger that threatened less competitive harm. In any event, the Department will consider such efficiencies only in resolving otherwise close cases.

The other defense that may protect a merger from challenge is the doctrine under which an otherwise anticompetitive merger might not be challenged if one of the merging firms is failing. Three conditions under which the failing firm doctrine might be accepted are: (1) if failure in the near future is imminent; (2) if reorganization under Chapter II of the Bankruptcy Act is not likely to succeed; and (3) if efforts to elicit alternative offers for acquisition have been made in good faith and have failed.

What emerges from the 1982 guidelines are that mergers are treated with less distrust than they were under the 1968 guidelines. First, both product and geographic markets are defined more consistently with the concept of workable competition than they were prior to 1982. Second, the HHI as a measure of market concentration is more clearly oriented to the issue of anticompetitive practices (particularly the extent of single-firm dominance of an industry) than the less sophisticated aggregative four-firm concentration ratio. Third, vertical mergers are less severely judged than they were when the HHI was not in place and when the presumption was that potential competition would be readily forthcoming. Fourth, defense to challenged mergers are made explicit. These four considerations lead to the inference that although the development of a marketing institution by merger continues to be governed by well worn (or outworn) existing Supreme Court precedents interpreting the statutory language of the amended Section 7 of the Clayton Act, which have almost entirely been rendered under the pre–1982 merger guides, the probability of action against mergers has been and will probably continue to be less than it was under early interpretations of the Act.

Premerger Notification Rules and Advisory Opinions Obviously a business considering a merger would be interested to know if a challenge is likely to be forthcoming under the merger guidelines and the Department's enforcement policy of them. Such a business might also be interested to know if other contemplated action (such as a joint venture for research and development) is likely to cause the Department of Justice or the Federal Trade Commission (FTC) to invoke action to prevent the merger or to prohibit the action. To provide some of this information, the Hart-Scott-Rodino Antitrust Improvements Act of 1976 provided for the promulgation of premerger notification rules by the Federal Trade Commission. The motivation of the Act was to provide the Federal Trade Commission with a means to stop mergers from being consummated without adequate time for the commission to take preventive action it might want to undertake. However, the effect of the Act is to provide a device by which a business may learn whether the FTC is likely to institute an antimerger case or whether the business will be required to provide additional information before a decision is made by the relevant governmental agency.[46]

For securing a Federal Trade Commission opinion on whether a non-merger action is likely to be challenged, the Federal Trade Commission has created an informational procedure. It is the Business Advisory Opinion in which a business may submit a "proposed course of action" to the Commission for its opinion.[47] The commission is not obligated to render an opinion. Nor is it precluded from taking other action "as may be appropriate." However, if a business has provided full and accurate information and the commission renders an opinion, the commission will not take action against a firm relying on the opinion in good faith. The procedure also provides for the publication of letters requesting advisory opinions and of the advisory opinions.

The Department of Justice also has a Business Review Procedure similar to the advisory opinion procedure of the Federal Trade Commission.[48] Under the business review procedure, written requests are submitted to the attorney general asking whether a contemplated business proposal will be challenged. The Department of Justice examines the request and may refuse to consider it, may indicate its enforcement intentions such as "no present intent to institute criminal proceedings," indicate an intent to take action if the proposed course of action is carried out, or, as in the case of a proposed merger, that it does not intend to challenge the merger. Businesses should, however, note carefully the dual jurisdiction of the Department of Justice and the Federal Trade Commission over proposed mergers. A business review opinion of the Department of Justice that action is not intended does not preclude action by the Federal Trade Commission under premerger guidelines, merger guidelines, and Section 7 of the Clayton Act.

Yet, marketers, interested in expanding their marketing organizations, should be cognizant of the possibility of securing guidance from the regulatory agencies prior to undertaking such action.

JOINT VENTURES

Monopoly, whether the result of economic forces beyond reproach or by conscious and illegal activity, and the equivocal merger in its cocoon of restrictions, represent the more common devices for altering business organization when internal growth is not undertaken. The third method is the joint venture—sometimes considered a form of merger since Section 7 of the Clayton Act is applicable to it. However, since a joint venture does not culminate in a single new business entity through disappearance of a previously existing firm, logically it should be considered separately.

A joint venture arises when, for compelling business reasons, two firms that retain economic independence and control of their own assets, join and create a jointly owned business enterprise. Joint ventures, not widely used before 1950, offer a number of economic advantages.[49] First, pooling of resources by two separate firms may enable the achievement of marketing advantages or economies of scale and thereby enable entry into an otherwise foreclosed market. Second, the joining of assets may enable—indeed, it may be the only way to accomplish this end—the entry of a foreign market. Third, research and development may be facilitated if two separate firms cooperate. Yet joint ventures are not free from the surveillance of regulatory agencies for the possibilities of the fixing of common prices, the foreclosure of potential entrants, and the sequestering of technological developments inhere in joint action.

Historically the most famous pre–Section 7 case involving a joint venture was the *Terminal Railroad Association of St. Louis* case.[50] That case, brought under the Sherman Act, involved a joint venture by thirty-eight defendants who had created the Terminal Railroad Association to combine all the independent terminal companies of St. Louis into a single operating system. What the promoters hoped to accomplish was, as was explicit in the original organizing document, "to obtain control of every feasible means of railroad access to St. Louis." Yet the Supreme Court found that the combination might be of "the greatest public utility" and, if the terms of joint venture were modified so that future entrants into the market were not excluded from participating in the joint ownership and so entrants not wishing to join joint venture might have access to the consolidated railway facilities, then the joint venture would not be held to violate the Sherman Act. Significance inheres in the Court's recognition of and the need to protect firms from illegal and anticompetitive exploitation by the consolidated power of a joint venture. However, in the *Associated Press* case,[51] also decided under the Sherman Act, the Court supported the government's request for an injunction because a "cooperative news gathering agency of the principal newspapers of the country organized under bylaws which permit any member to impose onerous conditions on the admission to membership of competitors, thus discouraging or preventing competition" was an illegal combination in restraint of trade.[52]

While the 1912 *Terminal Railroad* and *Associate Press* decisions governed for a long period of time, the *Penn-Olin* case[53] of 1964 is much more important because it reflects the increasing use of joint ventures after 1950 and their subjection to the jurisdiction of the Celler-Kefauver amendment to the Clayton Act. The *Penn-Olin* case still provides the basic guidance for those firms contemplating joint ventures and, unlike the mergers discussed previously, such ventures are not subject to the *Merger Guidelines* of the Department of Justice.

Pennsalt Chemicals and the Olin Mathieson Chemical Corporation formed Penn-Olin in 1960 as an equally owned joint venture. Penn-Olin was built to sell sodium chlorate in the southeastern United States where neither Pennsalt nor Olin sold the product in significant amounts. Pennsalt had over 57 percent of the sales west of the Rocky Mountains with minor sales in the southeast. Olin, although not a producer of sodium chlorate, used sodium chlorate extensively in its chemical applications. The joint-venture plant costing $6,500,000 was operated by Pennsalt with all sales handled by Olin.

Prior to the joint venture, both Olin and Pennsalt had undertaken studies of the feasibility of entering the southeastern United States market. These studies prompted the Supreme Court to quote with approval the finding of the district court that "the possibility of individual entry into the southeastern market has not been completely rejected by either Pennsalt or Olin before they decided upon the joint venture." Even so, the joint venture participants held that Section 7 did not apply to joint ventures but the Supreme Court held this was not consistent with the Congressional purpose in enacting and amending Section 7. What remained was to decide whether and on what grounds the antimerger provisions applied.

Although the Court found that, as we have noted, joint ventures do have advantages, it added that they "create anticompetitive dangers." Then the Court applied the doctrine of potential competition and noted that the district court had concluded that both Pennsalt and Olin possessed the resources and the motivation to build profitable plants independently in the southeastern United States. At issue was not whether *both* companies might have entered the market but the probability that *one* might have done so. The Court then remanded the case to the district court for that court to determine the probability that one of the joint venturers would have entered the market. It was to do this, said the Court, following these guiding criteria:

the number and power of the competitors in the relevant market; the background of their growth; the power of the joint venturers; the relationship of their lines of commerce; the competition existing between them and the power of each in dealing with the competitors of the other; the setting in which the joint venture was created; the reasons and necessities for its existence; the joint venture's line of commerce and the relationship thereof to that of its parents; the adaptability of its line of commerce to noncompetitive practices; the potential power of the joint venture in the relevant market; an appraisal of what the competition in the relevant market would have been if one of the joint venturers had entered it alone instead of through Penn-Olin; in the event of this occurrence of the other joint venturer's potential competition; and such other factors as might indicate potential risk to competition in the relevant market. In weighting these factors the court should remember that the mandate of the Congress is in terms of the probability of lessening of substantial competition, not in terms of tangible restraint.

Somewhat ironically, when the district court examined the case when the Supreme Court returned it, the court found that there was no reasonable probability that either Pennsalt or Olin would have entered the market independently. When the Supreme Court reviewed this decision of the district court, the district court's disposition was affirmed, though by a divided court.[54]

Thus the conclusions about joint ventures are reasonably clear. Despite the advantages they have, they are subject to the jurisdiction of the antimerger provisions of Section 7 of the Clayton Act. The relevant criteria, extensive in scope as outlined in the *Penn-Olin* case, indicate that if challenged, proof of legitimacy is difficult though not impossible as the outcome of that case demonstrates. Moreover, as noted in the analysis of merger programs, the institution of a case against a joint venture may be the crucial decision. Guidelines do not exist to alert the marketer to probabilities that a joint venture will be challenged.

SUMMARY

If, as I have argued, the goal of the marketing organization is to respond to the perceived needs of the consumers, then marketers are faced with choosing the most effective marketing structure. Yet, as we have seen, a body of statutes governing court precedents and administrative rules and regulations has developed that conditions and restricts the marketing structures businesses may choose. Much of this growth reflects historical forces that are both economic and noneconomic. Marketers, however, must conform to those constraints or risk legal penalties that may threaten even the existence of their organizations. Changing times bring changing constraints, but at any time marketers do not have the luxury of prospective compliance; theirs is but to face immediately prevailing rules and to respond to them.

The appropriate marketing organization, wishing to attain its optimum size, first is constrained by prohibitions on monopolization or attempts to monopolize. While clarity may not characterize either the terms of the governing statutes or the court interpretations of monopolization, marketers should recognize that most interpretations are structure oriented. Benign performance resulting from growth that achieves an ambiguous level of size that might be attacked as monopoly will not excuse the firm from having grown too large in the eyes of the regulators. Second, organizational size is constrained by prohibitions on mergers and a prevailing body of legal precedents that are highly restrictive or resulting structures that do not meet with regulator's acceptance. Guidelines may change and become more favorable toward mergers, but present trends remain opaque. Judicial precedents, nevertheless, still restrict mergers significantly. Third, joint ventures, recognized by regulatory bodies to have characteristics that may be desirable economically, encounter, as do mergers, the application of structural restrictions. In short, the available methods of altering the marketing organization by routes other than internal growth, are suspect.

Business firms, contemplating the reorganization of the marketing structure by merger or joint venture or even expansion into an ancillary production line, should utilize the advisory opinion procedure of the quasi-judicial Federal Trade Commission and the business review letter procedure of the Department of Justice. These methods of obtaining information in advance of making an actual decision are limited in scope and effectiveness. There is no guarantee that an alteration of the marketing organization can be made on the basis of the marketer's autonomous analysis of the change's impact on perceived economic performance. Indications may, however, abound and whenever the marketer can do it, they should be obtained.

NOTES

1. Matthew Josephson, *The Robber Barons* (New York: Harcourt Brace Jovanovich, 1962).

2. Marketers and historians will object that other statutes such as the National Industrial Recovery Act and the Securities and Exchange Act led to major changes in the American economy. Though they are correct in their objections, a marketing analyst cannot isolate with clarity or accuracy the impact of these and similar statutes on marketing itself.

3. The United States Supreme Court's decision in *Cantor v. Detroit Edison Co.*, 428 U.S. 579 (1976) is illustrative. There the use of monopoly power in distribution of electricity, which restrained competition in the sale of light bulbs in the Detroit Edison Company market, was prohibited.

4. References to the major federal statutes and to specific sections of them can be found in this book's Appendix, Selected Excerpts from Statutes Affecting Marketing.

5. Dominick T. Armentano, *Antitrust and Monopoly: Anatomy of a Policy Failure* (New York: John Wiley & Sons, 1982), p. 42.

6. *United States v. E. C. Knight Co.*, 156 U.S. 1 (1895).

7. *Northern Securities Co. et al. v. United States*, 193 U.S. 197 (1911).

8. *Standard Oil Company of New Jersey v. United States*, 221 U.S. 1 (1911).

9. *United States v. American Tobacco Co.*, 221 U.S. 106 (1911).

10. Armentano argues effectively that in neither case did the Supreme Court undertake an economically discriminating analysis of the reasonableness of the restraints or they would not have applied Section 2 to the companies. See Dominick Armentano, *Antitrust and Monopoly: Anatomy of a Policy Failure* (New York: John Wiley & Sons, 1982), pp. 55–95.

11. *United States v. U.S. Steel Corporation*, 251 U.S. 417 (1920).

12. *United States v. Aluminum Company of America*, CA-2, 148 F 2d 416 (1945). This case was certified to the Court of Appeals for the Second Circuit because the Supreme Court lacked a qualified quorum to hear the case. The decision has the status of a Supreme Court decision.

13. Cross-elasticity measures the change in price of a supposedly competitive product. Clearly if a one-percent increase in price brings a very great increase in sales of the rival product, other things such as consumer incomes and consumer perceptions of the relative usefulness of the alternative product remaining substantially unchanged, the two products are in the same relevant market. If a one-percent change in price brings no change in quantity sold as the supposedly rival product, the products are not in the same relevant market. Actually securing these data is a monumental task not often met successfully. Nor do other things such as the overall income levels of consumers or their perceptions of the desirability of alternative products for example, remain substantially unchanged.

14. Henry Adler Einhorn and William P. Smith, eds., *Economic Aspects of Antitrust* (New York: Random House, 1968), p. 9.

15. *United States v. E. I. du Pont de Nemours & Co.*, 351 U.S. 377 (1956). This case has been the subject of extensive analysis since its filing in 1947. See George W. Stocking and Willard F. Mueller, "The Cellophane Case and the New Competition," *American Economic Review* (March 1955), pp. 31–63 or Don E. Waldman, "The duPont Cellophane Case Revisited," *The Antitrust Bulletin* (Winter 1980), pp. 805–30.

16. The Supreme Court has been faulted for its analysis of the evidence contained in the 7,500 pages of testimony and 7,000 exhibits introduced at the District Court level. For example, du Pont's ability to control its cellophane prices independent of the price movements of other flexible wrapping materials did not indicate competitive behavior. In the same way, internal profit comparisons of du Pont's cellophane division with its rayon division utilizing basically similar production, management, and accounting techniques were indicative of abnormally high profits in du Pont's cellophane division. See Stocking and Mueller cited above.

17. *United States v. United Shoe Machinery Corp.*, D.C. Mass., 110 F Supp. 295 (1953) affirmed by the Supreme Court per curiam, 347 U.S. 521 (1954). On appeal of the remedy of the lower court in this case, see *United States v. United Shoe Machinery Corp.*, 391 U.S. 244 (1968).

18. The origin of the company was adjudged legal by the Supreme Court in 1918 in *United States v. United Shoe Machinery Corp.*, 247 U.S. 32 (1918).

19. *United States v. Grinnell Corp.*, 348 U.S. 563 (1966).

20. Accredited central station service operates by sending electrical signals on a twenty-four hour basis to a manned service center, which in the event a signal indicating a fire or burglary is occurring is received, dispatches guards or other equipment to the site. Additionally, such central service stations are approved by insurance underwriters and hence users receive lower insurance rates than users of nonaccredited forms of protection.

21. The Supreme Court had, in fact, followed an analogous concept in its earlier *Philadelphia Bank* case. See *United States v. Philadelphia National Bank*, 374 U.S. 350 (1963). However, the Court developed the concept in the unique regulatory setting of national banking and did not expand it as the Court did in the Grinnell case.

22. Michael Kirk-Duggan has observed that the Court came close to adopting by inference such a "cluster" of laundry products in the government's attack

on Procter & Gamble's acquisition of Clorox as a violation of the antimerger provisions of the Celler-Kefauver Amendment to the Clayton Act. See *Federal Trade Commission v. Procter & Gamble Co.*, 356 U.S. 568 (1967).

23. Some evidence of a moderation of the judiciary's attitude toward Section 2 cases can be found in *Telex Corp. v. International Business Machines Corp.*, 510 F 2d 894 (1975) and *California Computer Products, Inc. v. International Business Machines Corp.*, CA–9, 613 F 2d 727 (1979). In addition, the *California Computer Products* case includes a review of the general doctrines underlying cases presented under Section 2 of the Sherman Act.

24. The text of these provisions is found in the Appendix.

25. Indicative of the differences are the Department of Justice Merger Guidelines released on May 30, 1968, and the Department of Justice Guidelines issued by a new political administration on June 14, 1982. The 1982 guidelines classify all mergers simply as horizontal or nonhorizontal.

26. The Department of Justice did bring sixteen antimerger cases between 1914 and 1949; the Federal Trade Commission brought thirteen cases between 1914 and 1949. The cases are noted in Michael A. Duggan, *Antitrust and the U.S. Supreme Court, 1829–1980*, 2d ed., (New York: Federal Legal Publications, 1981) and *Supplement to Antitrust and the U.S. Supreme Court, 1829–1980) including 1980– 1981 and 1981–1982 Terms* (New York: Federal Legal Publications, 1982). The importance of these cases seems to lie in their existence more than in their significance for the regulation of the legal environment of marketing.

27. *United States v. E. I. du Pont de Nemours & Co.*, 353 U.S. 586 (1957).

28. This decision, it is worth noting, was a 4–2 decision with three Supreme Court justices not participating in the consideration of the case.

29. In its review of the legislative history of the amendment of Section 7, the Supreme Court in *Brown Shoe Co. v. United States*, 370 U.S. 294 (1962), discussed the meaning it gave to the Act and indicated that "unchecked corporate expansions" detailed in the Federal Trade Commission's 1948 publication on corporate mergers motivated Congress to provide protection against the increasing "threat to other values" than economic values. The Act, as visualized by the Supreme Court, was a structuralist-oriented, not a performance-oriented law.

30. *Brown Shoe Co. v. United States*, 370 U.S. 294 (1961).

31. While the important issue for marketers is the utilization of submarkets in merger analysis, subsequent analysis of this case by John L. Peterman, "The Brown Shoe Case," *The Journal of Law and Economics* (April 1975): 81–146, demonstrates that in the category of 118 cities of 10,000 and over, when government data are adjusted to exclude wholesale sales to independent dealers, Brown's actual share at retail was insignificant. In three specific cities cited as indicative of the merger's adverse effect—Batavia, New York, Hobbs, New Mexico, and Dodge City, Kansas—Brown's actual market share at retail was zero!

32. According to the Court's decision, Kinney sold only 1.6 percent of the national shoe pairage with only 7.9 percent of Kinney's needs supplied by Brown. Hence the merger could have foreclosed only 7.9 percent of 1.6 percent of the shoe market or .001264 percent of national pairage to other manufacturers. Despite the problems these considerations raise for this case, the fact remains that this evidence did not deter this Court from finding that a "substantial

lessening" of competition might occur. Ironically, Kinney was later sold, without government objection to the national merchandising giant, Woolworth's.

33. *United States v. Continental Can Co.*, 378 U.S. 441 (1964).

34. *United States v. Aluminum Company of America*, 377 U.S. 271 (1964).

35. *Federal Trade Commission v. Consolidated Foods Corp.*, 380 U.S. 592 (1965).

36. *United States v. Von's Grocery Co.*, 384 U.S. 270 (1966).

37. For a detailed analysis, see Ray O. Werner, "The Economics of the Joint Antitrust Dissents of Harlan and Stewart, " *Washington Law Review* 48 (1973): 577–79.

38. For an analysis of the marketing economies, particularly discriminatorily lower television advertising rates, flowing from the Clorox-Procter merger, see John L. Peterman's critique, "The Clorox Case and the Television Rate Structures," *The Journal of Law and Economics*, (October 1968): 321–422.

39. *United States v. Falstaff Brewing Corp.*, 386 U.S. 568 (1973).

40. An entry by acquisition of a small industry member is known as a "toehold" (sometimes "foothold") acquisition. The Federal Trade Commission explained a "toehold" acquisition in an FTC opinion, *In the Matter of the Bud Company*, 86 FTC 518 (1975) thus: "in as highly concentrated, sluggish market, the acquisition of a small industry member by a powerful, innovative firm which, by building upon the base of the smaller firm can pose a more effective competitive challenge to the industry giants and may promote competition. Such procompetitive mergers are not only not forbidden by Section 7, they are positively encouraged." Then, in rationalizing its position, the FTC added that "the threat of a toehold merger by a powerful firm may often serve as a much greater incentive to competitive performance in the affected market than the prospect of more costly and slower internal, *de novo* expansion."

In deciding, in the *Bud* case, what was a "smaller firm," the FTC approached making a guiding rule in declaring: "We believe it to be desirable to observe a general rule in potential competition cases that firms possessing no more than 10 percent in a target market (where . . . the four-firm concentration is approximately 60 percent or more) should ordinarily be presumed to be toehold or foothold firms. The presumption by no means is conclusive, and the inference of lack of anticompetitive effects flowing from the acquisition of such a firm can be rebutted in particular cases . . . The 10 percent demarcation is supported by the prior Commission cases . . . and is not inconsistent with the Department of Justice Guidelines."

41. *Cargill, Inc. and Excel Corp. v. Monfort of Colorado, Inc.*, 90 L Ed 2d 176 (1986).

42. *Phototron Corp. v. Eastman Kodak Co., Fuqua Industries and Colorcraft Corp.*, CCH ¶67,951 (CA–5), *Trade Regulation Cases, 1988–1*, (Chicago: Commerce Clearing House, 1988).

43. It is interesting to note that had the merger guidelines been in existence at the time the *Von's Grocery* case was decided, the case would have fallen outside the prohibited limits of the guidelines and would not have been challenged. However, the guidelines do contain an exception to the general percentage guides in that markets with a trend toward concentration ("when the aggregate market share of any grouping of the largest firms in the market from the two

largest to the eight largest has increased by approximately 7% or more of the market over a period of time extending from any base year 5–10 years prior to the merger . . . up to the time of the merger").

44. The index was pioneered separately by Orris G. Herfindahl in *Concentration in the Steel Industry*, unpublished Ph.D. dissertation (New York: Columbia University, 1950), and by Albert O. Hirschman, *National Power and the Structure of Foreign Trade* (Berkeley: University of California Press, 1945).

45. Eleanor M. Fox, "The New Merger Guidelines—A Blueprint for Microeconomic Analysis," *The Antitrust Bulletin* (Fall 1982): 519–92. Additional elaboration of the HHI is found in Richard A. Miller, "The Herfindahl-Hirschman Index as a Market Structure Variable: An Exposition for Antitrust Practitioners," *The Antitrust Bulletin* (Fall 1982): 593–618.

46. The Federal Trade Commission's Premerger Notification Rules and interpretations of them are found in Commerce Clearing House, *Trade Regulation Reports*, vol. 4 (Chicago: Commerce Clearing House, 1982), pp. 42,203–42,296.

47. For details about Federal Trade Commission Advisory Opinions, see Commerce Clearing House, *Trade Regulation Reports*, vol. 3 (Chicago: Commerce Clearing House, 1984), pp. 17,515–17,517. A list of advisory opinions is contained in Commerce Clearing House, *Trade Regulation Reports*, vol. 1, section 50.

48. The Department of Justice Business Review procedure was initiated in 1968 and published in the *Code of Federal Regulations*, vol. 28, section 50.6, p. 413 and amended in *Federal Regulations*, vol. 38, 1973, pp. 34,804 and in *Federal Regulations*, vol. 42, 1977, pp. 11, 831. A review of this procedure and a digest of all the Antitrust Divisions Business Review Letters to 1982 can be found in Bureau of National Affairs, *Special Supplement*, vol. 45, no. 1124, July 21, 1983, (Washington D.C.: Bureau of National Affairs, 1983).

49. Stanley E. Boyle, "An Estimate of the Number and Size Distribution of Domestic Joint Subsidiaries," *Antitrust Law and Economics Review* (Spring 1968): 81.

50. *United States v. Terminal Railroad Association of St. Louis*, 224 U.S. 283 (1912).

51. *Associated Press v. United States*, 326 U.S. 1 (1945).

52. Michael A. Duggan, *Antitrust and the U.S. Supreme Court, 1829–1980*, 2d ed. (New York: Federal Legal Publications, 1981), pp. 51–52. Professor Duggan's compilation of Supreme Court decisions decided under the federal antitrust laws is the single most valuable reference source for relevant court decisions impinging on marketing decisions. The compilation contains extensive cross-references by topic and by specific statute. It has been supplemented through the sessions of the Supreme Court through 1982.

53. *United States v. Penn-Olin Chemical Co.*, 378 U.S. 158 (1964).

54. See *United States v. Penn-Olin Chemical Co.*, 246 F Supp. 917 (DC Del., 1965) and *United States v. Penn-Olin Chemical Co.*, 389 U.S. 308 (1967).

4

The Legal Regulation of
Marketing Operations: Pricing

Marketers, once the product line and the organizational structure is chosen, correctly consider pricing of the product to be crucial. Not only does the profit of the business firm depend upon skillful pricing but continuing acceptance of the firm is contingent upon consumer acceptance. Legal regulations that direct and constrain the autonomy of the marketer in pricing are crucial in determining the success of the firm. The marketer's knowledge of those regulations is vital.

MARKETER'S INDEPENDENCE OF PRICING ACTION

The historical independence of the firm in making pricing decisions has withered as statutory and judicial controls have expanded. The earlier consideration of the populist-progressive distaste for enterprises—feared for their largeness and leading to limitations on growth leading to monopoly, either from combinations, mergers, or joint ventures—manifested itself in specific prohibitions of pricing autonomy. The underlying rationale that "fair competition" was an underlying premise of the American system was adopted in enactment of laws and in court interpretations.

Whether or not this bias toward unilateral and "fair" pricing is, in fact, most conducive to the consumer's long-run well-being is well grounded is debatable. The awkward question facing legislators, judges, and other protectors of the public interest is whether the result of extensive pricing regulation has not led to protection of competitors rather than competition. Current controversy surrounds the question of whether the model of perfect competition was ever desirable let alone attainable.[1]

The basic consideration is, however, that the judgmental problem of whether or not greater pricing autonomy would secure greater consumer satisfaction than rigorous legal regulation achieves, is largely irrelevant. The controls of legislatures, courts, and administrative agencies are extensive, and no significant indications that the controls will be lessened to any degree of operational significance exist.

PRICE-FIXING AND THE RESTRAINT OF TRADE

The major prohibitions on pricing are contained in the laws either explicitly dealing with restraints of trade or in laws that have, by indirection, incorporated those prohibitions.

The Sherman Antitrust Act

Section 1 of the Sherman Antitrust Act of 1890 embodies the major significant provision prohibiting marketing devices and actions that result in "price-fixing." The key provisions of Section 1 declare illegal "every contract, combination in the form of trust or otherwise, or conspiracy in restraint of trade or commerce." Under the Act as amended "every person" who shall make such contract or engage in a contract or conspiracy in violation of the law is "guilty of a felony, and on conviction thereof, shall be punished by fine not exceeding one million dollars if a corporation, or, if any other person, one hundred thousand dollars, or by imprisonment not exceeding three years, or by both said punishments, in the discretion of the court."[2]

Early Interpretations of the Sherman Act Although the Sherman Antitrust Act was adopted in 1890, initially there were few restrictions imposed on pricing activities of marketers. This may reflect the intent of the Act's supporters to codify the common law under which a number of marketing practices now held to be illegal as a result of court interpretation were then considered legal. Moreover, as the Supreme Court noted in the famous *Standard Oil Company of New Jersey*[3] case, its interpretation of the Act was based on the common law as it existed prior to the passage of the Act. The Court declared:

It is certain that those terms [of Section 1 and 2 of the Sherman Act], at least in their rudimentary meaning took their origin in the common law, and were also familiar in the law of this country prior to and at the time of the adoption of the act in question.

We shall endeavor then, first to seek their meaning . . . by making a very brief reference to the elementary and indisputable conceptions of both the English and American law on the subject prior to the passage of the Antitrust Act.[4]

Since the common law judged business policies in "the light of reason," the Court refused to find many business policies in violation of the Sherman Act.[5] The enunciation and general judicial adherence to the rule of reason precedent operated to allow pricing actions that subsequently were rejected.

The Development of the Per Se Rule   The rule of reason was replaced by the general principle that practices of marketers that led to fixed prices were per se illegal when the Supreme Court handed down its famous *Trenton Potteries* decision in 1927.[6] With only a slight deviation from that rule during the Great Depression, the basic interpretation has followed the guidelines of that decision.[7]

The facts in the *Trenton Potteries* case indicated clearly that the members of the Sanitary Potteries Association had adopted practices "to fix and maintain uniform prices" for their product. The evidence was almost incontrovertible since 82 percent of the producers of the product defined as relevant agreed to maintain the agreed-upon prices. However, the association members argued that the pricing practice should have been decided at every stage of the judicial proceedings under the rule of reason they had enunciated: "The essence of the law is injury to the public. It is not every restraint of competition and not every restraint of trade that works an injury to the public; it is only an undue and unreasonable restraint of trade that has such an effect and is deemed to be unlawful."

The district court had refused to charge the jury as the association requested, but the court of appeals from which the case was appealed did accept the association's view that its statement of the rule of reason governed.

The Supreme Court embraced the per se rule holding that a restraint of trade in and of itself violates the Sherman Act. It adopted the instruction of the district court to the jury: "the law is clear that an agreement on the part of members of a combination controlling a substantial part of an industry, upon the prices which the members are to charge for their commodity, is *in itself* an undue and unreasonable restraint of trade and commerce" (emphasis added). Then the Court undertook an analysis unique in the development of the earlier price-fixing interpretations of the Sherman Act. In a lengthy but precedent-setting statement, the Court declared:

The aim of every price-fixing agreement, if effective, is the elimination of one form of competition. The power to fix prices, whether reasonably exercised or not, involves power to control the market and fix arbitrary and unreasonable prices. The reasonable price fixed today may through economic and business changes become the unreasonable price of tomorrow. Once established, it may be maintained unchanged because of the absence of competition secured by the agreement for a price reasonable when fixed. Agreements which create such potential power may well be held to be *in themselves* unreasonable or unlawful restraints without the necessity of minute inquiry whether a particular price is reasonable or unreasonable as fixed and without placing on the Government in enforcing the Sherman Law the burden of ascertaining from day to day whether it has become unreasonable through the mere variation of economic conditions. Moreover, in the absence of express legislation requiring it, we should hesitate to adopt a construction making the difference between legal and illegal conduct in the field of business relations depend upon so uncertain a test as whether prices are reasonable—a determination which can be satisfactorily made only after a complete survey of our economic organization depend on a choice between rival philosophies. [emphasis added]

Such a lengthy statement is essential to indicate not only the nature of the per se rule but to indicate the logic that has dominated judicial interpretations since that time.

The marketer is given the clear message: if an offense is found to fall under the jurisdiction of the Sherman Act, there are no redeeming characteristics. All price-fixing in restraint of trade is illegal; the courts will not inquire as to the existence of justifications nor will they accept them. There is probably no more certain and invariable guideline to guide marketers than this.

The definitive elaboration of the per se rule prohibiting price-fixing of any kind was made by Justice Douglas in 1940 in the *Socony-Vacuum* case.[8] Although the elaboration is in footnote 59 to the case, that footnote has since been quoted extensively as evidence of the extent of coverage of the Sherman Act. Justice Douglas declared: "Under the Sherman Act, a combination formed for the purpose and with the effect of raising, depressing, fixing, pegging, or stabilizing the price of a commodity in interstate or foreign commerce is illegal *per se.*"

It would be difficult to conceive of any coordinated marketing practice that leads to a common price or system of prices that is not covered by this elaboration. However, in developing the Court's rationale further, Justice Douglas explained the Court's view of what "fixing" meant: "prices are fixed . . . if the range within which purchases or sales will be made is agreed upon, if the prices paid or charged are to be at a certain level or on ascending or descending scales, if they are to be uniform, or if by various formulae they are related to the market prices. *They are fixed because they are agreed upon*" (emphasis added).

Justice Douglas noted that the law had held that the power to commit an offense was not relevant to finding a conspiracy in violation of the Sherman Act. Instead, he declared, "the amount of interstate or foreign trade is not material since [Section] 1 of the Act brands as illegal the character of the restraint not the amount of commerce affected." Consistent with this view, the Court explicitly declared that illegal price-fixing activity, "whether the concerted activity be wholly nascent or abortive . . . or successful" fell under the per se prohibition of the *Trenton Potteries* case, which it had endorsed.

Emphasis to the interpretation of the *Socony-Vacuum* case was supplied in 1951 when the Supreme Court was faced with the specific question of whether an agreement to fix maximum prices should not constitute an exception to its broad dictum. Agreements to fix maximum prices would seem to protect consumers from excesses of marketers at stages in the channels of distribution where consumer exploitation is possible. But the Supreme Court was firm and in the *Kiefer-Stewart* case held that "an agreement to fix maximum resale prices . . . no less than those to fix minimum prices" was a violation of Section 1 of the Sherman Act.[9]

The summary of the law governing price-fixing by marketers is best embodied in Justice Douglas's footnote 59. Justice Douglas declared succinctly: "Whatever economic justification particular price-fixing agreements may be thought to have, the law does not permit an inquiry into their reasonableness. They are all banned because of their actual or potential threat to the central nervous system of the economy."

No more specific warning to marketers can be given than to emphasize: *Do not even contemplate making agreements to fix prices. All such agreements are illegal.*

Elaboration of the Per Se Illegality of Price-Fixing Despite the emphatic position taken by the Supreme Court in enforcing the Sherman Act, price-fixing has remained one of the most persistent problems facing the Department of Justice, which is specifically empowered to enforce the Act.[10] Yet, either because the balancing of potential fines against the gains from fixing prices induces violations or because there is a concern to protect goodwill accruing from consumer inference of quality inherent in a well-established trade name, marketers persist in price-fixing. Marshall Howard's evaluation of the evidence on price-fixing leads to the conclusion that over the past three decades, over one-half of the cases filed by the Department of Justice have been for price-fixing.[11] As Howard also notes, in 1977 a publication of the Department of Justice characterized price-fixing in many industries as "virtually institutionalized."[12]

The unwillingness of judges to imprison offenders may accentuate the willingness of business to engage in price-fixing. Evidence is overwhelming that imprisonment has been rare, the duration of imprisonment when imposed is relatively short, and the alternative deterrent of fines unsuccessful. In recent years the Department of Justice under the impetus provided by the increased penalties provided in 1974 has secured increasingly severe penalties but so-called "creative sentencing" developed in the extensive attack on bid-rigging in interstate highway construction has somewhat weakened the potential deterrent effect of the law.[13]

Extensive controversy about the merits of allowing some price-fixing in the form of resale price maintenance contracts has existed for a number of years.[14] The controversy still exists. The basic issue revolves around the answer to the question: is competition among producers of different brands of product so effective that to allow any seller of its unique brand of product to fix the resale price will not cause a significant reduction of effective protection of the consumer against excessive prices? Clearly an affirmative answer would allow for some resale contracts allowing marketers to fix prices. The per se prohibition against them would, thereby, be abandoned. However, even the advocates of the affirmative position such as William Baxter, former Attorney General for Antitrust, who advocated it in his brief before the Supreme Court in the *Monsanto* case recognize that some abuses may occur if vertical price-fixing by manufacturers and distributors is allowed.[15] Consequently, the proposals provide that any price-fixing that marketers implement will be judged under the rule of reason.

Historical Experience with Legalized Price Maintenance   Previous analysis indicates that resale price contracts or agreements fall under the per se rule rather than the rule of reason. But an exception is the use of resale price maintenance contracts. As early as 1910 in the *Dr. Miles Medical* case, the Supreme Court declared such contracts "invalid both at common law and under the act of Congress of July 2, 1890 [the Sherman Act]."[16]

In response to the pressure of both retailers who were being undersold by chain stores whose price cutting allegedly imperiled their existence and sellers who feared the loss of goodwill resulting from cut prices allegedly weakening the product quality consumers were thought to infer from their trademarks, states adopted "fair trade" laws. However, the state fair trade laws were applicable only within the states adopting the laws. Some states also adopted the "nonsigner" clause under which every retailer was legally bound to abide by the provisions of a resale price agreement if even a single retailer signed an agreement with the manufacturer. In 1936 the Supreme Court held state resale price agreements were constitutional.[17] However, even prior to the passage of the Miller-Tydings Act, a manufacturer was required to incorporate in each state in which he wished to utilize fair trade contracts. The Supreme Court, in effect, simply legalized intrastate fair trade agreements.

Since sales in interstate commerce could not be protected adequately by state laws, Congress adopted the Miller-Tydings Act validating resale price maintenance agreements in interstate commerce.[18] In 1951, the Supreme Court held that the Miller-Tydings Act did not, however, legalize the nonsigner clause.[19] In response, Congress passed the McGuire-Keogh Act.[20] By 1941, forty-five states had passed legislation legalizing resale price maintenance agreements. The McGuire-Keogh Act was challenged in the courts of appeals, its constitutionality was sustained, and the Supreme Court denied certiorari in 1953.[21] However, in response to the growing consumer movement of the late 1960s and early 1970s and to the repeal of fair trade enabling laws by some state legislatures, Congress in 1975 passed the Consumer Goods Pricing Act.[22] This Act eliminated all resale price exemptions from the prohibitions of the Sherman Act. Convoluted history notwithstanding, vertical price-fixing by resale price maintenance agreements has returned to the same status as all other price-fixing: it is illegal per se as a violation of Section 1 of the Sherman Act.

Delivered Price Systems and the Law on Price-Fixing One of the specific devices businesses have utilized to achieve control of prices is a delivered pricing system. Delivered pricing systems, whether they be the single basing point system or the multiple basing point system, are illegal per se.

Delivered pricing systems lead to uniform prices since all the firms adhering to the system will quote identical delivered prices to any customer at any delivery point. It is irrelevant that the locations of the sellers are different or that the costs of the sellers may differ. The delivered prices are based on transportation costs by rail from the agreed-upon "base" (or multiple bases in the more complicated schemes) plus a single "base price." The most famous of the basing point systems was the "Pittsburgh Plus" system in which all steel producers, no matter where located, quoted a price for steel based on an easily accessible delivered price in Pittsburgh (where no freight charges were incurred) plus the rail freight to any location. Even if delivery utilized alternative transportation methods, the quoted price for all producers was based on equally accessible rail freight charges. In response to a challenge by the Federal Trade Commission that the single basing point delivered price system in the steel industry was an antitrust violation, the steel industry adopted a more complex delivered price system.[23]

The more complex multiple basing point system achieved uniform delivered prices by choosing several sellers as base mills. To the lowest price of any one of the several basing-point sellers, any producer would add the easily accessible rail freight charges from that base to the delivery destination. Sellers, thereby, achieved uniform prices; buyers who might secure lower prices by buying the product at the seller's point of production and shipping it themselves by alternate (cheaper) means of transportation such as truck or water, were denied legitimately lower prices. Sellers who might deviate from the uniform price system by attempting to quote a lower price when their costs plus actual transportation costs were below the base mill price were restrained by punitive pricing. Such punitive pricing, extensively used in the cement industry that also utilized multiple basing point pricing, was usually implemented and policed by the leading sellers.[24]

It was not until 1948, however, that the multiple basing point system of delivered pricing was held to violate the antitrust laws. Then it was an attack by the Federal Trade Commission under Section 5 of the Federal Trade Commission and not by the Department of Justice under the Sherman Act that led to the holding that multiple basing point pricing systems,[25] constituted illegal price-fixing under the antitrust laws.[26]

Trade Associations and Illegal Pricing   Trade associations were involved openly in the *Trenton Potteries* case and in the *Cement Institute* case as devices to implement the illegal fixing of prices. The related and broader question that inheres in these cases is whether all pricing activities of trade associations are prohibited under the Sherman Act and the Federal Trade Commission Act. Since firms that are normally marketing competitors are often members of the same association, the possibility for deliberate or inadvertent pricing conduct that violates the antitrust laws is always a dangerous possibility. Innocuous activities such as the establishment of industry advertising of the generic product or the dissemination of historical statistics do not immunize trade associations from scrutiny and prosecution by enforcement agencies for illegal activity.

Trade associations' conduct that facilitates price-fixing through the gathering and distribution of statistics have been illegal since the Supreme Court decision in *American Column and Lumber* in 1921.[27] The trade association in that case controlled one-third of the hardwood in the United States and not only gathered and distributed information on sales and prices but also published suggestions on future prices. Although the Court did not find an explicit agreement to adopt uniform prices, it inferred from the expressed goal of securing " 'harmonious' individual action," a violation of the Sherman Act.

Competition requires information for price to vary to the benefit of the consumer. Certainly trade association activities may provide such information. To the extent they do, trade associations are probably legal although legality may be unclear and capable of resolution only on a case-by-case basis. To the extent that individual competitor's identity is revealed in information disseminated and increasingly to the extent that the information supports the inference that fixing, maintaining, or stabilizing prices is invited or intended, the trade association activities are suspect. Trade association can best follow the admonition that they, like Caesar's wife, must act to be above suspicion. Marketers should participate in their industry trade associations only if caution, discretion, and openness characterize it.

Professional Associations and Pricing Regulation   Professional associations in law, medicine, engineering, accounting, and psychiatry confront legal surveillance of their pricing behavior. In an attempt ostensibly, to assure ethical practices and the protection of the public, professional associations have adopted fee schedules and other restraints. Minimum fee schedules adopted by bar associations are the clearest illustration of the practice. Fee schedules also exist widely in the medical profession and recently have gained prominence as a technique by which the goal of reducing rapidly rising medical care costs might be attained.

The application of price-fixing prohibitions to professional associations was not decided by the Supreme Court until 1975 in the *Goldfarb* case.[28] That case, however, was not initiated by the Department of Justice or the Federal Trade Commission. Instead, the Goldfarbs as private individuals instituted a class action because, in attempting to buy a home, they discovered that the title examination which was a prerequisite to obtaining necessary title insurance to secure a loan, was priced identically by twenty different lawyers. They also discovered that the minimum price quoted was never lower than the minimum fee schedule of the local bar association. Any lawyer who might have charged less than the prescribed fee risked being disciplined by the Virginia Bar Association which had been empowered by the Virginia legislature to regulate legal practice in Virginia.

The Supreme Court, in deciding in favor of the Goldfarbs and others similarly situated, held that the Sherman Act applied to professions. The mere fact that law (and presumably other similar professions) was believed to be a "profession" in which competition was not appropriate did not exempt it from the reach of the Sherman Act. Nor was the fact that the regulation was undertaken under authority from the state sufficient to exempt it from the jurisdiction of the Act.[29]

Accounting has been brought under the Sherman Act and the practice of the American Institute of Certified Public Accountants in prohibiting competitive bidding for public accounting jobs held to be illegal price-fixing.[30] Prohibitions against the American Society of Civil Engineers were imposed in 1972 for expelling members who submitted price quotations on projects. In 1978, the National Society of Professional Engineers were denied price-fixing exemption, and its contention that the rule of reason should apply would find competition itself unreasonable, was rejected.[31] In the medical profession in 1982, the Supreme Court held that maximum-fee agreements of an Arizona local medical society were per se illegal under the Sherman Act.[32] The utilization by Blue Cross and Blue Shield of a procedure under which psychologists would be reimbursed by Blue Cross and Blue Shield only if the charges were submitted through a participating physician was held to constitute an interference with the pricing mechanism and hence was illegal.[33] Finally, peer review committees of chiropractor's associations designed to implement medical cost containment procedures utilized by insurance companies were held to be prohibited by the Sherman Act.[34] In 1986, the Supreme Court in *Federal Trade Commission v. Indiana Federation of Dentists* reinforced its limitations on price tampering by professional associations—in this case a dental association—undertaken under the guise of "cost containment" activities in the public interest.[35] Following its dictum that antitrust exemptions should be "narrowly construed," the Court has now made very clear the guidelines marketers must adopt. Price-fixing by professional organizations, as by trade associations, cannot be undertaken in any form with impunity. The Court will accord the central nervous system of the economy absolute protection.

LEGAL CONTROL OF OLIGOPOLY PRICING

Closely related to the question of whether the law prevents behavior that leads to price uniformity and parallel pricing is the question of how individual firms in an oligopolistic industry operate. If individual and completely unilateral business decisions motivated by nothing more sinister than an attempt to maximize profits (or even business growth while achieving satisfactory but not maximum profits) lead to uniform prices, do the statutes, the court decisions, or the rules of administrative agencies constrain them?

Oligopoly Theory and Price Rigidity

Economists have continued the analysis of the behavior of industries in which a few firms have dominated sales (or productive capacity, shipments, or some other relevant measure of total industry activity) for well over one hundred years.[36] Professor F. M. Scherer, a foremost analyst of oligopoly behavior, has observed that "economists have developed literally dozens of oligopoly pricing theories—some simple, some marvels of mathematical complexity."[37]

The importance of oligopoly for the marketer is that under certain conditions the adoption of a common price, no matter how a noncollusive price is determined, may be in the interest of the firms in the industry. The common and most persuasive case of such a situation is an industry with very few large firms producing a homogeneous product.[38] Under such conditions, a firm that raises its price above the prevailing market price may find buyers shifting away in very large numbers if other firms do not meet the increase. If a firm lowers its price, however, it will gain a large share of its rival's market if the rivals do not respond to the price reduction. Rivals, however, aware of this potential result of a price cut, will respond. At the lower price, all rivals will share in the increase in the market demand that will result at the lower price. Significantly, however, in an industry in which costs are similar, marketing estimates of the product demand are similar, and common goals exist, this oligopoly scenario will lead to a uniform price, no matter who set the prevailing price or how it was set.

As product differentiation exists in an oligopolistic industry, prices may increasingly diverge. If product differentiation becomes great enough so that buyers can perceive no substitution of any product for another product, monopoly has come into existence giving rise to the problems of monopoly discussed earlier. To the extent that product differentiation exists but consumer perception of the significance of differences is not great, deviation of the price of one product from that of its rivals increasingly approximates the oligopolistic situation of homogeneous products. Even in those cases in which advertising and other techniques of product differentiation have been relatively successful, a structure of prices is likely to prevail. Departures from the structure may evoke pricing responses from marketers similar to those of homogeneous oligopoly.

This view that oligopolistic firms will pursue nonprice marketing strategies and adopt uniform prices has led to the conclusion that wise marketers will, without collusion, achieve price uniformity identical with that which would result if they overtly colluded. In several cases, this view has been accepted by the government enforcement agencies and has caused Lloyd Reynolds to characterize oligopoly as "the tough nut" for legal and regulatory policy to crack.[39] To the extent that the view of oligopoly outlined above characterizes an industry, to that extent the economic results are identical with those that would have resulted from a violation of Section 1 of the Sherman Act if a contract, a combination, or a conspiracy had fixed the price.

Although the Department of Justice embodied an explicit recognition in its 1984 *Merger Guidelines* revision that a few firms might approximate monopoly pricing such as might result from collusion, the view of the Department of Justice is relevant to analysis of the legal control of oligopoly pricing. The Department of Justice declared: "where only a few firms account for most of the sales of a product, those firms can in some circumstances *either explicitly or implicitly coordinate their actions in order to approximate the performance of a monopolist*" (emphasis added.)[40] The significance of this view lies in the official recognition, at least to some degree, of the theoretical view of oligopoly that accepts the results of implicitly achieved price uniformity as similar to the results of overt price-fixing. Clearly, then, the Department of Justice—and as will be seen, the Federal Trade Commission—have been unwilling to attempt to even police the pricing of oligopolies.

Judicial Interpretation of Pricing under Oligopoly

In 1920 in an attack on the United States Steel Corporation, the government charged United States Steel with violations of both Sections 1 and 2 of the Sherman Act.[41] The attack under Section 1 charged that because of its great size and its share of the steel market, United States Steel had attempted to lead rival producers to price their steel at the same levels as did U.S. Steel. But the Court did not find this identity of prices, by itself, adequate proof that Section 1 of the Sherman Act had been violated. It noted that the government had argued that imitating rivals had "ascend[ed] to opulence by imitation [United States Steel's] prices which they could not do if at a disadvantage from the other conditions of competition; and yet confederated action is not asserted by the government." The Court clearly discerned oligopolistic price uniformity motivated by the pursuit of profit in an industry producing a homogeneous product.   The Court ended its analysis by an often-quoted statement: "the law does not make mere size an offense or the existence of unexerted power an offence. It . . . requires overt acts and trust to its prohibition of them and its power to repress or punish them. It does not compel competition nor require all that is possible." With that summary, the Court effectively dismissed attacks on noncollusive oligopoly pricing as being beyond the reach of the Sherman Act.[42]

Not until 1939 did the Supreme Court again encounter, albeit obliquely, the problem of oligopoly pricing. Then an attack by the government under Section 1 of the Sherman Act again raised the issue of whether a conspiracy could be inferred from a common pricing pattern. Although the case was, in fact, strengthened by overt behavior of the alleged conspirators, the Court issued a rationale that led commentators to believe that the *Interstate Circuit* case had brought conscious parallelism of pricing action under the prohibition of the Act.[43] The Court declared: "It is elementary that an unlawful conspiracy may be and often is formed without simultaneous action or agreement on the part of the conspirators. Acceptance by competitors, without previous agreement, of an invitation to participate in a plan, the necessary consequence of which, if carried out, is restraint of interstate commerce, is sufficient to establish an unlawful conspiracy under the Sherman Act."

In 1954 governmental reliance on *Interstate Circuit* as a basis for attacking implicit oligopoly price coordination was effectively weakened, if not destroyed, in the *Theatre Enterprise* case.[44] The Court defined the crucial legal issue in declaring:

The crucial question is whether . . . pricing conduct . . . stemmed from independent decision or from an agreement, tacit or express. To be sure, business behavior is admissible circumstantial evidence from which the fact finder may infer agreement. But this Court has never held that proof of parallel business behavior itself constitutes a Sherman Act offense. Circumstantial evidence of consciously parallel behavior may have made heavy inroads into the traditional judicial attitude toward conspiracy but "conscious parallelism" has not yet read conspiracy out of the Sherman Act entirely.

With that declaration the attempts to reach the marketing practice of independently pricing a product at the same level as rivals was apparently freed from governmental prohibition.[45]

Oligopoly and FTC Attack on "Shared Monopoly" Although the Department of Justice seemingly denied a basis for blocking independent oligopoly pricing, the Federal Trade Commission, adopting the concept of "shared monopoly" popularized by consumer-activist Ralph Nader, attempted to reach oligopolistic conduct in several areas by invoking Section 5 of the Federal Trade Commission Act.[46] That section, prohibiting "unfair methods of competition in commerce, and unfair or deceptive acts or practices in or affecting commerce" had been held to cover violations of the Sherman Act that could also be prevented by the Department of Justice. The Federal Trade Commission, attempting to broaden the reach of Section 5 to block several alleged oligopolistic actions, instituted action against the cereal industry.

In the case In re Kellogg Co., the FTC contended that among the unacceptable oligopolistic practices of the cereal industry was that its members with over 80 percent of the output was the avoidance of "various forms of price competition" by using promotional activities and brand diversification as alternative forms of competition.[47] On September 1, 1981, the administrative law judge hearing the FTC case ordered its dismissal. The case then came under review by the entire commission. In a 3–1 decision (one commissioner dissenting, one commissioner "disassociating" herself from the decision) on January 15, 1982, the FTC "dismissed with prejudice" the proceeding.

The decision is instructive in its elaboration of the economic theory upon which the FTC initiated the case. It was explained by Commissioner David Clanton who noted that the FTC counsel contended "that an *implied conspiracy* to monopolize can be inferred from respondent's course of dealing over the past twenty years" (emphasis added).

Clanton, however, dismissed the shared monopoly theory declaring: "As for the separate shared monopoly theory, I do not believe such a theory, however characterized, can serve as a predicate for the Commission to restructure an industry, at least in the absence of clear predatory behavior."

Further analysis, however, added a cautionary note that marketers must mark carefully even though Section 5 has not yet reached independent but uniform pricing (or other related actions) that is nonconspiratorial. Clanton cautioned:

It is quite clear . . . that Section 5 can reach anticompetitive behavior that is not covered by the Clayton or Sherman Acts. And . . . such authority extends to noncollusive, marketwide behavior that may not involve traditional forms of predation. Presumably this could include behavior that would not be illegal for a single firm to engage in, but, due to the industry wide nature of the practice could lead to significant anticompetitive effects.

Clanton's statements seem to embody the current status of oligopoly pricing under Section 5 of the Federal Trade Commission Act. Nonconspiratorial pricing has not yet been prohibited but the possibility is still real that the practice may, at some later and unpredictable date, again be attacked. Marketers, therefore, can only conclude that single-minded and totally unilateral but conscious parallelism of pricing can be undertaken but with some risk that can be inferred from the *Interstate Circuit* case. Economic and legal challenges to such pricing continue with increasing erosion of the unwillingness to regulate such pricing behavior.[48]

PREDATORY PRICING AND ITS LEGAL CONTROL

Predatory pricing has long been one of the most difficult issues of marketing operations. In a general sense, the most elementary ideas of predation are likely to be offensive to American business persons. Predators devour others unable to defend themselves. This view, borne of the animal world, has been transferred to the world of business. Legal aversion to predatory pricing hardly surprises either laypersons or marketers.

The Concept of Predatory Pricing

Problems of definition and of proof are more elusive than developing a prohibition against predatory pricing. That problem of definition has plagued analysts of legitimate pricing behavior for years and continues as one of the knottier problems facing the enforcement agencies and the judicial systems today. The definition is crucial, however, since if marketers are to make available to the consumer lowering prices resulting from production or marketing efficiencies, then some other less efficient firms may be destroyed. For the end of economic activity is not the protection of competitors; it is the protection of a process called competition. If competition succeeds, then some firms inevitably will fail. In fact, capitalism has even been characterized as "a system of failure."[49]

Immediate impressions of pricing suggest that sales below cost are predatory if the intent is malevolent. As with most first impressions this one is faulty. Sales below cost occur frequently and without malicious intent when inventories must be liquidated during a recession in order to eliminate expensive interest costs of carrying the inventories. Similarly, product promotion, especially of new products, seems to find below-cost sales acceptable. Excess capacity with heavy sunk costs justify sales below costs if variable cost items can be more than covered so that revenues above those items can be applied to the coverage of at least part of the sunk costs. Clearly, too, developing product obsolescence seems to justify sales below costs. Consequently, a number of common marketing situations exist in which sales below cost clearly are not predatory.

Some economists have argued that predation is a nonrational exercise in "commercial folly."[50] Certainly, Robert Bork's analysis is accurate if rational behavior is assumed. Bork explains:

Predation may be defined, provisionally, as a firm's deliberate aggression against one or more rivals through the employment of business practices that would not be considered profit maximizing except for the expectation either that (1) rivals will be driven from the market, leaving the predator with a market share sufficient to command monopoly profits, or (2) rivals will be chastened sufficiently to abandon competitive behavior the predator finds inconvenient or threatening.[51]

In continuing elaboration, Bork notes the requirement for predation to be a rational business practice:

Any realistic theory of predation recognizes that the predator as well as his victims will incur losses during the fighting, but such a theory supposes it may be a rational calculation for the predator to view the losses as an investment in future monopoly profits (where rivals are to be killed) or in future undisturbed profits (where rivals are to be disciplined). The future flow of profits, appropriately discounted, must then exceed the present size of the losses. So stated, there seems nothing inherently impossible in the theory. The issue is the probability of the occurrence of predation and the means available for detecting it.[52]

Losses imposed on a predator may discourage predation especially if the intended victim finds a source of funds to enable survival. Rational lenders, noting the losses imposed on the predator, and the fact that if the victim is supported until the predator's losses signal failure, the survivor will be a viable competitor, would be willing to make funds available. As Stigler has noted, because capital is one of the most fungible and mobile of all commodities, the availability of capital to intended victims is likely to be available.[53] In addition, if the predator must experience rising unit costs as output is expanded to supply the increased market demand resulting from the lowered and predatory unit price, losses will mount. Or, if the industry (and especially the firm of the intended victim) has low unit-fixed costs, the victim can simply close the operation temporarily while the predator paves the path of its own ruin.[54]

In short, contemporary economic theory indicates that predatory pricing is not likely to be an effective marketing strategy. Despite extensive controversy about the appropriate legal rule to determine when predatory pricing occurs and therefore should be subjected to regulatory constraint, the developing rule seems to be that formulated by Phillip Areeda and Donald F. Turner.[55]

The Areeda-Turner rule is, in theory, relatively simple. Application of the rule is complicated. As Areeda and Turner formulated the rule, it provides: "Unless at or above average cost, a price below reasonably anticipated (1) short-run marginal costs or (2) average variable costs should be deemed predatory, and the monopolist may not defend on the grounds that his price was 'promotional' or merely met an equally low price of a competitor."[56]

Reference to "the monopolist" is indicative of the generally held view that attempts to utilize predatory pricing are closely linked with an attempt to attain monopoly in violation of Section 2 of the Sherman Act. It should be noted, however, that Rolland Koller's study identifies only twenty-three cases of convictions for predatory price cutting, but that Koller's analysis concluded that in only seven cases was predation actually attempted with only four successful instances.[57] The conclusion that emerges is that the usually unsound pricing practice of predation is not common, usually fails, and can, if successful, be reached under Section 2 of the Sherman Act.

The Current Status of the Law Regulating Predatory Pricing

The Areeda-Turner rule is rapidly emerging as the test of predatory pricing, but the Supreme Court has not yet issued an opinion in which it has been utilized. As a result, the most that can be said is that in the circuit courts of appeal from which such a case will eventually emerge, the rule has been used in a manner that can best be described as ambiguous. In twenty-four cases identified from 1974 to 1984, defendants were usually absolved of predatory pricing charges when the Areeda-Turner rule was applied and convicted when it was rejected.[58]

Indicative of the circuit court application of the Areeda-Turner rule is the *O. Hommel Case*.[59] That case led ultimately to the Supreme Court's denial of certiorari, thus leaving the circuit court's holding stand. However, in 1986 in the *Matsushita* case, the Supreme Court outlined the four requirements of illegality if a firm is to establish injury resulting from monopolization by predatory pricing.[60] As Kirk-Duggan has summarized them:

A plaintiff who charges attempted monopolization by predatory pricing must prove the alleged monopolist did four illegal things:

The alleged monopolist intended specifically to control prices or destroy competition in some part of interstate or foreign commerce.

The alleged monopolist directed predatory or anticompetitive conduct toward achieving monopoly.

The alleged monopolist's conduct indicated a dangerous probability of success.

The monopolist caused injury to the plaintiff because of actions which specifically violate the antitrust laws.[61]

Significance resides in the growing reliance on the Areeda-Turner rule found in the cases as they continue to evolve.

Predatory Pricing and the Marketer's Synthesis

Thus, all the difficulties of the determination of marginal cost in actual business practice and the probable need to utilize average variable cost as a surrogate for marginal cost notwithstanding, pricing below marginal cost is the guideline the marketer can adopt with the least legal danger. The serious related issue of accompanying conduct should, however, be emphasized.

Without more relevant evidence, probabilities of success against a charge of predatory pricing are grounded in careful adherence to the marginal cost standard.[62]

REGULATION OF DISCRIMINATORY PRICING

Legal regulation of pricing practices that may be considered discriminatory has been one of the burdens that plague the lives of marketers. The Robinson-Patman Act adopted in 1936 was an amendment to Section 2 of the earlier Clayton Act. Ostensibly it was created to protect relatively weak sellers from the coercive abuses associated with chain store buying during the 1930s. The Act, sometimes known derisively as the anti-chain store act, has not been clear either in its legislative language or in its judicial interpretations. The clamor for its repeal or extensive modification is, therefore, not surprising. Yet until change is effected, the law against price discrimination continues in force and marketers have no alternative but to adhere to its ambiguous provisions as best they can.

Historical Background of the Robinson-Patman Act

Lengthy studies of the Robinson-Patman Act provide much of its relevant historical background. The original version in the Clayton Act of 1914 was interpreted by the Supreme Court in the *Van Camp* case in 1929. [63] The case limited the ability of the government to reach the abuses against which the Act was directed since the substantial lessening of competition, which was the predicate to the application of the original Clayton Act, was narrowly interpreted. The decision appeared to limit the Act's usefulness in reaching apparent abuses only to the very large buyers whose inducements of price advantages had been one of the abuses the Act was designed to reach. [64] The success of the chain stores in avoiding prohibitions of the Clayton Act was great enough that in a 1934 report the Federal Trade Commission contended that because of induced discriminatory prices, chain stores had secured an approximate 15 percent advantage over smaller rivals. [65]

With the full impact of the Depression falling on small retailers, the congressional response to the perceived chain-store abuses was not surprising. Yet the protection embodied in the Robinson-Patman amendment to the Clayton Act's original Section 2 against buyers that induced price discriminations was more an afterthought than the designing of the key element of a protective provision. [66] Subsequent Court interpretations indicate the narrow protection afforded sellers abused by the inducement of discriminatory prices by powerful buyers. Moreover, as numerous critics have argued, the history of the Act suggests that it has not been used to protect competition but individual competitors who, in the crucible of capitalistic rivalry, are expected to lose when they cannot maintain their effectiveness.

Economics of Price Discrimination

The analysis of the economics of price discrimination is complicated, but it is also frequently misunderstood. A prerequisite for its successful application requires that, in F. M. Scherer's succinct phrase, "the seller . . . have some control over price—some monopoly power." [67] Implicit in this statement is the probability that price discrimination cases are likely to invoke consideration of other sections of antitrust laws such as those governing monopolization, attempts to monopolize, price-fixing, or predatory pricing.

In competitive situations, however, price discrimination tends to be ineffective. Persons being charged higher prices in one market will simply buy in the market with discriminatorily lower prices and transfer the purchases in the lower-priced market to the higher-priced market. The effect is simple: the resulting increase in the supply in the higher-priced market will force down price; the resulting increase in the demand will drive up price in the lower-priced market. This process of arbitrage will equalize prices net of transportation cost. In noncompetitive situations, the economic effects may be great and price discrimination may be effective.

THE APPLICATION OF THE ROBINSON-PATMAN ACT TO PRICING

Although economic and historical complications abound, marketers must, nevertheless, attempt to adhere to the law's prohibitions and directions. Increasingly, however, the application of the law has arisen from private civil actions for damages invoked by individuals against alleged violators of the Act. Less and less has the government through the Department of Justice or the Federal Trade Commission attempted to invoke the provisions of the Act.[60]

Prohibition on Granting Discriminatory Prices

The core of the Robinson-Patman Act is found, not in Section 2(f) prohibiting the inducement or the attempted inducement by buyers of discriminatory prices, but in Section 2(a) prohibiting the granting by sellers of discriminatory prices. The first issue that must be confronted in either case, however, is what for the purposes of the Act constitutes a "discrimination in price."

Interpretations have been extensive yet they all can be reduced to the simple proposition that a price discrimination "within the meaning of [Section 2(a)] is merely a price difference."[69] Moreover, price differences can be effected not only in the quoted price but also in a variety of ancillary marketing devices such as differences in credit terms or promotional devices.[70]

Product Coverage of the Act The prohibition of price differences applies only to "commodities of like grade and quality." This seemingly innocuous phrase provides a major difficulty for the marketer. While the Supreme Court's frequent self-congratulation for its recognition of "commercial realities" would seem to indicate no inherent difficulty, the *Borden* case of 1966 raises major questions about how well commercial realities govern.[71] In that case, the Court held that physical and chemical identity was the test of "like grade and quality"; distinctions grounded in the commercial reality of marketing techniques were held to be insufficient to distinguish commodities. That definition still holds, although in the Borden case the court of appeals held that if the price difference of two products of like grade and quality represented merely the difference of two products of like grade and quality represented merely the difference in consumer "preferences," no punishable anti-trust injury resulted.[72] The definition raises problems for the marketer pricing the identical product sold under the producer's own label and the private label of another purchaser.

Functional Levels Covered by the Act   The price differences that may be granted to one buyer but not to another buyer to drive a competitor of the price discriminator from business represents "primary line injury." This "primary line injury," is best represented by geographic price discrimination when the price discriminator seems intent on destroying a rival seller in a separate and distinct geographic location and falls clearly within the ambit of Section 2(a).

The Act has been extended to cover "secondary-line injury" when a seller lowers his price to one buyer but not to another competing buyer. In this case, the buyer not receiving the price concession will be competitively injured. In a like manner, "third line injury," which occurs at a third level in the distributional chain when customers of customers are injured because a seller three steps up the channels of distribution offers differential price concessions is a violation of Section 2(a) of the Act. Finally, "fourth line injury" (described by Earl W. Kintner as "injury suffered by a disfavored customer in his competition with a customer of a customer of the supplier's favored customer"[73]) is also prohibited by the Act.[74] Marketer's awareness of the long reach of the price discrimination prohibitions down the distributional channels must be acute. Even more important must be their recognition not only of the difficulties posed for them in policing the resale practices of distant resellers of their product but also the associated dangers of damage actions from distant buyers.

Injury to Competition as a Prerequisite to Violation   The Robinson-Patman prohibitions apply only "where the effect of such discrimination may be substantially to lessen competition or tend to create a monopoly." This language, similar to that found in other statutes examined previously, raises the question of when and under what conditions the incipient threat invokes the Act.

As with other provisions, the line of cases is long and complicated but the classic denouement developed in the interpretation in the *Utah Pie* case.[75] In that treble-damage suit brought by Utah Pie against Continental Baking and other major rivals in the Salt Lake City frozen pie market under Sections 4 and 16 of the Clayton Act, the full extent of the reach of the Clayton Act was revealed. The Court declared in its summary statement: "the Act reaches price discrimination that erodes competition as much as it does price discrimination that is intended to have immediate destructive impact." A related view was expressed in the *Anheuser-Busch* case in which the Court ruled that even if the price difference offered by a seller does not result from a discriminatory pricing pattern, and even if all the competing purchasers are charged the same price, injury to competition may be inferred.[76]

The Act and its judicial interpretations have been attacked in what Bork characterizes as "a cascade of vituperation."[77] The usual culminating acidulous remark is that the Act has been so interpreted that it is being used to "protect competitors, not competition."[78] Small solace in this exists for marketers who must recognize that price differences invite attack under the Robinson-Patman Act, if not from the government then from greedy private seekers of treble damages.

Seller's Defenses to Price Discrimination Charges

Ostensibly sellers may defend against charges of price discrimination in violation of Section 2(a) by invoking the provision that allows different prices "which make only due allowance for differences in the cost of manufacture, sale, or delivery resulting from the differing methods or quantities in which such commodities are to such purchasers sold or delivered [('cost justification')]" They may also "rebut" a prima facie case of a price difference otherwise violative of Section 2(a) by "showing that [the seller's] lower price . . . to any purchaser or purchaser was made in good faith to meet an equally low price of a competitor." These defenses, while logical and economically realistic, have proved to be more illusory than real.

Cost Justification Defense The application of cost justification as a defense requires that the discriminating seller provide conclusive proof that any classifications of customers are realistic and not intended to subvert the intent of the law. Classifications must include homogeneous groupings of buyers paying different prices, and the evidence must indicate that in each grouping the price differences do reflect general cost differences. Moreover, the Supreme Court has made it clear that it is the seller's responsibility to provide satisfactory cost justification. The Court, in a narrowing of the provision, declared: "The Robinson-Patman Act was passed *to deprive* a large buyer of [a competitive advantage over a small buyer solely because of the large buyer's quantity purchasing ability] except to the extent that a lower price could be justified by reason or a seller's *diminished costs* due to quantity manufacture, delivery or sale"[79] (emphasis added).

In developing adequate evidence of cost justification, moreover, the Supreme Court will not accept a cost justification defense that estimates average costs of selling to differing classes of customers, especially if the classes include too few firms in one or more of the classes. Likening these cost justification techniques to "averaging one horse and one rabbit," the Court called for class groupings that are "so homogeneous as to permit the joining together of these purchasers for cost allocations purposes."[80] The marketing conclusion, too often encountered in the application of this Act, is that danger lurks in the Act and little protection is afforded.

Meeting Competition Defense   The second defense of Section 2(b) would seem to be a relatively simple provision without hidden pitfalls. Such is not the case. Much of the difficulty that inheres in developing the evidence to support a cost justification defense reappears when a meeting competition defense is invoked. But there are added difficulties.

First of all, a seller "meeting an equally low price of a competitor" cannot invoke price discriminations to prevent one of its competitors from being destroyed by a rival whose prices are unlawful. The classic case involved an attempt of an oil refiner to offer price concessions to a gasoline service station marketing its gasoline and faced with destruction by a price-cutting rival service station in a price war. The Supreme Court in the *Sun Oil* case held such a price concession not offered by the refiner to all its other outlets in the marketing region was not legitimate cost-justified pricing conduct.[81]

Second, the question arises whether "meeting" an equally low price must be defensive to retain old customers or whether it may also be used to attempt to gain new customers. Although the recent Supreme Court decisions plowed little new antitrust ground, the Court's decision in the *Falls City Industries* case gave previously unavailable support to the use of meeting competition to gain new customers.[82] Said the Court: "Section 2(b) . . . does not distinguish between one who meets a competitor's lower price to retain an old customer and one who meets a competitor's lower price in an attempt to gain new customers."

Third, what constitutes "good faith" is a knotty problem in establishing a "meeting competition" defense. Generally, the line of decisions is clear that the seller must demonstrate that the legal fiction, the reasonable and prudent person, would have undertaken an effort to discover the existence of a legal price of his competitor and its general implementation.[83] Good faith, therefore, becomes a pragmatic exercise in which no adequate guidance exists for the marketer. Again the marketer is at sea in a rudderless boat.[84]

Buyer's Inducement of Discriminatory Prices

Although, as we have noted, the genesis of the Robinson-Patman Act is the desire to protect weak sellers from rapacious buyers, Section 2(f) was a weak afterthought. While the Act provides that it is illegal for a buyer "knowingly to induce or receive a discrimination in price which is prohibited by this section," the section has been used infrequently and has labored under a heavy burden of restrictive Court interpretations.[85] With relatively little use, generally the marketer needs only limited acquaintance with this provision of the Act.

The Supreme Court's decision in the *Automatic Canteen* case in 1953 seriously damaged buyers' ability to utilize the protection of Section 2(f).[86] For then the Court noted that illegally induced price concessions had to be proved, first, to be "prohibited by this section." This requirement that proof be developed that Section 2(a) prohibiting the granting of an illegally discriminatory price reduced the effectiveness of the Section 2(f) prohibition. The Court, in a succinct statement, declared "a buyer is not liable under Section 2(f) if the lower prices he induces are either within one of the seller's defenses such as the cost justification or not known by him not to be within one of those defenses." The Court agreed with Automatic Canteen also that only if the seller contended that an induced price discrimination was *not* justified and the buyer still insisted on the price concession was a violation of Section 2(f) clearly proved.

A series of cases intervened before the *Kroger* case.[87] In that case, the Federal Trade Commission dismissed the case against the seller for violating Section 2(a) but reinstituted a case against Kroger, which the administrative law judge had dismissed. Kroger was held to have violated Section 2(f) independent of a violation by the seller, Beatrice Foods, because Kroger's legitimate "hard bargaining" had misrepresented facts to the seller, which if it had known them, would have also known that the price discrimination was illegal. Yet the basic conclusion that the requirements to establish a violation of Section 2(f) are difficult to meet remains. The agency or person charging knowing inducement or receipt of a price discrimination must demonstrate not only that the buyer received price concessions that were illegal but that the buyer had a reasonable basis for believing they were illegal.[88]

Some modifications of this general rule may follow from the 1988 decision of the Court of Appeals for the District of Columbia in the *Boise Cascade Corp. v. FTC* analyzing the application of Section 2(f) of the Robinson-Patman Act.[89] Boise was alleged to have received wholesale discounts from its suppliers whether it sold the supplies at wholesale or retail. The FTC alleged that other retail buyers did not receive a favorable price equal to that Boise received from its suppliers. The Court of Appeals remanded the case to the FTC. The Commission decided 3–2 in its own earlier decision, but the Court of Appeals asked the FTC to determine if Boise Cascade's dual distribution system (operating both as a wholesaler and a retailer) injures competition through Boise's receipt of the lower price on all its purchases whether Boise resells at wholesale or at retail.

Buyer's pressure to secure price concessions and seller's acquiescence to it present difficult problems. Sellers are not, however, well protected from buyer's pressure. Whether enforcement of Section 2(f) to broaden protection of sellers from rapacious buyers (allusions to "lying buyers" to describe purchasing agents for very large buyers are frequently substituted) or to dual distributors is not likely to be forthcoming soon given the limiting language and judicial interpretations that currently characterize it.

Summary of the Legal Regulation of Price Discrimination

Marketing conclusions that follow from an examination of price discrimination and its regulation, as they follow from the examination of other pricing techniques, is that caution must be the watchword. For even though the Robinson-Patman Act may be widely damned both legally and economically, it continues to be the law of the land. The interpretations indicate that restrictions on marketing autonomy are pervasive ostensibly to protect competition and to aid the consumer. That they may fail to achieve these ends should be apparent. Bork may be correct in concluding that the law should not attempt to deal with the marketing economics inhering in price discrimination.[90] Yet the marketer must live with the law and the myriad difficulties implicit in it.

EXEMPTIONS FROM PRICE-FIXING PROSECUTION

Specific congressional enactments exempt pricing practices from the strict coverage of traditional prohibitions. Three exemptions should be explicitly recognized.

The first major exemption, grounded in the long United States history of labor-management adversarial relations, was included in the Clayton Act. Section 6 of that Act exempted from the antitrust acts labor organizations, agricultural, and horticultural organizations whose goals were the joint action of their members to improve their economic position. The National Labor Relations Act of 1935 buttressed the antitrust exemptions of labor organizations.

The second major exemption, grounded in the agricultural roots of early America, is the freedom of agricultural cooperatives under the Capper-Volstead Act of 1922 from antitrust prosecution. There are two basic requirements. First, such exempt agricultural cooperatives (surprisingly Ocean Spray Cranberries, Sunkist citrus products) must be clearly "agricultural" (producers of eggs may band together but marketers who are not also producers may not). Second, the activities of such cooperatives must not "unduly enhance" the products of authorized cooperatives.

The third major exemption provided by the Webb-Pomerene Act of 1918 authorizes American producers to form export associations that may fix prices. Price-fixing activities become illegal if the prices affect the prices of the commodities in the United States market either intentionally or artificially. Such Webb-Pomerene associations carry the potential for undetectable but very real mischief in domestic pricing, but current concern with sizeable foreign trade deficits and international competition probably militate against changes in the exemption.[91]

The conclusions about these exempt organizations and their operations do not seem difficult. Their extent is not great and their importance measured by their total volume of sales is relatively small. But for the marketer operating in one of the three fields, the general antitrust prohibitions on pricing do not apply.

UNILATERAL ACTION AND FREEDOM FROM PRICE-FIXING REGULATION

Marketers to this point may feel that they have no control over their own pricing destiny. This view is too extreme. For the United States Supreme Court as long ago as 1919 in *United States v. Colgate & Co.*, recognized that unilateral decisions to select customers and the pricing terms under which sales might be made were a marketer's right.[92] The Court expressed the view thus: "In the absence of any purpose to create or to maintain a monopoly, the act does not restrict the long recognized right of trader or manufacturer engaged in an entirely private business, *freely to exercise his own independent discretion* as to parties with whom he will deal; and, of course, he may announce *in advance* the circumstances under which he will refuse to sell" (emphasis added). This Colgate Doctrine is supported by the rhetoric of the Court in almost any case before it. Shortly thereafter an additional paragraph beginning with "But..." indicates the limited nature of this protection of the unilateral refusal to deal with firms who do not adhere to pricing programs outlined by the seller.

The issue of "unilateralness" is the crucial one. If significant evidence emerges during the preparation of a case alleging price-fixing and in which the charged party pleads the Colgate Doctrine that other dealers urged the termination of a seller not following the manufacturer's fixed prices, a conspiracy to violate Section 1 of the Sherman Act may be inferred. Certainly resale price maintenance contracts fail the test of "unilateralness." In fact, in specific situations in cases arising after *Colgate*, the Court was very rigorous in its analysis and found most cases thought to be "unilateral actions" outside the coverage of the doctrine.[93]

Recently, however, the erosion of the Colgate Doctrine has prompted attempts to give the doctrine new life. In the *Russell Stover Candies* case the Court of Appeals for the Eighth Circuit considered a final order of the Federal Trade Commission holding that Russell Stover had violated Section 1 of the Sherman Act.[94] Stover's defense was that its actions were protected under the Colgate Doctrine.

Specifically, Russell Stover designated and communicated its established resale prices for all its candies; all its retailers were aware of those prices. Prior to accepting a retailer, Stover announces that it would refuse to sell to the retailer if it "reasonably believes that a prospective retailer will resell at less than designated prices; and whenever an existing retailer has resold at less than designated prices." Stover's policy was announced, but no contracts nor even "express assurances" from prospective or existing retailers respecting resale prices are required.

The administrative law judge who first heard the Federal Trade Commission case dismissed the complaint because he found Russell Stover's actions totally unilateral. The actions, therefore, were immunized under the Colgate Doctrine. The Federal Trade Commission reversed the decision of the administrative law judge and appealed. It contended that "*Colgate* only protected a manufacturer's right to initially select its customers and not to conditioning continued dealing on announced policies." Stover argued this contention to "overturn" the Supreme Court's holding in *Colgate*. The Commission even granted to the appellate court that "its [the Commission's] interpretation of *Colgate* is not free from doubt." At issue is whether *Colgate* requires "plus factors" to bring otherwise unilateral and legal action under the prohibitions of the antitrust acts. The appellate court concluded: "If *Colgate* no longer stands for the proposition that a 'simple refusal to sell to customers who will not sell at the prices suggested by the seller is permissible under the Sherman Act' . . . it is for the Supreme Court, not this court to declare."

The Supreme Court in the related *Monsanto* case expressly accepted a previously rejected opinion of the Court of Appeals for the Seventh Circuit that "an antitrust plaintiff can survive a motion for a directed verdict if it shows that a manufacturer terminated a price-cutting distributor in response to or following complaints by other distributors.[95]

The Supreme Court expressed its interpretation of the Colgate Doctrine declaring: "Under *Colgate*, the manufacturer can announce its resale prices in advance and refuse to deal with those who fail to comply. And a distributor is free to acquiesce in the manufacturer's demand in order to avoid termination." The Court added: "If an inference [of a price-fixing agreement] may be drawn from highly ambiguous evidence, there is a considerable danger that the doctrines enunciated in *Sylvania* and *Colgate* will be seriously eroded."

If evidence is not developed that the manufacturer and nonterminated distributors are acting collusively, then the Court's view is, somewhat lengthily, summarized thus:

Permitting an agreement to be inferred merely from the existence of complaints, or even from the fact that termination came about "in response to" complaints, could deter or penalize perfectly legitimate conduct. As Monsanto points out, complaints about price-cutters "are natural—and from the manufacturer's perspective, unavoidable—reactions by distributors to the activities of their rivals." Such complaints, particularly where the manufacturer has imposed a costly set of nonprice restrictions, "arise in the normal course of business and do not indicate illegal concerted action." Moreover, distributors are an important source of information for manufacturers. In order to assure an efficient distribution system, manufacturers and distributors constantly must coordinate their activities to assure that their product will reach the consumer persuasively and efficiently. To bar a manufacturer from acting solely because the information upon which it acts originated as a price complaint would create an irrational dislocation in the market. . . . In sum, "[t]o permit the inference of concerted action on the basis of receiving complaints alone and thus expose the defendant to treble damage liability would both inhibit management's exercise of independent business judgment and emasculate the terms of the statute."

This decision of the Supreme Court operates in such a way as to create a virtual per se legality for pricing conduct that is unilateral as it seems to have been practiced in the Russell Stover case and as the requisite conditions for utilizing the Colgate Doctrine are outlined. The Court defined the correct standard in *Monsanto* thus: "there must be evidence that tends to exclude the possibility of independent action by the manufacturer and the distributor."[96]

In January 1988, the Supreme Court clarified its position on termination of a price-cutting dealer. In the *Business Electronics* case, the Court, in effect, refused to apply a per se standard in holding that an agreement of a manufacturer and a dealer to terminate another price-cutting dealer was legal if the dealer and the manufacturer did not go further and engage in a price-fixing agreement.[97] If this precedent holds, marketers may, therefore, cut off offending price-cutting dealers with some feeling of safety from legal prosecution only if they are also careful to be able to reply negatively to the question. "Will this action, if the courts see it as arising from joint action, result in significant loss of interbrand competition?" As the Supreme Court observed in the *Business Electronics* case: "interbrand competition [in contrast to intrabrand competition] is the primary concern of the antitrust laws" This, the Court also noted, followed from its 1984 decision in *Monsanto v. Spray-Rite Service Corp*, which adopted a rule of reason to a manufacturer's termination of a dealer who violated territorial restrictions imposed by the manufacturer.[98]

Justice Scalia, in his decision for the majority in the *Business Electronics* case, dismissed the danger in the agreement to terminate the price-cutting retailer. He explained:

Any assistance to cartelizing that such an agreement might provide cannot be distinguished from vertical nonprice agreements like the exclusive territory agreement in *GTE-Sylvania* and is insufficient to justify a per se rule. Cartels are neither easy to form nor easy to maintain. Uncertainty over the terms of the cartel, particularly the prices to be charged in the future, obstructs both the formation and adherence by making cheating easier. . . . Without an agreement with the remaining dealer on price, the manufacturer both retains its incentive to cheat on any manufacturer-level cartel (since lower prices can still be passed on to consumers) and cannot as easily be used to organize and hold together a retailer-level cartel.

Furthermore, in *Monsanto*, Justice Brennan explicitly noted the Court refused the Justice Department's invitation to reject the traditional rule of the 1911 precedent in the *Dr. Miles* case. Dr. Miles had held simply that all vertical price-fixing such as took place in the *Business Electronics* case was to be resolved under a per se interpretation. Nevertheless, from the ambiguities and vagueness of current legal interpretations, marketers seemingly could conclude that decisions are pointing toward a rebirth of the rule of reason in interpreting antitrust laws—the natural outgrowth of the Court's holding in the *Continental TV* case, which explicitly reversed a line of precedents embodied in the *Schwinn* decision.

The present freedom of marketers to price their products unilaterally and with noncoercive announcement that refusal to deal if adherence to those prices does not occur is ambiguous. The latest judicial rule of the Supreme Court by an 8–0 decision (though Justice Brennan's concurring opinion is quixotic) and its 1988 elaboration seem to indicate that increasing autonomy in pricing is being allowed to marketers. The entire question is so explosive, however, that continued watchfulness is demanded.

CONCLUSION

A journey through the thickets of the legal regulation of pricing can hardly be equated to a stroll in emerging springtime. Competition and the protection of the central nervous system of the economy have led to a long, involved, and evolving catalog of legislation and court elaborations of it. The evidence suggests that collusion in pricing will, as it has in the past, be a per se violation of the antitrust and the Federal Trade Commission laws. Coverage extends beyond physical commodities to cover professional associations. Oligopolistic pricing, free from collusion, seems immune to price-fixing attack despite the body of opinion that contends that such immunity is socially undesirable.

Price discrimination, burdened by a poorly written law and hampered by judicial interpretations that protect competitors but not the competition intended to assure the economic well-being of the American consumer, remains a sword of Damocles for marketers.

Exemptions free some businesses from the restraints on the crucial operational decision that pricing is. And autonomy of pricing practices, grounded in the Colgate Doctrine and recent expositions of them, are in a state of flux. Marketers, however, cannot plead ignorance either from the rules of the past or the developments of the future. Such a plea would abdicate the central marketing decision they confront.

NOTES

1. An interesting explanation and evaluation of an emerging theory of "perfect contestability" as a substitute for "perfect competition" is found in Elizabeth E. Bailey and William J. Baumol, "Deregulation and the Theory of Contestable Markets," *Yale Journal on Regulation* 1 (1984): 111–37. The development of the theory is noted in footnote 1, p. 111 of this article. Since this theory has not yet been accepted explicitly by legislators or the judicial system, further analysis of it will not be incorporated here.

2. Prior to the 1974 Antitrust Procedures and Penalties Act, 88 Stat. 1706, violations were misdemeanors with fines not exceeding $50,000 and imprisonment for one year, or both. The $50,000 fine was adopted in 1955. Prior to that time the maximum fine was $5,000.

3. *Standard Oil Company of New Jersey v. United States*, 221 U.S. 1 (1911).

4. A discussion of the background of the Sherman Act and the common law as it existed is found in Donald Dewey, *Monopoly in Economics and Law* (Chicago: Rand McNally & Company, 1959), especially Chapter X. See William Letwin, *Law and Economic Policy in America: The Evolution of the Sherman Antitrust Act* (New York: Random House, 1965).

5. An especially instructive price-fixing case under the per se interpretation is *United States v. Joint Traffic Association*, 171 U.S. 505 (1898).

6. *United States v. Trenton Potteries Co.*, 273 U.S. 392 (1927).

7. During the Great Depression the Codes of Fair Competition authorized by the National Industrial Recovery Act (NIRA), 48 Stat. 195, 1933, allowed industries to adopt techniques to fix, stabilize, and maintain prices ostensibly to alleviate chaotic conditions characterizing those industries. The NIRA was declared unconstitutional in *Schechter Poultry Corp. v. United States*, 295 U.S. 495 (1935). Another aberration was the Supreme Court's decision in *Appalachian Coals, Inc. v. United States*, 288 U.S. 344 (1933) in which the Court seemed to allow an exclusive selling agency to fix the prices for 137 member producers to achieve "reasonable prices" in an industry otherwise subject to cutthroat competition and chaos. These aberrations are, however, probably best explained by the tragic economic conditions facing the nation, which seemed to call for unconventional measures.

8. *United States v. Socony-Vacuum Oil Co.*, 310 U.S. 150 (1940).

9. *Kiefer-Stewart Co. v. Seagram & Sons, Inc. et al.*, 340 U.S. 211 (1951); rehearing denied, 340 U.S. 939 (1951).

10. Walter B. Erickson provides some explanation for the prevalence of price-fixing in "Economics of Price Fixing," *Antitrust Law & Economics Review* (Spring 1969): 85.

11. See Marshall Howard, *Antitrust and Trade Regulation: Selected Issues and Case Studies* (Englewood Cliffs, N.J.: Prentice-Hall, Inc., 1983), pp. 57–62.

12. U.S. Department of Justice, *The Investigation of White-collar Crime* (Washington, D.C.: U.S. Government Printing Office, 1977).

13. Michael A. Duggan, *United States v. Wm. Anderson Co., Inc.*, in "Legal Developments in Marketing," *Journal of Marketing* (Spring 1983): 121; and Michael A. Duggan, "Creative Probations Are Beneficial in Punishing Corporate Wrongdoers," *The Marketing News* (March 30, 1984): 6.

14. Mary Jane Sheffet and Debra L. Scammon trace the detailed history of resale price maintenance and its regulation in "Resale Price Maintenance: Is It Safe to Suggest Retail Prices?" *Journal of Marketing* 49 (Fall 1985): 82–91. They include recommendations for marketing actions under the laws and precedents through the *Monsanto* decision.

15. *Monsanto v. Spray-Rite Service Corp.*, 465 U.S. 752 (1984). Then the Department of Justice argued its view that price-fixing should be judged under a rule of reason standard (thereby reversing the Court's position that the standard should be per se) in an amicus curiae brief. However, the United States Congress, in its appropriation bill for the Department of Justice explicitly denied the Department the use of any funds to appear before the Court to argue its position.

16. *Dr. Miles Medical Co. v. John D. Park & Sons Co.*, 220 U.S. 373 (1911).

17. *Old Dearborn Distributing Co. v. Seagram Distillers Corp.*, 299 U.S. 183 (1936).

18. Miller-Tydings Resale Price Maintenance Act, 26 Stat. 209 (1937). This Act was an amendment of Section 1 of the Sherman Act exempting resale price maintenance contracts from that Act. The Act also denied the Federal Trade Commission jurisdiction to attack such contracts under Section 5 of the Federal Trade Commission Act.

19. *Schwegmann Bros. v. Calvert Distillers Corp.*, 299 U.S. 183 (1936).

20. McGuire-Keogh Act, 66 Stat. 631 (1952). This act was an amendment of Section 5 of the Federal Trade Commission Act although it was applied specifically to all federal antitrust acts.

21. *Eli Lilly & Co. v. Schwegmann Bros.*, 205 F 788 (1953); certiorari denied at 346 U.S., 856 (1953). The effect of a denial of certiorari, while not affirming the lower court decision, is to validate the lower court holding by inaction.

22. Consumer Goods Pricing Act, 89 Stat. 801 (1975). By 1979, none of the states had a fair trade law applying to intrastate sales, *Topical Law Reports: Trade Regulation Reporter*, vol. 2 (Chicago: Commerce Clearing House, 1982), pp. 9,011–12. Texas, Missouri, and Vermont never authorized fair trade contracts. Neither did the District of Columbia where Congressmen also make their purchases!

23. *In the Matter of the United States Steel Corporation et al.*, 8 FTC 1 (1924).

24. An old but detailed and definitive study of basing-point pricing is Fritz Machlup, *The Basing-point System* (Philadelphia: The Blaikston Company, 1949).

25. *Federal Trade Commission v. Cement Institute*, 333 U.S. 683, rehearing denied 334 U.S. 839 (1948). This case is instructive because it explains in detail how punitive basing-points can be utilized to discipline recalcitrant sellers and how dominant sellers utilize the system to gain supranormal profits.

26. Both single-base and multiple-base delivered pricing systems were also found to violate Section 2 of the Robinson-Patman Act discussed below. The success of an attack on the basing-point system had been foreshadowed by two Supreme Court decisions in 1945 holding that basing-point pricing systems violated the Robinson-Patman Act. The cases were *Corn Products Refining Co. v. Federal Trade Commission*, 324 U.S. 726 and *Federal Trade Commission v. Staley Mfg. Co.*, 324 U.S. 746.

27. *American Column and Lumber Co.*, 257 U.S. 377 (1921). A related decision complicated by the use of a price-fixing system to abolish unfair trade practices existing in an industry was *Sugar Institute v. United States*, 297 U.S. 553 (1936). The Court disallowed the attempt to justify the price-fixing by that trade association and held the program was a violation of the Sherman Act. A later case involving price-fixing similar to the trade activities of the Cement Institute was *Triangle Conduit & Cable Co. v. FTC*, 168 F. 2d 175 (1948), which was affirmed by an evenly divided Supreme Court under the case name of *Clayton Mark & Co. v. FTC*, 336 U.S. 956 (1949).

28. *Goldfarb et ux. v. Virginia State Bar et al.*, 421 U.S. 773 (1975).

29. The Supreme Court authorized the exemption of state action (otherwise legal regulations promulgated and actively supervised by agencies of state government) from application of the antitrust laws in *Parker v. Brown*, 317 U.S. 341 (1943).

30. *United States v. Texas State Board of Accountancy*, 592 F 2d (1979), certiorari denied, 445 U.S. 925 (1979).

31. *National Society of Professional Engineers v. United States*, 435 U.S. 679 (1978).

32. *Arizona v. Maricopa County Medical Society et al.*, 457 U.S. 465 (1978).

33. *Blue Shield of Virginia et al. v. Carol McCready*, 457 U.S. 465 (1982).

34. *Union Labor Life Insurance Company v. Alexander Pireno; New York State Chiropractic Association v. A. Alexander Pireno*, 458 U.S. 119 (1982). The Court also held that the McCarran-Ferguson Act (59 Stat. 33 [1945]) exempting the "business of insurance" from the Sherman Act did not apply in this case

35. *Federal Trade Commission v. Indiana Federation of Dentists*, 90 L Ed 2d 445 (1986).

36. The theoretical foundation is generally agreed to be in Augustin Cournot, *Researches into the Mathematical Principles of the Theory of Wealth*, N. T. Bacon, trans. (Homewood, Ill.: Irwin, 1957).

37. Probably the best summary of oligopoly theory and its nuances is found in F. M. Scherer, *Industrial Market Structure and Economic Performance*, 2d ed. (Chicago: Rand McNally College Publishing Co., 1980), chapters 5–8. Extensive bibliographical citations are found there. Briefer analyses of oligopoly as seen by lawyers are found in George C. Thompson and Gerald P. Brady, *Antitrust Fundamentals: Text, Cases and Materials*, 3rd ed (St. Paul, Minn.: West Publishing Co., 1979), pp. 61–66, and John G. Ranlett and Robert L. Curry, "Economic

Principles: The 'Monopoly,' 'Oligopoly,' and 'Competition' Models," in Michael A. Duggan, *Antitrust and the U.S. Supreme Court, 1829–1980*, 2d ed., (New York: Federal Legal Publications, 1981), pp. 353–78.

38. Product homogeneity is a tricky concept as a subsequent examination of the concept of a product of "like grade and quality" embodied in Section 2(a) of the Robinson-Patman Act will show. Suffice it to note that products may be differentiated by differences in service, credit terms, and similar devices not intrinsic to the physical composition of the product itself. For legal purposes, however, these techniques for differentiation may be considered by some courts to be irrelevant.

39. Lloyd G. Reynolds, *Economics*, 3rd ed. (Homewood, Ill.: Irwin, 1969).

40. Bureau of National Affairs *Antitrust and Trade Regulation Report*, Special Supplement 1169 (June 14, 1984): S–1.

41. *United States v. U.S. Steel Corporation*, 251 U.S. 417 (1920). This case was decided by a 4–3 vote with two justices not participating.

42. Ironically the Court also found that the attempt of U.S. Steel to fix prices had been unsuccessful.

43. *Interstate Circuit v. United States*, 306 U.S. 208 (1939).

44. *Theatre Enterprises v. Paramount Film Distributing Corp.*, 346 U.S. 537 (1954). This was a private case for treble damages under Sections 4 and 16 of the Clayton Act but was based on an alleged violation of the Sherman Act.

45. In both the *Interstate Circuit* case and the *Theatre Enterprises* case, the Court upheld a jury verdict. Thus, conscious parallelism may lead to the presumption that an offense has occurred but it is not, in and of itself, an offense. Moreover, when conscious parallelism is found, the presumption of illegal behavior that may be inferred from it may be rebutted by the accused party.

Two related cases, though technically distinguishable because of seemingly overt arrangements to exchange price information but without an agreement to adhere to the prices, are *United States v. Container Corp.*, 393 U.D. 33 (1969) and *United States v. United States Gypsum Co.*, 438 U.S. 422 (1978). Neither, however, contains the requisite elements to invoke the Sherman Act prohibition of unilaterally adopted price uniformity.

46. Mark J. Green with Beverly C. Moore, Jr., and Bruce Wasserstein, *The Closed Enterprise System* (New York: Grossman Publishers, 1972), pp. 7–9.

47. In re Kellogg Co., FTC Dkt. 883 (1972). General Mills, General Foods Corporation, and The Quaker Oats Company were also parties to this case.

48. A recent and significant attack on economic and judicial theories governing oligopoly and monopoly is Robert Bork, *The Antitrust Paradox*, (New York: Basic Books, 1978), chapter 8. Bork was later a federal judge and an unsuccessful nominee for the United States Supreme Court, but his failure to achieve confirmation reflects more clearly congressional disenchantment with his civil rights and minority group views than his economic expertise.

49. Lester Thurow, *The Zero Sum Society* (New York: Basic Books, 1980), p. 21.

50. John S. McGee, "Predatory Price Cutting: The Standard Oil (N.J.) Case," *Journal of Law and Economics* (October 1958): 137–69. See also Bork, *The Antitrust Paradox*, pp. 144–60; Kenneth Elzinga, "Predatory Pricing: The Case of The Gunpowder Trust," *Journal of Law and Economics* (April 1970): 233–40; Richard Zerbe, "The American Sugar Refining Co.," *Journal of Law and Economics* (October, 1969): 351–75.

51. Bork, *The Antitrust Paradox*, p. 144.

52. Bork, *The Antitrust Paradox*, p. 145.

53. George Stigler, "Imperfections in the Capital Market," *Journal of Political Economy* (June 1967): 287–92.

54. Bork notes that in the relevant industry ease of entry and ease of exit are likely to be symmetrical. If entry is easy and a predator drives a victim from market, abnormally high profits will lead to quick and easy entry of new firms. Bork, *The Antitrust Paradox*, p. 153.

55. Phillip Areeda and Donald F. Turner, "Predatory Pricing and Related Practices under Section Two of the Sherman Act," *Harvard Law Review* 88 (1975): 697–733. The literature on predatory pricing is extensive and usually presupposes or requires a knowledge of price theory. Some indication of the controversy is found in Paul L. Joskow and Alvin K. Klevorick, "A Framework for Analyzing Predatory Pricing Policy," *Yale Law Journal* (December 1979): 213–70; or Joel B. Dirlam, "Marginal Cost Pricing Tests for Predation: Naïve Welfare Economics and Public Policy," *The Antitrust Bulletin* (Winter 1981): 769–813; John S. McGee, "Predatory Pricing Revisited," *Journal of Law and Economics* (October 1980): 289–330; Roland Koller, "The Myth of Predatory Pricing: An Empirical Study," *Antitrust Law and Economics Review* (Summer 1971): 105–23. An interesting unpublished analysis is Polly Swartzfager, *Economic and Administrative Evaluation of the Areeda-Turner Predatory Pricing Rule*, thesis (Colorado Springs: The Colorado College, 1984).

56. Areeda and Turner, *Harvard Law Review*, 733.

57. Koller, *Antitrust Law and Economics Review*, 105.

58. Joel B. Dirlam, *The Antitrust Bulletin*, 777–79, as expanded by Swartzfager, *Economic and Administrative Evaluation of the Areeda-Turner Predatory Pricing Rule*, p. 59.

59. *O. Hommel Co. v. Ferro Corp.*, 659 F 2d 340 (1982), certiorari denied, 455 U.S 1017 (1982). The Court of Appeals for the Third Circuit cited growing reliance on the Areeda-Turner rule and cited *Janich Brothers, Inc. v. American Distilling Co.*, 570 F 2d 848 (1974), certiorari denied, 439 U.S. 829 (1978).

60. *Matsushita Electric Industrial Co., Ltd. v. Zenith Radio Corp.*, 475 U.S. 574 (1986). This case involved the application of the international law to damages alleged to have resulted from the actions of a foreign-owned multinational corporation and was decided by a 5–4 vote. The basic holding of the case that antitrust law did not apply in this case was limited in its reach and was unique to the case itself. The broader statement of the standards of predation is more important than its application in this case.

61. "Collusive Practices" in "Legal Developments in Marketing," *Journal of Marketing* 51 (Janaury 1987): 110.

62. No amount of simplification can avoid the inevitable conclusion that finally a specific case of pricing likely to evoke predatory pricing charges require consultation with both lawyer and economist. A single prefatory analysis might begin with *The Journal of Reprints for Antitrust Law and Economics: Predatory Pricing* (New York: Federal Legal Publications, 1980).

63. *George Van Camp & Sons v. American Can Co.*, 278 U.S. 245 (1929).

64. Extensive analyses of the Robinson-Patman Act including its history abound. See Corwin Edwards, *The Price Discrimination Law* (Washington, D.C.:

Brookings Institution, 1959); Earl W. Kintner, *A Robinson-Patman Act Primer* (New York: Macmillan, 1970); and Frederick M. Rowe, *Price Discrimination under the Robinson-Patman Act* (Boston: Little Brown, 1962).

65. U.S. Federal Trade Commission, *Final Report on the Chain Store Investigation* (Washington, D.C.: Government Printing Office, 1934).

66. Ray O. Werner, "The Knowing Inducement of Discriminatory Prices," *Journal of Purchasing* (May 1968): 5–16.

67. Scherer, *Industrial Market Structure and Economic Performance*, p. 315. Scherer's analysis of price discrimination in chapter 11 is encyclopedic, well documented, and definitive.

68. Scherer, *Industrial Market Structure and Economic Performance*, p. 581, notes that between 1966–1970 the FTC instituted an average of 5.6 cases yearly with a further drop in the 1970s.

69. *Federal Trade Commission v. Anheuser-Busch, Inc.*, 363 U.S. 536 (1960).

70. Indicative of how the judiciary considers indirect price inducements is a recent case (albeit involving the Sherman Act), *Catalano, Inc. v. Target Sales, Inc.*, 446 U.S. 643 (1980).

71. *Federal Trade Commission v. Borden Company*, 383 U.S. 637 (1966).

72. *Borden Company v. Federal Trade Commission*, 381 F 2d (1967).

73. Kintner, *A Robinson-Patman Primer*, p. 97.

74. *Perkins v. Standard Oil Co.*, 395 U.S. 642 (1969) created the "fourth line injury" coverage and also discussed earlier Supreme Court holdings on levels of injury covered by the Act. See also *Federal Trade Commission v. Fred Meyer, Inc.*, 390 U.S. 341 (1968) in which application of Section 2(a) to "third line injury" was established.

75. *Utah Pie Co. v. Continental Baking Co.*, 386 U.S. 568 (1968).

76. *Federal Trade Commission v. Anheuser-Busch, Inc.*, 363 U.S. 536 (1960).

77. Bork, *The Antitrust Paradox*, p. 385. Two illustrations of the bitter attack on the *Utah Pie* case are found in Ward S. Bowman, "Restraint of Trade by the Supreme Court: The Utah Pie Case," *Yale Law Journal* (November 1967): 70–85 and in Kenneth G. Elzinga and Thomas F. Hogarty, "Utah Pie and the Consequences of Robinson-Patman," *Journal of Law and Economics* (October 1978): 427–34.

78. See the unusually virulent dissent of Justices Harlan and Stewart in the *Utah Pie* case.

79. *Federal Trade Commission v. Morton Salt Co.*, 334 U.S. 34 (1948). Extensive discussion of cost categories that may be employed in developing cost justifications are found in Kintner, *A Robinson-Patman Primer*, pp. 172–77.

80. *United States v. Borden Co.*, 370 U.S. 460 (1962)

81. *Federal Trade Commission v. Sun Oil Co.*, 371 U.S. 505 (1963).

82. *Falls City Industries, Inc. v. Vanco Beverage, Inc.*, 460 U.S. 428 (1983).

83. In *Forster Mfg. Co. v. Federal Trade Commission*, 355 F 2d 47 (1964), certiorari denied 380 U.S. 906 (1965), it was held that diligence was a requisite not only in determining the existence of lower prices that were being met but the same diligence was required in ascertaining that those rival price offers were cost justified.

84. In 1978 in *United States v. United States Gypsum Company*, 438 U.S. 422, an attempt of members of a trade association allegedly for the purpose of verifying

a rival's "equally low prices" so that compliance with the Robinson-Patman Act could be assured was tolerated. However, the Supreme Court cautioned that such exchange of price information should be scrutinized very closely to avoid violation of price-fixing prohibitions of the Sherman Act.

85. See Edwards, *The Price Discrimination Law*, p. 66; and "Robinson-Patman: Dodo or Golden Rule?" *Business Week* (November 12, 1966): 72.

86. *Automatic Canteen v. Federal Trade Commission*, 346 U.S. 61 (1953).

87. *The Kroger Co. v. Federal Trade Commission*, CCH Trade Reg. Rept. 63,489 (February 1971) discussed at length in Ray O. Werner, "A New Look at the Inducement of Discriminatory Prices," *Journal of Purchasing* (August 1971): 5–10.

88. The classic case involving Section 2(f) of the Robinson-Patman Act is *Great Atlantic & Pacific Tea Co. Inc. v. Federal Trade Commission*, 440 U.S. 69 (1979), in which A&P was absolved of a violation since the Court held that there was no "duty upon a buyer to affirmatively disclose that the seller's bid has 'beaten' competition. A buyer is not liable under Section 2(f) if the seller has any affirmative defense to a charge of a 2(a) violation (such as a meeting competition defense)."

89. *Boise Cascade Corp. v. FTC*, (CA-DC, 1988) CCH ¶67,870 Trade Cases 1988–1, (Chicago: Commerce Clearing House, 1988); Bureau of National Affairs, *Antitrust and Trade Regulation Reporter*, vol. 54, no. 1351 (February 4, 1988): 155, 186, 209.

90. Bork, *The Antitrust Paradox*, p. 401. Bork's analysis of price discrimination, as is his analysis of other topics, is unusually illuminating and convincing.

91. See David A. Larson, "An Economic Analysis of the Webb-Pomerene Act," *Journal of Law and Economics* (October 1970): 461–500.

92. *United States v. Colgate & Co.*, 250 U.S. 300 (1919).

93. See *Frey & Sons, Inc. v. Cudahy Packing Co.*, 256 U.S. 208 (1921); *Federal Trade Commission v. Beech-Nut Packing Co.*, 257 U.S. 441 (1922); *United States v. Bausch & Lomb Optical Co.*, 321 U.S. 707 (1944). In this context, *Dr. Miles Medical Co. v. John D. Park & Sons Co.*, 220 U.S. 373 (1920) is historically relevant.

94. *Russell Stover Candies, Inc. v. Federal Trade Commission*, (CA–8, 1983), CCH ¶65,540, Trade Cases 1983–2, (Chicago: Commerce Clearing House, 1983).

95. *Monsanto Co. v. Spray-Rite Service Corp.*, 465 U.S. 752 (1984), Bureau of National Affairs, *Trade Regulation Reports Extra Edition No. 140* (March 21, 1984): 1–15.

96. Ironically, in applying the test it had enunciated in the *Monsanto* case, Monsanto was held to have engaged in an illegal price-fixing plan violative of Section 1 of the Sherman Act.

97. *Business Electronics Corp. v. Sharp Electronics Corp.*, 100 L Ed 2d 92 (1988); Bureau of National Affairs *Antitrust and Trade Regulation Reporter*, no. 1329 (January 21, 1988): 83; no. 1364 (May 5, 1988): 777, 797; no. 1366 (May 19, 1988): 851.

98. The uncertain status of vertical price-fixing has led the Senate Judiciary Committee to draft a Retail Competition and Enforcement Act (S. 430) codifying the per se rule for vertical price-fixing. See Bureau of National Affairs, *Antitrust and Trade Regulation Reporter* 54, no. 1351 (February 4, 1988). 156, 210–16.

5

The Legal Regulation Of Marketing Operations: Methods of Distribution

Pricing may be the most important variable for the ultimate financial success of an enterprise. Yet experienced marketers know that other operational decisions are intertwined with that of pricing. Success in marketing a product or a service may be dependent on the contractual arrangements that govern the distribution of the product or the territorial controls that may be utilized to distribute the product effectively and economically.

Some of the methods of controlling distribution are closely tied to the marketing organization. Monopolies, mergers, joint ventures, and even interlocking directorates between firms exert a major influence on the distributional techniques of the marketing division. Limitations on the organization of the marketing institution have been noted. Marketers—as well as other decision makers of a business—should never lose sight of the holistic nature of an enterprise. Coordination is the last best guarantee of the success of an enterprise in delivering products and services of high quality, low price and expanding variety to its consumers.

MAJOR LAWS REGULATING THE DISTRIBUTION OF COMMODITIES AND SERVICES

Marketers should not be surprised to learn that the three major statutes, the Sherman Act, the Clayton Act, and the Federal Trade Commission Act, are the dominant laws regulating distribution. Other acts applicable to a single industry or to a unique marketing situation such as the Automobile Dealers Franchise Act,[1] the Soft Drink Interbrand

Competition Act,[2] and even the unlikely Racketeering Influenced and Corrupt Organization Act (RICO)[3] all impact on the distributional procedures of specific industries or regulate specific practices employed in distribution. In addition, the Uniform Commercial Code, which lies outside the scope of this analysis, also exerts a significant impact on the distribution of commodities and services.

Yet the Sherman Act is the major regulatory statute controlling distributional methods. Sections 2's prohibitions on monopolizing or attempts to monopolize may be utilized to prevent marketing methods that the Department of Justice believes might prevent achievement of the goal of workable competition. Section 1, making illegal contracts, combinations, or conspiracies that might restrain trade can clearly be invoked not simply to reach price-fixing methods discussed earlier but also to reach methods that contain no pricing provisions but nevertheless "chill the vigor of competition."

The Clayton Act's convoluted restrictions on price differences considered discriminatory are augmented by Section 3, which renders unlawful a variety of marketing techniques. Section 3 provides:

That it shall be unlawful for any person engaged in commerce, in the course of such commerce, to lease or make a sale or contract for the sale of goods, wares, merchandise, machinery, supplies or other commodities, whether patented or unpatented, for use, consumption or resale . . . or fix a price charged therefore, or discount from or rebate upon, such price, on the condition, agreement or understanding that the lessee or purchaser thereof shall not deal in the goods, wares, merchandise, machinery, supplies, or other commodities of a competitor or competitors of the lessor where the effect of such lease, sale, or contract for sale or such condition, agreement or understanding may be to substantially lessen competition or tend to create a monopoly in any line of commerce.

Immediately apparent from a careful reading of this section is the omission of services from the catalog of covered activities. This difficulty can be remedied by the government whenever it wishes to reach a practice involving a service by invoking the Sherman Act since restraints of trade violative of Section 1 inevitably "lessen competition" and tend to create a monopoly and attempts to monopolize can be made congruent by a minimum of legal imagination. Hence, the omission of services from Section 3 of the Clayton Act and also from Section 2 is of no practical importance to the marketer.

Were there any question of whether distributional techniques were subject to federal regulation, the breadth of Section 5 of the Federal Trade Commission should obviate it. For since the prohibition of Section 5 on unfair or deceptive practices in or affecting commerce has been interpreted to reach other practices that violate the antitrust laws (unless the enforcement of a specific antitrust act is given exclusively to another agency), the FTC can also control distribution.

In short, in the arsenal of federal weapons, there is a plethora of devices. Analysis of the application of the regulatory devices will cause the marketer to conclude that the range of weapons is from a pea-shooter to a megaton neutron bomb. Little incipient action, well subject to the specific language of the Clayton Act and the precedents of the judiciary, can escape the potential control of the law.

REGULATION OF EXCLUSIVE DEALING AND REQUIREMENTS ARRANGEMENTS

Marketers' concerns with assuring strong outlets for their products are understandable and economically defensible. Methods of achieving this goal include exclusive dealing arrangements and the closely allied technique of requirements contracts. An exclusive dealing arrangement is an agreement, usually in contractual form, whereby a producer and a seller of the producer's good agree that the seller will not "use or deal in the goods . . . supplies, or other commodities" of a competing producer. Such an agreement necessarily has the effect of foreclosing some part of the market to rivals of the producer securing the agreement. The loss of access to a market by the contracting firm's competitors may be very small but every exclusive dealing arrangement is, to some degree, anticompetitive.

Exclusive Dealing Arrangements and the Law

Although there is a vigorous debate as to whether all exclusive dealing arrangements deserve the harsh treatment accorded them under the law, only one characteristic of such an arrangement will enable it to survive government prohibition.[4] That exculpatory characteristic is the failure of the arrangement to lessen competition "substantially." Moreover, substantiality is easily discovered by regulatory agencies. The conclusion that emerges is that exclusive dealing arrangements fare harshly under the regulatory laws.

The initial legal interpretation of Section 3 of the Clayton Act to exclusive dealing agreements came in 1922 in the *Standard Fashion* case.[5] In that case a Boston retailer agreed to sell only the fashion patterns of Standard; the retailer violated the contract; Standard attempted to enforce it. Noting that Standard and the other major producers controlled approximately 40 percent of the output in an industry with approximately 52,000 pattern agencies, the Supreme Court held that the foreclosure of the market by the exclusive dealing contract had the possibility of substantially lessening competition in violation of Section 3 of the

Clayton Act. Instructive is the fact that the Court's decision notes neither what percentage of the outlets selling fashion patterns were foreclosed to Standard's competitors by the contracts nor does it emphasize the fact that Standard's contracts were for two years.

In 1949 the Supreme Court, confronting again an exclusive dealing contract in what has become known as the "The Standard Stations Case," analyzed the question of whether a distributional method that is a defensible and normal marketing technique was exempt from Clayton Act prohibition because of redeeming virtues.[6] The exclusive dealing contract in the form of a requirements contract (under which a buyer agrees to purchase all of the covered commodity from the buyer and under which the buyer agrees, on specified contract terms, to provide all the commodity needed by the buyer) was evaluated by the Court. The Court reasoned:

Requirements contracts . . . may well be of economic advantage to buyers as well as to sellers, and thus indirectly of advantage to the consuming public. In the case of the buyer they may assure supply, afford protection against rises in price, enable long-term planning on the basis of known costs, and obviate the expense and risk of storage in the quantity necessary for a commodity having a fluctuating demand. From the seller's point of view, requirements contracts may make possible the substantial reduction of selling expenses, give protection against price fluctuations, and—of particular advantage to a newcomer to the field to whom it is important to know what capital expenditures are justified—offer the possibility of a predictable market. . . . They may be useful, moreover, to a seller trying to establish a foothold against the counterattacks of entrenched competitors.

The Court, having noted these advantages which may ultimately benefit the public, also noted that if such agreements were disallowed the outcome might well be the vertical integration of producer and outlets for selling the product. It noted that this possibility might "be a greater detriment to the public interest than the perpetuation of the system." However, Congress's determination of the appropriate policy was accepted and the Court reached its conclusion:

It cannot be gainsaid that observance by a dealer of his requirements contract . . . does effectively foreclose whatever opportunity there might be for competing suppliers to attract his patronage . . . [u]se of the contracts creates . . . a potential clog on competition as it was the purpose of Section 3 to remove wherever, were it to become actual, it would impede a substantial amount of competitive activity.

With this interpretation, however, the Supreme Court made explicit the coverage of exclusive dealing and requirements contracts under Section

3 of the Clayton Act. Yet there was a loophole in the decision that later was to become apparent. In 1953, the Federal Trade Commission case against a producer and distributor of motion picture advertisements reached the Supreme Court. In the *Motion Picture Advertising Service Company* case, the FTC attacked the producer-distributor for an exclusive dealing arrangement charging it was an "unfair method of competition" prohibited by Section 5 of the Federal Trade Commission Act.[7]

The Court agreed that Section 5, which was "designed to supplement and bolster the Sherman Act and the Clayton Act," gave the FTC jurisdiction over exclusive dealing arrangements. Some of the exclusive dealing arrangements that prompted the FTC to institute the suit ran for as long as five years. The Court accepted the FTC's delineation of its power: "a device which has sewed up a market so tightly for the benefit of a few falls within the prohibitions of the Sherman Act and is therefore an 'unfair method of competition' within the meaning of Section 5(a) of the Federal Trade Commission Act." Thus, exclusive dealing arrangements were brought within the coverage of Section 3 of the Clayton Act, Section 1 of the Sherman Antitrust Act, and Section 5 of the Federal Trade Commission Act. The only unresolved question was what appropriate remedy the FTC might recommend. It recommended not the complete dissolution of all exclusive dealing arrangements, but a limitation on their duration. The FTC recommended that such contracts be limited to one year. The Court accepted this limitation declaring:

The point where a method of competition becomes "unfair" within the meaning of the Act will often turn on the exigencies of a particular situation, trade practices, or the practical requirements of the business in question. Certainly we cannot say that exclusive contracts in this field should have been banned in their entirety or not at all, that the Commission exceeded the limits of its allowable judgment . . . in limiting their term to one year.[8]

Only one major step remained before exclusive dealing arrangements and requirements contracts were brought within a de facto rule of reason approach. The decision had already been made that a reasonable length did not constitute an indefensible clog on competition; the Court needed only hold that some measure of market foreclosure would be so small as to excuse the agreement as not lessening competition *substantially*. That situation arose in 1961 in the *Tampa Electric* case.[9]

The Tampa Electric case was a private antitrust action by Nashville Coal to void as illegal and unenforceable a twenty-year contract it had made with Tampa Electric. Under the contract Nashville was obligated to provide the coal requirements of a Tampa electric generating facility for twenty-years. The Court found the contract to be an exclusive dealing arrangement, but it defined the market widely for 100 percent of the

Florida market for the supplier rather than the customer. It outlined the considerations it considered relevant in this market:

To determine substantiality in a given case, it is necessary to weigh the probable effect of the contract on the relevant area of effective competition, taking into account the relative strength of the parties, the proportionate volume of commerce involved in relation to the total volume of commerce in the relevant market area, and the probable immediate and future effects which preemption of that share of the market might have on effective competition. . . . It follows that a mere showing that the contract itself involves a substantial number of dollars is ordinarily of little consequence.

The Court then undertook the relevant market definition and after lengthy analysis concluded that the accurate figure of market preemption that would flow from the contract "even assuming preemption to the extent of the maximum anticipated total requirements . . . would be .77 percent." The Court reached the obvious conclusion. Since the agreement "did not fall within the broader proscription of Section 3 of the Clayton Act," neither did it fall within the narrower proscriptions of Sections 1 and 2 of the Sherman Antitrust Act.

Regulation of Reciprocity and Exclusive Dealing

A technique for foreclosing markets to competitors without exclusive contracts is reciprocity. While reciprocity is usually associated with a number of related and frequently legally anticompetitive devices (a notable illustration is the conglomerate merger), its chameleon-like nature suggests that it may lead to exclusive dealing arrangements, though not necessarily in contract form.[10]

Reciprocity in its simplest form involves no more than one marketer dealing with another marketer who purchases requisite products from the initial producer. Such "you-buy-from-me-and-I'll-buy-from-you" practices are everyday occurrences. Prevention of them would probably prove totally impossible and, enforcement costliness aside, probably not desirable. If the consensual basis is merely doing "nice things" for one another, there is probably no offense. However, if the reciprocity involves the granting of discriminatory price-cutting as a technique for achieving market control, the already-examined price-discrimination law may be violated and the prohibitions of the Robinson-Patman Act brought into play. If, on the other hand, the seller who is attempting to foreclose a market to competitors by the threat to withhold purchases from a buyer unless purchases are made from it, may use coercion. Coercive reciprocity becomes under the Federal Trade Commission Act clearly illegal, and, if as in the *Consolidated Foods* case a conglomerate merger has been the motivating and implementing method of market foreclosure, a remedy as severe as divestiture may be imposed on the offender.[11]

Status of the Regulation of Exclusive Dealing Since exclusive dealing contracts, of which requirements contracts are a variant, are a considered undesirable marketing techniques by Congress, the enforcement agencies, and the judiciary, the marketer has no option but to use them only with the greatest care. The redeeming virtues of the contracts, though admitted, and the rarity of the cases in which anticompetitive conditions flowing from them are encountered do not alter this conclusion. Substantiality of market foreclosure is a prerequisite for conviction for use of exclusive dealing, but the precedent in which substantiality was absent involved a complicated Court analysis of the relevant market. Exclusive dealing and requirements contracts are, according to the Court, subjected to pragmatic testing, but as the tests have been applied, only exclusive dealing arrangements of short duration are likely to survive regulatory scrutiny. As for reciprocity, coercion will lead to its destruction as a marketing device to build and to maintain vital product outlets.

REGULATION OF TYING CONTRACTS AS A MARKETING TECHNIQUE

Tying contracts show a marked similarity to exclusive dealing contracts and, like them, are treated severely under the antitrust laws. Under some conditions, tying contracts can exert a more anticompetitive influence than exclusive dealing contracts. However, to the extent they can be utilized, they afford marketers an opportunity to facilitate the distribution of their products and services.

Requisites of a Tying Contract

A tying contract is an agreement under which a buyer agrees as a condition of purchasing one distinct commodity or service of a seller to purchase another distinct commodity or service. A requirements contract, which requires a buyer to buy an array of products (such as tires, batteries, and accessories) from a seller of another desirable product (such as an assured supply of gasoline), is one of the extended varieties of such a contract.[12]

The initial step in demonstrating the existence of a tying contract is the demonstration that two distinct products are involved. One of the products over which the seller exerts control to induce or coerce the buyer to accept a second product is the tying product. The second product, the purchase of which is induced or coerced, is the tied product. Although the Supreme Court made its first definitive ruling involving tying contracts in the *International Salt* case[13] in 1947, it did not face a major case deciding the threshold question of whether or not two products existed until the *Times-Picayune* case in 1953.[14] In that case, general and classified advertising sold in the morning paper could be purchased only if the same advertising were purchased in the evening paper; the converse was also true. The government charged the dominant position occupied in the morning market by the single paper accorded it a monopoly position forcing advertisers to take advertising lineage in the evening paper which faced a rival evening newspaper. This unit advertising contract, assured by the morning paper's monopoly, was held to violate the Sherman Act.

The analysis of the Supreme Court provided two key insights. First, the Supreme Court did not find the existence of two products requisite for a tying contract. It declared succinctly: "for the present purposes the products [national display advertising and classified advertising] are identical and the market the same." Second, the Supreme Court held that the circumstances that would support a finding that the Sherman Act was violated were more demanding than the circumstances that would support a finding that Section 3 of the Clayton Act had been violated. The absence of adequate proof that a per se illegal practice in violation of the Sherman Act was based on the Court's indication that the *Times-Picayune* did not possess "monopoly power" or "dominance" over the tying product. Yet the instructive message to marketers of the *Times-Picayune* case remains that if products are so interrelated that they are, as a matter of commercial reality, one, then no tying contract under any of the governing laws can be sustained.

A step backward to the *International Salt* case in which the question of the number of products involved was incontrovertible and in which both Section 1 of the Sherman Act and Section 3 of the Clayton Act were invoked reveals the full scope of the Court's reasoning about tying contracts. In that case, International Salt with monopolistic patent control over industrial salt dispensing machines, required both lessees or purchasers (the least frequent method of providing them to users) to purchase the salt used with the machines from itself. The added proviso in the leases and contracts of sale of the machines provided that the lessee or purchaser was free to buy salt in the open market "unless [International Salt] would furnish the salt at an equal price." This guaranteed International Salt "at all times a priority on the business at equal prices."

The Supreme Court had little difficulty in finding the requisite elements of a violation of the antitrust laws. First, the Court found that International Salt's legitimate patent on the salt dispensing machines conferred adequate power to foreclose competitors from a substantial market in salt. The evidence of the substantiality of foreclosure was the sale of 119,000 tons of salt with a value of approximately $500,000. No measure of the percentage of the market foreclosed such as was adduced in the *Tampa Electric* requirements case was mentioned by the Court. The Court's generalized conclusions declare:

Not only is price-fixing unreasonable, *per se*, but also it is unreasonable, *per se*, to foreclose competitors from any substantial market. The volume of business affected by these contracts cannot be said to be insignificant or insubstantial, and the tendency of the arrangement to accomplishment of monopoly seems obvious. Under the law . . . it is immaterial that the tendency is a creeping one rather than one that proceeds at a full gallop, nor does the law await arrival at the goal before condemning the direction of the movement.

The *International Salt* decision is instructive for it made clear to marketers that both the Sherman Act and the Clayton Act provisions could be used to reach tying contracts. Its rationale was clear: a contract that affords a seller a priority on business at prices equal to a rival (when competition would suggest some dispersion of sales) forecloses markets to rivals illegally. Moreover, in the mere "large" dollar volume of sales foreclosed, the regulatory agencies may find "substantiality" sufficient to bring the contract under the prohibition of the Clayton Act. Yet, as we have noted, in *Times-Picayune* with its failure to cross the threshold, a tying contract under Section 1 of the Sherman Act was to be adjudged under a rule of reason analysis while this case indicated that Section 3 of the Clayton Act supported a finding of illegality on lesser proof.

Any distinction between the treatment of tying cases under the Sherman Act and the Clayton Act was effectively destroyed in the *Northern Pacific Railway* case of 1958.[15] The case was brought under Section 1 of the Sherman Act since Northern Pacific was alleged to have tied "preferential routing" clauses into leases of land adjoining its railway. The routing clause required that the lessees of the land ship produce from the land over the rail lines of Northern Pacific "provided that its rates (and in some instances services) were equal to those of competing carriers." This clause clearly afforded Northern Pacific a priority on the business at equal prices. As a result, the evil of tying contracts the Court had explicated in *International Salt* was present. However, since railroad transportation and related services were not a "commodity," the Clayton Act was not applicable. Theoretically, therefore, since *Times-Picayune* had suggested that the circumstances supporting a finding of illegality of a tying contract under Section 1 were more severe than would be required under the Clayton Act, the issue appeared to be whether Northern Pacific's restrictive contract would be considered legal.

In its argument demolishing Northern Pacific's preferential routing clauses, the Supreme Court, in effect, demolished any differences under the Sherman Act and the Clayton Act. The Court declared: "[Tying agreements] are unreasonable in and of themselves whenever a party has sufficient economic power with respect to the tying product to appreciably restrain free competition in the market for the tied product and a 'not insubstantial' [*sic*] amount of interstate commerce is affected." Tying contracts were thus made illegal per se. The fact that the tying product in the precedent, *International Salt,* involved the monopoly control afforded by patents, was dismissed in the Court's declaration that "[w]e do not believe this distinction has, or should have, any significance." Marketers must remember that if they have either a patent or a copyright involved, the government needs make no further market inquiry—a definition of a product or a geographic market is not required. Because so many products are patented or copyrighted, marketers must be constantly aware of this fact.

Asserting that "competition rules the marts of trade," the Court provided a ringing statement of its requisites for finding an illegal tying contract:

While there is some language in the *Times-Picayune* opinion which speaks of "monopoly power" or "dominance" over the tying product as a necessary precondition for application of the rule of *per se* unreasonableness to tying arrangements, we do not construe this general language as requiring anything more than *sufficient economic power to impose an appreciable restraint on free competition in the tied product* (assuming . . . that a "not insubstantial" amount of interstate commerce is affected). [emphasis added]

Then the Court, rationalizing *International Salt* with *Times-Picayune* came to its final point of analysis: "the vice of tying arrangements lies in the use of economic power in one market to restrict competition on the merits in another, *regardless of the source from which the power is derived and whether the power takes the form of a monopoly or not*" (emphasis added).

Thus the evolution of the regulation of tying contracts had proceeded to the point at which tying contracts were per se illegal and at which adequate control of the tying product could be inferred from "sufficient economic power." It remained for the *Fortner* cases to demonstrate how far marketing was to be restrained by the line of decisions on tying contracts.[16]

In *Fortner I,* a real estate developer secured a loan from United States Steel to develop land upon which prefabricated homes to be purchased from United States Steel were to be erected. The loan was large, it covered the full development costs and it was at a very favorable interest rate. Fortner later in a dispute with United States Steel alleged that the prefabricated homes were both overpriced and of inferior quality. Fortner sued for treble damages alleging injury resulting from a tying contract violative of the Sherman Act.

The knotty issue was not whether a tying product—in this case alleged to be the credit extended by United States Steel—was within the coverage of the Sherman Act but whether credit could be separated from the purchase of commodities resulting from its extension. If it could not be separated, the threshold question of whether two products prerequisite for a tying contract existed was answered negatively. In such a case, as *Times-Picayune* had made clear and, as *Northern Pacific* had reinforced, the law indicated there was no tying contract.

The Supreme Court separated the extension of credit from the purchase of product to be financed by it. The Court noted that the credit extended to Fortner was not used to finance Fortner's purchases from United States Steel but rather to make Fortner's homes more attractive to Fortner's customers. It was on this basis that the Court held that two products existed. Justice Black, speaking for a 6–3 Court, argued:

There is, at the outset of every tie-in case, including the familiar cases involving physical goods, the problem of determining whether two separate products are ...involved. In the usual sale on credit the seller, a single individual or corporation, simply makes an agreement determining how much he will be paid for his product. In such a sale the credit may constitute such an inseparable part of the purchase price for the item that the entire transaction could be considered to involve only a single product.

Unfortunately the majority of the Court did not outline the criteria by which "separability" could be ascertained.

Fortner's case was predicated, however, on the contention that the credit terms given his customers were "unusually and uniquely" favorable with 100 percent financing and no down payment required. The Court, somewhat ambiguously, then explained its view: "We do not mean to accept [Fortner's] apparent argument that market power can be inferred simply because the kind of financing terms offered by a lending company are 'unique and unusual.' We do mean, however, that uniquely and unusually advantageous terms can reflect a creditor's unique economic advantage over his competitors." A footnote elaboration did little to clarify the ambiguity surrounding uniqueness from which the power to impose a burden on a buyer of the allegedly tied product arose. The Court said:

Uniqueness confers economic power only when other competitors are in some way prevented from offering the distinctive product themselves. Such barriers may be legal . . . or physical. . . . It is true that the barriers may also be economic, as when competitors are simply unable to produce the distinctive product profitably, but the uniqueness test in such situations is somewhat confusing since the real source of economic power is not the product itself but rather the seller's cost advantage in producing it.

Sensing the morass into which it was about to tumble, the Court avoided the whole issue of whether sales on credit at favorable terms were not imperiled if it declared credit a tying product. Its neat equivocation was that "[i]t will be time enough to pass on the issue of credit sales when a case involving it actually arises."

The Court did, however, find that the extension of credit was the tying product and that the prefabricated homes were tied to it. It accomplished this by noting that United States Steel was legally (if not economically) divided into a credit corporation, which in effect extended the favorable loan to Fortner's customers, and the separate corporation from which the homes were purchased.[17] The opaque language of the Court held: "Whatever the standards for determining exactly when a transaction involves only a 'single product,' we cannot see how an arrangement such as that present in this case could ever be said to involve only a single product." Having, therefore, declared that two products were involved and that credit could be a tying product, the Court remanded the case for a decision whether United States Steel, as "a big company with vast sums of money in its treasury [and that] could wield very substantial power in a credit market," possessed "economic power over the tying product."

The acidulous dissents of Justices White, Harlan, Fortas, and Stewart found this extension of tying contract regulation a distortion. Justice White emphasized:

A seller who is willing to take credit risks which no one else finds acceptable is simply engaging in the hard and risky competition which it is the policy of the Sherman Act to encourage. And if he may not do so, then those businesses and entrepreneurs who depend for their survival and growth or for the initiation of new enterprises on the availability of credit from sellers may well fail for lack of credit availability.

The full extension of the Court's opinion was made in Justice Fortas's reasoning. He observed with perceptive marketing insight:

Almost all modern selling involves providing some ancillary services in connection with making the sale—delivery, installation, supplying fixtures, servicing, training of the customer's personnel in the use of the material sold, furnishing display material and sales aids, extension of credit. Customarily—indeed almost invariably—the seller offers these ancillary services only in connection with the sale of his own products, and they are often offered without cost or at bargain rates. It is possible that in some situations, such arrangements could be used to restrain competition or might have that effect, but to condemn them out-of-hand under the "tying" rubric is, I suggest, to use the antitrust laws themselves as an instrument in restraint of competition.

These dissenting statements are indicative of the extent to which normal marketing activities have been imperiled by these interpretations of tying contract law.

It remained for *Fortner II* to extricate, but to a very limited degree, the Court from its position threatening an extensive array of normal marketing practices. *Fortner II* arose when the remanded case was resolved for Fortner by the district court and was supported by the Court of Appeals. Both those courts found that the contract between Fortner and United States Steel was a tying contract and that Fortner was, therefore, entitled to treble damages.

The Supreme Court, on appeal, reiterated its argument that credit could be a tying product, but it held that United States Steel did not possess differentiated advantages over its competitors that would provide it with unique power over credit. The Court did not find this power declaring: "Quite clearly if the evidence merely shows that credit terms are unique because the seller is willing to accept a lesser profit—or to incur greater risk—than its competitors, that kind of uniqueness will not give rise to any inference of economic power in the credit market. Yet this is, in substance, all that the record in this case indicates." This extricated the Court from the legal quagmire into which it had wandered in *Fortner I* but, unfortunately, it left marketers faced with uncertainties. Marketers cannot be certain of what products or services will be separated from a related product or service and an illegal tie-in be declared. Since a tie-in, if declared illegal in a private damage action will give rise to treble damages, the potential liability arising from innocuous and even traditional marketing practices remains.

Emergence of a New Doctrine of Tying Contracts

The survival powers of the mischievous tying contract regulations appeared to come under attack in 1984 in the *Jefferson Parish Hospital* case. [18] Although the case was decided by a 9–0 decision, the exact status of tying contracts remains unclear because of two separate opinions concurring in the outcome of the case but offering additional caveats and rationales.

The case involved the provision of anesthesiologists' services by a professional association associated with a hospital in a New Orleans parish. Because the arrangement involved services, it was filed under Section 1 of the Sherman Act. Hyde, an unassociated practitioner, charged that Jefferson Hospital had tied its services to the tied product, the services of the anesthesiologists' association. Hyde charged that this injured him in his "business or property" and therefore, as an illegal tying contract, entitled him to treble damages.

The Court's majority opinion bowed in the direction of traditional tying contract precedents, saying: "It is far too late in the history of our antitrust jurisprudence to question the proposition that certain tying arrangements pose an unacceptable risk of stifling competition and therefore are unreasonable 'per se' " The Court, in a statement presaging a new line of argument, continued:

It is clear . . . that every refusal to sell two products separately cannot be said to restrain competition. If each of the products may be purchased separately in a competitive market, one seller's decision to sell the two in a single package imposes no unreasonable restraint on either market, particularly if competing suppliers are free to sell either the entire package or its several parts.

Our cases have concluded that the essential characteristic of an invalid tying arrangement lies in the seller's exploitation of its control over the tying product to force the buyer into the purchase of a tied product that the buyer either did not want at all, or might have preferred to purchase on different terms. When such "forcing" is present, competition on the merits in the market for the tied item is restrained and the Sherman Act is violated.

Accordingly, we have condemned tying arrangements when the seller has some special ability—usually called "market power"—to force a purchaser to do something that he would not do in a competitive market.

This extensive elaboration of the doctrine of "forcing" is crucial for it inserts into the regulation of tying contracts a much-needed economic concept. This concept led the Court to add: "When the seller's power is just used to maximize its return in the tying product market where presumably its product enjoys some justifiable advantage over its competitors, the competitive ideal of the Sherman Act is not necessarily compromised." Having reached this point, the Court could not avoid the next step in its logic: "Per se condemnation—condemnation without inquiry into actual market conditions—is only appropriate if the existence of forcing is probable." In addition, the Court refused to accept "market imperfections"—the consumer's lack of price or quality consciousness or the consumer's indifference to those attributes—to represent legitimate elements of foreclosure on its merits resulting in illegitimate "forcing." The result was predictable—lacking the power to "force" the purchasers of hospital and anesthesiologists' services to purchase them separately and to the consumer's disadvantage, no illegal tying contract was found.[19]

Embedded in the concurring opinion announced by Justice O'Connor in which Justices Burger, Powell, and Rehnquist joined, is an indication that the Court's movement toward a new approach is significant. Justice O'Connor's signal of the disagreements within the present Court appeared in her suggestion for change:

The time has therefore come to abandon the "per se" label and refocus the inquiry on the adverse economic effects and potential economic benefits, that the tie-in may have. The law of tie-ins will thus be brought into accord with the law applicable to all other allegedly anticompetitive economic arrangements, except those few horizontal or quasi-horizontal restraints that can be said to have no economic justification whatsoever. This change will rationalize rather than abandon tie-in doctrine as it is already applied.

Then Justice O'Connor added: "The ultimate decision whether a tie-in is illegal under the antitrust laws should depend upon the demonstrated economic effects of the challenged agreement.... A tie-in should be condemned only when its anticompetitive impact outweighs its contributions to efficiency."[20] The test to be adduced in evaluating efficiency is the harm or benefit to the consumer. The rule of reason, openly advocated as the governing legal doctrine, and consumer sovereignty as the touchstone, may soon reappear in the regulation of tying contracts.[21]

Status of the Regulation of Tying Contracts

Marketers, faced with the evolution of the regulation of tying contracts, cannot conclude that the prevailing regulations are clear. They can be certain that the reach of the Sherman Act and the Clayton Act is long and that the exemption of services from that of the Clayton Act can be achieved with facility by application of the Sherman Act. They can be certain, too, that if an individual damage suit can demonstrate an illegal tie-in has caused damages, the full burden of treble damages (and associated court costs) will fall upon them. The fact that the existence of two separate and distinct products must be demonstrated as a prerequisite to finding a tie-in may provide little solace when the judiciary has gone so far as to separate ancillary services such as the provision of credit from the product or service secured using it. Some hope may arise from the present divided Supreme Court which seems willing to move toward a rule of reason analysis guided by consumer's needs and preferences. Yet the final devastating blow may be implicit in Justices Brennan and Marshall's concurrence in the *Jefferson Parish* case in which they note that with full knowledge of the Court's decisions, Congress, in whose hands change properly should rest, has not yet seen fit to alter prevailing doctrine.

REGULATION OF TERRITORIAL RESTRICTIONS

Implementation of territorial restrictions constitutes a method by which marketers may effectuate control of the distribution of their products. As a marketing device such restrictions may accomplish ends similar to those of exclusive dealing arrangements. Given the state of the current law governing territorial restrictions, they may be less vulnerable to regulatory harassment than other operational alternatives.

Rationale of Territorial Restrictions

Marketers, interested in maintaining a selling network that will promote and service their products efficiently and effectively, find the imposition of restrictions on the market areas of resellers an effective technique. If no rival marketer impinges on the allocated territory, effective marketing techniques by a seller can enhance the potential profits of the seller. This is especially a possible result if the product has wide name recognition, a well-established reputation for quality, and supplementary national promotion by the producer. The producer in return receives a relative assurance that the chosen reseller will service and maintain the product well, thereby protecting the producer's economically valuable goodwill.

One of the complaints of marketers against discounters as marketing outlets is the failure of those discounters to service the product after its sale. Reliance is placed on established outlets to provide the maintenance of products on which they have earned no profit and which, in fact, was lost to them because of the discounter's marketing methods. In theory, however, the consumer gains from the lower prices afforded by the marketing techniques of the discounter while experiencing no significant loss in servicing since nondiscount operations provide servicing. If those behavioral assumptions are met, then restrictions on the marketing of the product by allowing producers to adopt and enforce territorial restrictions will be anticompetitive.

The countervailing tendency that protects the consumer from the higher prices that ostensibly follow from restricting sellers to specific locations or territories is the existence of interbrand competition. It is clear that if sellers are effectively restricted to a given marketing area, then the absence of competition for the product with imposed restrictions can be expected to be higher in the controlled area than they might otherwise be. For the restricted brand, since intrabrand competition has been reduced, that tendency will exist. But if the competition from other brands (and assuming no product monopoly) is workably intense, then the consumer can expect the market price of the rival products to be driven to similar, though different by virtue of differentiation, levels.

Development of Legal Restrictions on Territorial Allocation Systems

The genesis of contemporary regulation of territorial restrictions is grounded in the *General Motors* case[22] and the *Sealy* case.[23] In the first case, Los Angeles Chevrolet dealers took action to induce General Motors to discipline (and even cancel) the dealerships of other Chevrolet dealers who were making Chevrolet automobiles available for resale by discount outlets. The government, proceeding under Section 1 of the Sherman Act, convinced the Supreme Court to declare:

It is of no consequence for purposes of determining whether there has been a combination or conspiracy under Section 1 of the Sherman Act, that each party acted in its own lawful interest. Nor is it of consequence for this purpose whether the "location clause" and franchise system are lawful or economically desirable. ... Elimination, by joint collaborative action, of discounters from access to the market is a *per se* violation of the Act.

In a similar way, the Supreme Court found that an arrangement for exclusive dealerships developed by licensees who controlled the producer who imposed the restraints was also a violation of Section 1 of the Sherman Act. In this *Sealy* case, the Court noted that the exclusive market territories that were to be judged by their substance accomplished effective and illegal price-fixing. The exclusive territories of Sealy were augmented by additional techniques (such as policing of retail prices), but all were found to constitute per se violations of the Sherman Act.

The *Topco* case decided by the Supreme Court in 1972 reaffirmed the holding that elimination of intrabrand competition of grocery products by territorial limitations, implemented by members of an association of Topco product retailers, constituted a per se violation of Section 1 of the Sherman Act.[24] The Court, cognizant of the argument that limiting intrabrand competition might intensify interbrand competition particularly with national marketers, repudiated the rule of reason analytical approach. The Court held that use of the per se approach eliminated the need to weigh "in an meaningful sense, destruction of competition in one sector of the economy against promotion of competition in another sector."

The Schwinn Per Se Rule on Territorial Restrictions   Even before the *Topco* case, however, the precedent-setting and definitive elaboration of the prohibition of territorial restrictions was developed in the *Schwinn* case.[25] Both distributors and retailers purchased products from Schwinn, which imposed territorial limitations as a condition of dealership. In its consignment or agency system, under which Schwinn retained "title, dominion, or risk with respect to the article, and where he completely retains ownership and risk of loss," the producer could legally restrict territorial outlets. But when the producer *sells* his product and "title, dominion, and risk" pass to the purchaser, any territorial or dealer restrictions by the producer violates, per se, Section 1 of the Sherman Act. In a too-little noted phrase, however, the Court added: "vertically imposed distribution restraints—*absent* price fixing and in the presence of adequate sources of alternative products to meet the needs of the unfranchised—may not be held to be *per se* violations of the Sherman Act." Thus, after *Schwinn*, the guiding rule of the judicial system effectively became that territorial and dealer restrictions imposed by a producer on seller-owned products constituted a per se violation of Section 1 of the Sherman Act.

Sylvania, the Rule of Reason, and Territorial Allocations

In 1977 the Supreme Court faced again the issue of the validity of territorial restrictions in the form of location clauses in the *Sylvania* case.[26] In that case Sylvania had included a contract clause in its franchise agreement with Continental limiting Continental's sales to a prescribed location. Continental, having purchased Sylvania television sets from Sylvania, then asked to move from its agreed-upon location in San Francisco to a new location in Sacramento after Sylvania had franchised a new San Francisco dealer near Continental. Sylvania denied this request; Continental nevertheless opened an outlet in Sacramento. Sylvania cancelled Continental's franchises. Continental filed suit against Sylvania alleging a violation of the Sherman Act's prohibition on territorial location agreements. The Court of Appeals for the Ninth Circuit held that because of distinctions between the *Schwinn* case and the *Sylvania* case the proper basis for decision was the application of the rule of reason.

Sylvania, however, argued that even if its case could not be distinguished from the *Schwinn* case, reconsideration of the *Schwinn* rule was needed. The Supreme Court agreed: "we are convinced that the need for clarification of the law in this area justifies reconsideration."

The Court in its reconsideration noted that "vertical restrictions reduce intrabrand competition by limiting the number of sellers of a particular product competing for the business of a given group of buyers." It also noted that "vertical restrictions promote interbrand competition by allowing the manufacturer to achieve certain efficiencies in the distribution of his products." Then the Court found "redeeming virtues . . . implicit in every decision sustaining vertical restrictions under the rule of reason."

Finding "economic utility" inhering in vertical restrictions, the Supreme Court faced the issue squarely. It declared:

we conclude that the per se ruled stated in *Schwinn* must be overruled. In so holding, we do not foreclose the possibility that particular applications of vertical restrictions might justify per se prohibition. . . . But we do make clear that departure from the rule-of-reason standard must be based upon demonstrable economic effect rather than—as in *Schwinn*—upon formalistic line drawing.[27] . . .

When anticompetitive effects are shown to result from particular vertical restrictions they can be adequately policed under the rule of reason, the standard traditionally applied for the majority of anticompetitive practices challenged under Section 1 of the Act.

Status of the Regulation of Territorial Allocations

Traditional guidelines now indicate to marketers that vertical territorial restrictions may be employed if analysis indicates their desirability. They are not, however, free from legal scrutiny but are subject to a weighing of economic gains and losses to competition under the rule of reason standard commonly employed in other antitrust cases. Freedom to implement such restrictions, therefore, leaves the marketer in the dilemma of having gained flexibility but at the expense of lost certainty. Marketers must recognize that increasing litigiousness characterizes our contemporary economy and challenges to territorial allocation systems can be expected even under the rule of reason. Yet, the knowledge that the per se rule of a "formalistic" nature has given way to the weighing of distributional methods will seem welcome to many marketers.

As in most situations where "there's good news and there's bad news," one overhanging and restricting consideration remains. If the use of territorial allocation systems are adopted or implemented to achieve results similar to those resulting from a price-fixing scheme illegal per se under existing precedents, those systems are candidates for early attack and demise. The intelligent use of the marketing freedom, having developed, still requires respectful acceptance of remaining restrictions.

REGULATION OF FRANCHISING AS A METHOD OF DISTRIBUTION

Franchising as a method of distribution is old and, for many years, was subject to the regulations of marketing techniques used by non-franchisers. Franchising is so pervasive today that even definition of it becomes so complex that virtually any method of distribution might be encompassed by it. Yet specific regulations that supplement those already examined necessitate some examination of them.[28]

Coverage of Franchising Regulations

Marketers who utilize franchising as a method of distribution are subject to the same legal regulations on methods of organization and operations as are individuals in other businesses. Therefore, collusive price-fixing is precluded, exclusive dealing contracts are prohibited, tying contracts are controlled. In addition, other regulations cover aspects of franchising as a method of distribution.

Franchising, as a marketing method, is not easily defined, but for the analysis of its legal environment, the definition of the Federal Trade Commission must be accepted. Even the process of drawing FTC regulations indicated how treacherous is the process of formulating generally applicable rules. When the definitions and other franchising guidelines were formulated, the hearings on the proposed FTC franchising disclosure rule lasted for thirteen days with a public record of 22,787 pages and a hearing transcript of 1,756 pages.[29] Even such extensive hearings did not soon lead to an FTC franchise rule. The regulatory Federal Trade Commission Franchise Rule did not become effective until July 21, 1979.[30]

The official language is extensive, involved, and complicated, but the relationships held to constitute a "franchise" under the Federal Trade definition embrace the following: Either of two types of continuing commercial relationships are defined as "franchises" and covered by the Rule. The first type involves three characteristics: (1) the franchisee sells goods or services that meet the franchiser's quality standards (in cases where the franchisee operates under the franchiser's trade mark, service mark, trade name, advertising or other commercial symbol designating the franchiser) or are identified by the franchiser's mark; (2) the franchiser exercises significant control over, or gives the franchisee significant assistance in, the franchisee's method of operation; and (3) the franchisee is required to make a payment of $500 or more to the franchiser or a person affiliated with the franchiser within six months after the business opens.

The second type also involves three characteristics: (1) the franchisee sells goods or services that are supplied by the franchiser; (2) the franchiser secures accounts for the franchisee, or secures locations or sites for vending machines or rack displays, or provides the services of a person able to do either; and (3) the franchisee is required to make a payment of $500 or more to the franchiser or a person affiliated with the franchiser within six months after the business opens.

Further elaboration emphasizes that the Rule covers relationships represented to be "franchises" even if some technical consideration would otherwise cause them to fall outside the definitions. Specific exclusions are "leased departmental arrangements" and "purely verbal agreements."

Required Franchise Disclosure Statements

Any franchiser covered by this Trade Regulation Rule must provide extensive information to potential franchisees about the franchise agreement. Twenty specific subjects are covered that detail the background, experience, past history involving litigation, financial arrangements, restrictions on the franchisee, ancillary services to be provided, and details on cancellation and renewal of the franchisee. In addition, the Rule details how the information about how disclosure should be made in a "Uniform Franchise Offering Circular." Finally, a detailed catalog of acts or practices that violate the rule are included.

Penalties for violation of the Rule are civil fines of $10,000 per violation. More important for the marketer proposing franchising as a method of controlling distribution is the FTC explanation of the rights of private damage actions that may arise from violations: "The Commission believes that the courts should and will hold that any person injured by a violation of the Rule has a private right of action against the violator under the Federal Trade Commission Act, as amended, and the Rule." The Federal Trade Commission has held itself forward as available for consultation on the question of compliance with the Rules and the Act. Because of the complex details required, marketers who do not avail themselves of this service are risking unnecessary and expensive delays and penalties. Subsequent behavior, after consultation, will not guarantee that no difficulties will be encountered but attempts to lessen them seem desirable.

Judicial Regulation of Franchising

Court decisions involving franchise relations, as distinct from those involving exclusive territories or tying contracts, are sparse at the Supreme Court level. One case is most often cited: the *Siegel v. Chicken Delight* case.[31] However, the most frequent bases for complaint remain the failure to disclose relevant factual information which leads to significant financial loss by the franchisee and the imposition of illegal tying agreements.

The *Chicken Delight* case was also an agreement charging an illegal tying arrangement. The evil was outlined by the Court of Appeals for the Ninth Circuit: "Chicken Delight required its franchisees to purchase a specified number of cookers and fryers and to purchase certain packaging supplies and mixes exclusively from Chicken Delight. . . . The prices fixed for these purchases were higher than, and included a percentage markup which exceeded that of, comparable products sold by competing suppliers." Chicken Delight argued vigorously that the franchise agreement and the cookers, packaging, and mixes constituted a single product and hence failed to pass the threshold requirement that tying agreements require the existence of two products. The Chicken Delight trademark was held to be indicative of the existence of a single product.

The Court of Appeals upheld the finding of the district court jury from which appeal had been taken. The unique issue addressed was whether the franchiser's need to preserve the "distinctiveness, uniformity and quality of its product" justified the tying arrangement. The court granted that protection of distinctiveness and quality were legitimate concerns but noted that "competent manufacturers of like products could consistently and satisfactorily" produce the requisite components. The tie-in, as a part of the franchise contract, foreclosed the market to other producers and hence violated Section 1 of the Sherman Act.

Since that time, as is indicated by a number of lower court decisions, franchisers have been accorded a measure of protection in specific cases. Complete elaboration is impossible; indicative is the *Baskin-Robbins* case in which a requirement that franchisees purchase all ice cream requirements from a Baskin-Robbins area franchiser was held to be legal.[32] In *New York v. Carvel* franchisees were required to buy ice cream mix from Carvel's agent with the court declaring it could find nothing to support the conclusion "that Carvel's trademark is something separate from its ice cream."[33] The Supreme Court in an appeal from a decision of the Court of Appeals for the Second Circuit refused to grant certiorari when a franchisee alleged that required purchases of ingredients and paper products from a designated supplier was illegal. In that *Mister Softee* decision, the Supreme Court found that since no damages had been established, no violation of regulatory law had occurred.[34] Apparent from the development of lower court cases is a relaxation of the rigor with which franchise abuses are found to exist.

Status of the Regulation of Franchising

Most important of the conclusions marketers may draw about the legal control of franchising is that franchiser-franchisee relations are subject to all the regulations that govern other marketing methods of distribution. Some, such as tie-in agreements, appear more frequently and certainly the constraints on action are not reduced.

The important added marketing consideration is that the Federal Trade Commission has created a bundle of requirements for the creation of a franchising network. The requirements are extensive and are designed to protect the franchisee from the abuses known to have occurred in franchising programs. Careful adherence to the regulations may be time-consuming and difficult, but the assurances they provide both parties to a franchise agreement suggest its social utility.

SUMMARY

Methods of distribution that may facilitate the marketing of products and services are, like pricing, subject to myriad controls that have evolved. Early reliance on common law rules of reason gave way to an expansion of the per se doctrines in such a way that under the Sherman, Clayton, and Federal Trade Commission Acts, tying contracts, exclusive dealing arrangements, and their allied requirements contracts were circumscribed by extensive limitations. Territorial restrictions fared badly and, governed by the same basic regulatory interpretations, franchising was controlled with rigor.

A new movement seems to be emerging giving rise to the extension of rules of reason in interpreting methods of controlling distribution. This affords marketers a flexibility and a freedom they frequently advocate but this development offers in its place uncertainty as to what courts and administrative agencies may do. It may seem somewhat incongruous to suggest in this context that "eternal vigilance is the price of liberty," but the ambiguities and uncertainties of the current regulation of distributional methods suggest its appropriateness.

NOTES

1. Automobile Dealers Franchise Act, 70 Stat. 1125 (1956).

2. Soft Drink Interbrand Competition Act, 94 Stat. 939 (1980).

3. Racketeer Influenced and Corrupt Organizations Act, 84 Stat. 941 (1970). Increasingly states are supplementing the federal law with RICO laws. See *Topical Law Reports*, vol. 5 (Chicago: Commerce Clearing House, 1982), pp. 56,055-3–56,060.

4. See Ward S. Bowman, "Tying Arrangements and the Leverage Problem," *Yale Law Journal* (November 1957): 19–36; Robert Bork, *The Antitrust Paradox* (New York: Basic Books, 1978), chapter 15.

5. *Standard Fashion Company v. Magrane-Houston Company*, 258 U.S. 346 (1922). Under the common law, tying contracts, a more virulent form of exclusive dealing, than a simple exclusive dealing contract, were analyzed legally under a rule of reason. The precedent usually cited is *Henry v. A. B. Dick Co.*, 224 U.S. 1 (1912).

6. *Standard Oil of California v. United States*, 337 U.S. 293 (1949).

7. *Federal Trade Commission v. Motion Picture Advertising Service Co.*, 344 U.S. 392 (1953).

8. In support of the Federal Trade Commission's power to fashion enforceable remedies, the Court cited *Jacob Siegel Co. v. Federal Trade Commission*, 327 U.S. 608 (1946) and *Federal Trade Commission v. Cement Institute*, 333 U.S. 683 (1948).

9. *Tampa Electric Company v. Nashville Coal Company*, 365 U.S. 320 (1961).

10. The theoretical conditions for reciprocity and a related bibliography are found in Scherer, *Industrial Market Structure and Economic Performance*, 2d ed., pp. 342–45.

11. *Federal Trade Commission v. Consolidated Foods Corp.*, 380 U.S. 592 (1965).

12. The product that the purchaser must buy may, in fact, be produced by a firm other than the one with which the contract is made. This distinction is

legally irrelevant as the Supreme Court indicated in *Federal Trade Commission v. Texaco, Inc.,* 393 U.S. 223 (1968).

13. *International Salt Company v. United States,* 332 U.S. 392 (1947).

14. *Times-Picayune Publishing Co. v. United States,* 345 U.S. 594 (1953).

15. *Northern Pacific Railway Co. v. United States,* 356 U.S. 1 (1958).

16. The first case, denominated *Fortner I,* is *Fortner Enterprises v. United States Steel,* 394 U.S. 495 (1969). The second case, *Fortner II,* is *United States Steel Corp. v. Fortner Enterprises,* 429 U.S. 610 (1977).

17. A related and unresolved issue was the extent to which separate legal entities of a single corporation should be treated legally as having a common and legitimate purpose. Some brief examination of this will be made later when the intra-enterprise conspiracy will be examined in the *Copperweld* case.

18. *Jefferson Parish Hospital District No. 2, et al. v. Edwin G. Hyde,* 466 U.S. 2 (1984).

19. Elaboration of the concept of forcing so central in the Court's analysis is M. L. Burstein, "A Theory of Full-Line Forcing," *Northwestern University Law Review* (March-April 1960): 62–95.

20. Marketers will recognize Justice O'Connor's statement as a pure and simple statement of the rule of reason rationale for antitrust decision making.

21. An interesting and only partially resolved issue is the extent to which a marketer such as an automobile manufacturer may condition the sale of its primary product (e.g., automobiles) on the requirement that the dealer buy all replacement parts from the manufacturer. In the *Mercedes-Benz* case *(Mercedes-Benz of North America, Inc. v. Metrix Warehouse Inc.,* (CA–9 828 F 2d 1033 1987), certiorari denied 100 L Ed 2d 215 (1988); Bureau of National Affairs, *Antitrust and Trade Regulation Reporter,* vol. 54, no. 1348 (January 14, 1988): 56; Bureau of National Affairs, *Antitrust and Trade Regulation Reporter,* vol. 54, no. 1366 (May 19, 1988): 85, the Supreme Court appeared to find the tying requirement illegal, but, after allowing an automobile trade association to file an *amicus curiae* brief, the Court refused to grant certiorari.

22. *United States v. General Motors Corp, et al.,* 384 U.S. 127 (1950).

23. *United States v. Sealy, Inc. et al.,* 388 U.S. 350 (1967).

24. *United States v. Topco Associates, Inc.,* 405 U.S. 596 (1972).

25. *United States v. Arnold, Schwinn & Co.,* 388 U.S. 365 (1967).

26. *Continental TV, Inc. v. GTE-Sylvania, Inc.,* 433 U.S. 36 (1977).

27. The Court's reference to "formalistic line drawing" is an indirect reference to the location of the title to the product.

28. A summary analysis of franchising is found in Shelby D. Hunt, "Franchising: Promises, Problems, Prospects," *Journal of Retailing* (Fall 1977): 71–84. A selective bibliography of high quality is appended.

29. Statement of William D. Dixon, assistant director, Rules and Guides, Bureau of Consumer Protection, Federal Trade Commission in *Franchising and Antitrust,* International Franchise Association's Sixth Annual Legal and Governmental Affairs Symposium (Washington, D.C.: International Franchise Association, 1973), p. 3.

30. The franchise rule is formally titled "Disclosure Requirements and Prohibitions Concerning Franchising and Business Opportunity Ventures," 44 *Fed-*

eral Register 31170 (May 31, 1979). An FTC summary of the rule follows the official text of the rule.

31. *Siegel v. Chicken Delight, Inc.*, 448 F 2d 43 (1971); certiorari denied, 405 U.S. 955 (1972).

32. *Kriehl v. Baskin-Robbins Ice Cream Co.*, 664 F 2d 1348 (1982).

33. *New York v. Carvel Corp.*, Case No. 42126/79, New York Supreme Court (1984) reported in *Antitrust & Trade Regulation Report* (April 12, 1984): 745.

34. *Esposito v. Mister Softee, Inc.* 465 U.S. 1026 (1984) reported in *Antitrust and Trade Regulation Report* (February 23, 1984), 287. Two additional decisions continuing the acceptance of tying contracts of franchisers are *Midwestern Waffles, Inc. v. Waffle House, Inc.*, Case No. 83–8424, CA–11 (June 18, 1984), reported in *Antitrust and Trade Regulation Report*, (June 28, 1984): 1243–44 and the *Fiske* case decided by the California Supreme Court relying on the *Jefferson Parish* case and reported in *Trade Regulation Reports Newsletter* (June 25, 1984): 3–4, in which a dietary supplement and the diet program franchise in which the supplement was used were not considered to be two separate products.

6

The Legal Regulation of Marketing Operations: Promotion and Product Characteristics

Marketers are keenly aware that a product that is optimally priced and for which the most effective methods of distribution have been chosen requires carefully chosen promotion. They know, too, that the products must inspire customer trust and that customers must be convinced that the marketer will support the product after the sale. Yet government will now allow marketers autonomy in deciding the operational questions that are associated with those decisions. Consequently, an extensive body of regulations control advertising and nonadvertising marketing techniques, product characteristics, and terms and conditions of sale. Regulators hope that these regulations will not only assure the consumer that the product quality is high, the price appropriate, and the variety safe but also that a concomitant will be the maintenance of fair and workable competition.

LAWS REGULATING PRODUCT CHARACTERISTICS AND PRODUCT PROMOTION

Analysis of the basic regulations of product characteristics and product promotion, in sharp contrast to the regulation of pricing and methods of distribution, does not emphasize the Sherman and Clayton Acts. Foremost among the regulatory techniques are the regulations developed and enforced by the Federal Trade Commission (FTC). The regulations, designed primarily to effectuate Section 5 of the Federal Trade Commission Act, are also enforced by the FTC augmented by the judicial system. In addition, there are a number of specific laws that the FTC administers that govern the marketing of specific kinds of products.

Finally, note should be made that the Food and Drug Administration is empowered to regulate the marketing of certain specific products.

Section 5 of the Federal Trade Commission Act, as it was adopted in 1914 provided simply: "[u]nfair methods of competition in commerce are hereby declared to be illegal." Section 5, in response to decisions of the judicial system, grew, when in 1938, the Wheeler-Lea Act amended Section 5 to provide: "Unfair methods of competition in commerce, and unfair or deceptive acts or practices in commerce, are hereby declared unlawful."[1] Even this modification, broad as it has proved to be, did not regulate as extensively as the FTC and Congress wished. As a consequence, in 1975, Section 5 was again amended by replacing the phrase, "in commerce," with the phrase, "in or affecting commerce" thus enabling the FTC to reach practices at the local level formerly beyond the jurisdiction of the FTC.[2]

Implementation of Section 5 has been augmented by allowing the Federal Trade Commission to develop Trade Regulation Rules. These Rules, as indicated in the examination of the franchising rule, are codifications of a number of decisions relating to a specific marketing practice or to a specific commodity. They become, thereby, the "law" of a quasi-judicial administrative agency as binding operationally as if they had been enacted by Congress itself.[3] Moreover, the number of such regulations and the authorizing statutes have grown sharply since the end of World War II.[4]

The more significant statutes enforced by the Federal Trade Commission are found in the Appendix. Specific examination of some of them will be necessary, but the list includes the Magnuson-Moss Warranty Act of 1975, the Fair Packaging and Labeling Act of 1966, the Wool Products Labeling Act of 1939, the Fur Products Labeling Act of 1951, the Flammable Fabrics Act of 1953, the Textile Fiber Products Identification Act of 1958, the Lanham Trade Mark of 1946, and four statutes governing the provision of credit to consumers.[5] The Webb-Pomerene Act is also enforced by the Federal Trade Commission. The Food and Drug Administration enforces the Pure Food Act of 1906 and the Federal Food, Drug and Cosmetic Act of 1938. However, the regulation of advertising of drugs and cosmetics is granted to the Federal Trade Commission.

Related to the question of marketing and advertising is the question of the liability of producers and sellers of products to consumers and to other producers and sellers who might be injured competitively. Product liability has grown until legal actions involving questions of its existence and, if found to exist, the damages consumers and competitors may have suffered are common knowledge. Illustrative is the bankruptcy petition of the Johns Mansville Company arising from potential liability actions arising from injury to health resulting from use of asbestos produced by the company. Expanding legal doctrines of product liability examined below promise marketers that in the absence of legislative limitations and in part because of sympathetic juries that make damage awards, the costliness of products found defective also promises to rise.

Current Conflict over Promotion by Advertising

Defining advertising broadly enough to encompass all the promotional activities the Federal Trade Commission regulates under that generic term is difficult. The American Advertising Federation favors the use of the term, "commercial speech," both because it suggests the issues arising under the protection of freedom of speech under the First Amendment to the United States Constitution and because regulated promotional devices such as door-to-door calling cards are otherwise excluded.[6] William Stanton defines advertising broadly emphasizing it is a process: "[which] consists of all the activities involved in presenting to a group a nonpersonal, oral or visual, openly sponsored message regarding a product, service, or idea. The message, called an *advertisement*, is disseminated through one or more media and is paid for by the identified sponsor" (emphasis in original).[7] No matter how broad the definition, however, promotional activities that may be reached by Federal Trade Commission regulation under the rubric of "advertising" may simply be considered all-encompassing, as the judicial system has applied the term.

Much of the controversy about advertising as a promotional method reflects sharp disagreement over the informational aspects of the process contrasted with the entry barriers advertising is alleged to raise against new business and the maintenance of workable competition. The literature on the controversy is voluminous.[8] Suffice it to note that in 1982 marketers saw fit to make advertising expenditures of an approximate $67 billion, more than a five-fold increase over the expenditures of 1960.[9] Neither marketers nor the American public even consider the possibility that advertising might not exist. So, the nature of its regulation is critical.

FEDERAL TRADE COMMISSION REGULATION OF ADVERTISING

Since unfair or deceptive acts or practices in or affecting commerce are unlawful, the interpretation of unfairness becomes critical. An act may deceive consumers and yet fail to injure competition as was observed by the United States Supreme Court in the *Gratz* case [10] and in the *Raladam* case.[11] In 1922 in the *Winsted Hosiery* case, however, the Court interpreted "unfairness" broadly, holding that labels that deceive purchasers attract customers by a fraudulent practice causing competitors who label goods honestly to be injured.[12] In 1934, in the *Keppel* case, the Supreme Court, while noting that each practice alleged to be unfair competition under Section 5 of the FTC Act, added that a practice that is not fraudulent or deceptive but is contrary to public policy may be prohibited.[13] But ambiguity characterized Section 5. Consequently, the Act was broadened with the 1937 passage of the Wheeler-Lea amendment to Section 5.

The legislative debate on the Wheeler-Lea amendment to Section 5 makes its full reach apparent. The House Report on the amendment noted: "This amendment makes the consumer, who may be injured by an unfair trade practice, of equal concern, before the law, with the merchant or manufacturer injured by the unfair methods of a dishonest competitor." The House Report then added:

the essential elements of a false advertisement are that it is misleading in a material respect. It places on the advertiser the burden of seeing that his advertisement is not misleading. The definition is broad enough to cover *every form of advertisement deception over which it would be humanly practicable to exercise government control. It covers every case of imposition on a purchaser for which there could be a practical remedy. It reaches every case from that of inadvertent or uninformed advertising to that of the most subtle as well as the most vicious type of advertisement.* [emphasis added][14]

There seems little doubt that the legislative history indicates Congressional intent to reach unfairness in the broadest sense conceivable. The interpretation received its Supreme Court validation in 1972 in the *Sperry & Hutchinson* case.[15] The classic quotation from that case indicating how far Section 5 reaches was announced by Justice White for a unanimous court (with Justices Powell and Rehnquist not participating): "legislative and judicial authorities alike convince us that the Federal Trade Commission does not arrogate excessive power to itself if, in measuring a practice against the elusive, but congressionally mandated standard of fairness, it, like a court of equity, considers public values beyond simply those enshrined in the letter or encompassed in the spirit of the antitrust laws." The Court added a footnote that seemed to embrace criteria used by the FTC in developing a cigarette industry advertising regulation:

The Commission has described the factors it considers in determining whether a practice that is neither in violation of the antitrust laws nor deceptive is nonetheless unfair:

"(1) whether the practice, without necessarily having been previously considered unlawful, offends public policy as it has been established by statutes, the common law, *or otherwise*—whether, in other words, it is within at least the penumbra of some common-law, statutory, or other established concept of unfairness; (2) *whether it is immoral, unethical, oppressive, or unscrupulous;* (3) whether it causes substantial injury to consumers (or competitors or other businessmen)." [emphasis added]

With that grant of power to apply the concept of unfairness, the Federal Trade Commission, restrained finally only by its collective interpretation of morality, ethics, oppression, and scruples, is free to restrain virtually any promotional advertising by marketers. Noteworthy, too, is the fact that the Supreme Court's dictum of "unfairness" as a concept is not explicitly limited to advertising. What remains to be considered is what the FTC has done in applying this broad grant of power to specific advertising and other promotional activities.

Trade Regulation Rules as a Method of Advertising Regulation

The Federal Trade Commission's power to regulate advertising it considers unfair or deceptive can arise from judicial action arising under the "gap filler doctrine."[16] Since 1975, under powers granted by the Magnuson-Moss Warranty–Federal Trade Commission Improvement Act, the authorization of trade regulation rules has been specifically authorized by Congress. Prior to 1975, the FTC had undertaken the issuance of trade regulation rules as early as 1963. However, in a challenge to the FTC practice, the National Petroleum Refiners Association secured a district court decision overruling the FTC power. The Court of Appeals reversed the lower court decision and the Supreme Court denied certiorari.[17] The Supreme Court's inaction was, however, rendered moot by the Congressional authorization of 1975.

The list of trade regulation rules adopted by the Federal Trade Commission is extensive and includes some trade regulation rules issued prior to the 1975 authorization. This was accomplished by Section 202(c)(1) of the Magnuson-Moss Act, which expressly permitted trade regulation rules completed or "substantially" completed when the Act was adopted. In addition, advertising through posting of minimum gasoline octane numbers was granted to the FTC in 1978 under provisions of the Petroleum Marketing Practices Act.[18] The list of the current trade regulation rules, the proposed rules, and the terminated rules is constantly changing both in response to the FTC's changing view of its responsibilities [19] and to specific Congressional mandates.[20] Moreover, the Regulatory Flexibility Act of 1981 requires periodic scheduled review of all trade regulation rules with significant economic impact on small businesses to cost-justify the rules.[21]

Marketers might infer, from the discussion thus far, that the marketing regulations the Federal Trade Commission might codify as trade regulation rules are limited to advertising and labeling rules. While it is true that the rules mentioned to this point have been primarily those impacting on advertising, the FTC indicated in 1976 that its thrust was to be directed at adopting and enforcing laws protecting consumers.[22] The course of the regulations may move increasingly toward detailing the affirmative requirements marketers must meet rather than toward specifying prohibited practices. Moreover, the changing political composition of the FTC may alter its rule-making propensity so that the marketer can, at any time, hope to understand the principles that appear to guide it.[23]

Federal Trade Commission Procedures to Regulate Advertising

Although detailed rules of procedure govern actual presentation of cases before the Federal Trade Commission and since the judicial rules contained in the Federal Rules of Civil Procedure govern the judicial controversies arising from actions of the FTC, those legal regulations are beyond normal marketing concern. Much more vital for the marketer is knowledge of the normal steps taken by the FTC in deciding if an action is appropriate and, if so, how it will proceed short of an actual hearing or a court case calling for the services of a legal specialist.

The basic guidelines governing the operation of the Commission are contained in the Appendix. The FTC, divided into three bureaus–Consumer Protection, Competition, and Economics—gather the data and make the decisions as to whether a violation of Section 5 of the FTC Act has occurred. Research and statistical information gathered by the Bureau of Economics may be supplemented by subpoenas of witnesses, documents, and required reports—all subject to judicial enforcement. If investigation suggests a violation requires correction, the alleged violator may be notified officially that a formal complaint is contemplated. The business, facing this complaint procedure, which may be long, involved, and very expensive, may, if the FTC agrees, accept a consent order agreeing to accept certain remedial provisions or to refrain from certain conduct considered illegal. If a consent order is accepted, it has full legal force as if a complaint had been issued and fully adjudicated.

If a consent order is not agreed to, then the formal complaint procedure is adopted. The general procedure at this point becomes judicial in nature with motions, pleadings, witnesses, depositions, and finally a hearing before an Administrative Law Judge (formerly called a hearing examiner and so characterized in early FTC cases and judicial reviews).

The decision of the Administrative Law Judge, if neither the business firm nor the Federal Trade Commissioners on their own initiative ask for review, becomes final. If review is undertaken, the FTC issues a "final order." This final order may be appealed to the circuit court of appeals and eventually to the United States Supreme Court. The dearth of advertising cases, however, is especially indicative, it must be emphasized, given the breadth of the *Sperry & Hutchinson* interpretation and in view of the virtually unlimited mandate extended to the FTC under Section 5.[24] Faced with the possibility a complaint order might be issued, however, the marketer can avoid expensive litigation with low probability of success by "consenting" to a cease-and-desist order. Marketers should also be aware, however, that settlement by accepting a cease-and-desist order is not their right; if the FTC believes consumer protection or competition may be better served by a formal proceeding, the Commission may so act. Finally, marketers should remember that accepting a consent order does not admit guilt for the conduct undertaken and, therefore, it may not be used as prima facie evidence by a private party in a damage action. In short, marketers should weigh very carefully the advantages that adhere in agreeing to a consent order if, in the course of their normal business practices, the FTC acts against them.

Federal Trade Commission Guides and Advisory Opinions Adherence to the accepted practices can be furthered if marketers will not only conform to the codified practices embodied in the trade regulation rules but also if they will examine the FTC "industry guides." These guides are issued by the FTC and focus on specific marketing situations that might arise and in which issues of the coverage of Section 5 are involved. Illustrative are guides covering such diverse practices as bait advertising, the use of secret coding in marketing research, and the assigning of model year designations to motor vehicles.[25] Not every marketing question can be expected to be resolved by reference to the guides, but, in a significant number of cases, they indicate what the FTC may or may not accept.

Supplementary to the trade regulations rules and the guides are advisory opinions. The provision of advisory opinions is discretionary with the Commission. The request for an opinion must be on a "proposed" course of action and, if an opinion is given, does not preclude later consideration of the opinion given or even recission of the opinion. However, a complete and full good-faith presentation of the facts relevant to an advisory opinion and good faith reliance on the opinion will protect marketers against proceedings against them while the opinion is current. Since 1970, advisory opinions have been published, eventually codified, and are now integrated into Title 16, Part 15 of the *Code of Federal Regulations*.

FEDERAL TRADE COMMISSION INTERPRETATION OF DECEPTION AND UNFAIRNESS

If all complaints, cease-and-desist orders, trade regulation rules, trade guides, and advisory opinions are grounded in the Federal Trade Commission's interpretation of unfairness and deception, marketers must attempt to know what those terms mean to the Commission. Since they lack quantitative precision, and since industry regulation has evolved historically, it is not surprising to discover that marketers are, at least to a degree, again at sea in a rudderless boat. The full extent of the ambiguity and ambivalence that characterize the interpretation of the operative terms are fully revealed in the extensive literature of them.[26] Some generalizations can be made, but alertness to changes currently is an absolute necessity, especially since unfairness and deception may be combined or may be treated separately as the Federal Trade Commissioners deem appropriate. An explicit limitation on the formulation of any FTC rule which "prohibits or otherwise regulates any commercial advertising on the basis that such commercial advertising constitutes an unfair act or practice in or affecting commerce" was included in the Federal Trade Commission Improvements Act of 1980 and applied to fiscal years 1980, 1981, and 1982.[27]

Current Federal Trade Commission Law of Deception

The current interpretation of "deception" was published on October 14, 1983, when the Federal Trade Commission replied to a letter from Representative John Dingell, Chairman of the Energy and Commerce Committee of the House of Representatives. Chairman James Miller presented the majority view noting:

Numerous Commission and judicial decisions have defined and elaborated on the phrase "deceptive acts or practices" under both Sections 5 and 12 [of the FTC Act]. Nowhere, however, is there a single definite statement of the Commission's view of its authority. . . .

We have therefore reviewed the decided cases to synthesize the most important principles of general applicability. We have attempted to provide a concrete indication of the manner in which the Commission will enforce its deceptive mandate. In so doing, we intend to address the concerns that have been raised about the meaning of deception, and thereby attempt to provide a greater sense of certainty as to how the concept will be applied.[28]

Chairman Miller also noted that Section 12, which prohibits advertising that might induce purchases of food, drugs, devices, or cosmetics, is encompassed in the prohibition of Section 5. Section 15, he added, defines false advertising prohibited by Section 12, as an advertisement that is "misleading in a material respect."

The majority view of deception, therefore, is the present definitive operative criteria of the Commission. However, controversy has surrounded the policy statement. Two commissioners, Patricia Bailey and Michael Pertschuk, filed a vigorous dissent. Representative John Dingell rejected the statement with the abrupt comment that the Commission statement "is not responsive and is, therefore, rejected and returned." Miller, reiterating that the enforcement policy statement was a "consistent synthesis" of the prevailing cases, defended the policy: "[the enforcement policy statement] represents the Commission's formal position on how it has exercised its deception authority in recent years."[29] Ironically, however, Chairman Miller in 1982 had urged Congress to amend Section 5 to define deceptive acts.[30] His proposal had been opposed by Commissioners Clanton, Bailey, and Pertschuk and supported Commissioner Douglas. Congress, if it wished, might resolve this conflict, but until a resolution is forthcoming, the key elements of deception under Section 5 are those outlined in the majority statement. Given no legislative mandate to change its interpretation, the initiation of cases and the enforcement of the Act rests on that uncertain foundation. The analysis that follows also rests on that foundation.

Three elements "undergird all deception cases."[31] First, there must be "a representation, omission or practice that is likely to mislead the consumer." The representation need not be explicit. It may be implied and may be deduced from "qualifying information" that is necessary to avoid misrepresentation from occurring, yet which is not supplied. Misleading price claims, bait-and-switch sales methods, failure to meet warranty obligations, sales of hazardous or defective products without revealing defects or hazards have all been included as covered misrepresentation. In a general sense, the guiding principle is found in the ITT Continental Baking Co. case: "In the final analysis, the question whether an advertisement requires affirmative disclosure would depend on the nature and extent of the . . . claim made in the advertisement."[32] It should be noted, however, that when application of the unfairness provision of Section 5 is not taken from the Commission, an act may be unfair even though it is not specifically deceptive.[33]

The second element of deception provides:

> The Commission believes that to be deceptive the representation, omission or practice must be likely to mislead reasonable consumers [or a particular group to which it is addressed] under the circumstances. *The test is whether the consumer's interpretation or reaction is reasonable.* . . . In evaluating a particular practice, the Commission considers the totality of the practice in determining how reasonable consumers are likely to respond. [emphasis added]

If several reasonable interpretations are possible, one of which is false while others are true, deception will still be found. However, the Commission disavows the attempt to make the advertiser liable for "every conceivable misconception, however outlandish, to which his representations might be subject among the foolish or feeble-minded." Nor will "puffery" be pursued as deceptive. The criterion of deception, however, seems to have reintroduced the concept of the "reasonable and prudent person" concept of tort law into the enforcement of Section 5. The Commission has approached the reacceptance of the Supreme Court's view in the *FTC v. Algoma Lumber Co.* case: "the public is entitled to get what it chooses, though the choice may be dictated by caprice or by fashion or perhaps by ignorance."[34]

The third requisite for a finding of deception is that "the representation, omission or practice must be material." A material representation is defined in the statement: "A 'material' misrepresentation or practice is one which is likely to affect a consumer's choice of or conduct regarding a product."

In other words, it is information that is important to consumers. If inaccurate or omitted information is material, injury is likely. Presumptions of materiality abound. Illustrative are presumptions that health or safety is involved, or that cost, durability, performance, or quality is expressed or implied. The Commission summarized its view on the relations of injury and materiality succinctly: "Injury to consumers can take many forms. Injury exists if consumers would have chosen differently but for the deception. If different choices are likely, the claim is material, and injury is likely as well. Thus, injury and materiality are different names for the same concept."

The dissenting views on the FTC law of deception presented by Commissioners Bailey and Pertschuk emphasize some aspects of deception not emphasized but not rejected by the majority statement.[35] The aspects are important for, as the minority view demonstrates, it is within the FTC's power to reach violations in their incipiency—if they have the "tendency or capacity" to mislead but actual deception cannot be demonstrated.[36] The majority's use of "likely" in its discussion of the relation of injury and materiality suggest that it, too, accepts this reach of the Act.

The dissenters would go beyond the "average" consumer in ascertaining injury. Noting that courts have accepted FTC actions based on "the normal inattentiveness of consumers to the subtleties of seller's communications," the minority suggests the protection of consumers who are not "average": "[The minority implies that protection should be accorded protection since] the consuming public includes many persons who are not sophisticated, well informed, or careful and that these groups may constitute a substantial number of consumers even though some of their members may not be 'average.' " Materiality would be inferred by the minority simply on a very simple basis: "When a fact is misrepresented intentionally, the Commission can normally infer materiality from the existence of the misrepresentations; the company's business decision to make the representation is a convincing basis for the inference that it is important to potential purchasers."[37]

The differences of the majority and the minority position on the FTC law of deception probably cannot be resolved at the personal level, but the marketer can reach a synthesis of views. The synthesis derives in part from the limited budget governing the FTC's choice of cases. First, the FTC must choose which cases it will attack. The minority defines "some of the traditional factors the Commission uses" as "the likelihood, nature and degree of consumer injury, the cost of the product or service in question, the prevalence of the allegedly deceptive practices, and the need for federal intervention."[38]

The second step in FTC action is the application of the law of deception to the alleged violations. The third step in the Commission's application of Section 5 is the determination and implementation of the appropriate remedy. The judicial system accords expertise to the deliberations of the FTC,[39] and, as the Supreme Court declared in the *Jacob Siegel* case, "[The Commission] has wide latitude for judgment and the courts will not interfere except where the remedy has no reasonable relation to the unlawful practices found to exist."[40]

In 1986, the United States Supreme Court added a noteworthy interpretation of advertising regulation but seemingly not of wide application. In the *Posados de Puerto Rico* case in 1986, the Court allowed states to ban even truthful advertising if the state also had the power to regulate or ban the activity (such as casino gambling) itself.[41]

Current Status of the Federal Trade Commission Law of Deception   Conclusions that the status of the law under Section 5 of the Federal Trade Commission Act is uncertain and in flux immediately commend themselves to marketers. Fortunately, they may safely conclude more. First, the latitude accorded to the FTC under judicial interpretations of Section 5 is so great that only self-imposed limitations, Congressional restrictions, and budget limitations exist. These restraints, however, are meaningful.

While egregious violations may lead to FTC complaints and the invocation of the less burdensome acceptance of consent orders, the FTC is something less than the ogre it has been pictured to be. The FTC focus of concern has shifted to two public policy considerations. The first consideration, congruent with the changing social milieu within which marketing operates today, is the protection of a vaguely defined consumer. The consumer to be protected is not less than a reasonable and prudent person; the only issue is that the consumer may be as unreasonable and imprudent as the members of the FTC decide needs protection. Second, the FTC believes it has a mandate to see that the consumer is provided honest information. To this end, it acts to eliminate

barriers to dissemination of information such as are embodied in restrictions on advertising by professional associations subject also to Department of Justice action.[42]

Marketers, wishing to know the FTC's opinion either on proposed
advertising or upon restrictions on advertising, may utilize the advisory
opinion process of the agency.

Penalties for Violations of Section 5 of the FTC Act

Violations of cease-and-desist orders issued by the Federal Trade Commission and enforced by the judicial system can be both costly and
burdensome. Violations of trade regulation rules carry the same penalties. A penalty of $10,000 may be levied for each violation, but each
day a firm fails to comply constitutes a violation. Failure to comply for
a period of ten days, therefore, might incur a penalty of $100,000. In
the case of mailing a proscribed advertising brochure (a simulated check),
each separate letter may be held to be a separate violation. In the *Reader's
Digest* case the court upheld the decision of the FTC that such an interpretation was valid and, although the FTC's penalty was modified, the
company was required to pay $1.75 million.[43]

Section 15 of the Magnuson-Moss Warranty–Federal Trade Commission Improvements Act of 1975 also authorizes FTC actions providing
for consumer redress for damages resulting from violating Section 5 of
the Act. A prerequisite for the assessment of such damages is the issuance of a cease-and-desist order against the alleged offender and subsequent proof that a reasonable man would have known the proscribed
acts were fraudulent or dishonest. Since the FTC does include consumer
redress provisions in the orders it issues, this penalty becomes a real
possibility and one that may grow increasingly costly. Damages are not
the only possible penalty; refunds and rescinding or reforming contracts
may also be used.

Advertising Substantiation   Since the purpose of the FTC is to protect
the consumer and honest competitors, it has implemented an advertising
substantiation program to facilitate achievement of those goals. Advertisers may, under this program, be required to submit evidence that
almost all product claims have been verified by reputable scientific meth-
odological studies prior to making of claims. This program has been
applied to a wide variety of industries and its extension to previously
untouched industries remains possible.[44]

Corrective Advertising   Remedial action against advertisements found
to be unsubstantiated or otherwise in violation of Section 5 may take
the form of corrective advertising. The initial action of the FTC to invoke
a corrective advertising requirement was adopted in 1971 in a case involving the advertising of Profile bread by ITT.[45] ITT accepted the FTC's

requirement that it spend 25 percent of its Profile bread advertising budget to inform consumers that Profile bread was not effective as a weight reduction product. However, it was not until 1978 that the Supreme Court, by refusing to grant certiorari in the case of Warner-Lambert's advertising of Listerine, left standing the decision of the Court of Appeals for the Ninth Circuit that a corrective advertising requirement was legal FTC action.[46] Since that time, subject to the specific criteria outlined in the Warner-Lambert *Listerine* case, the FTC's authority to require corrective advertising has been accepted.[47] The extent of the FTC's corrective advertising regulatory power extends not only to the amount of money required to accomplish correction but also to the type size and even the text of the corrective advertisement. Marketers might feel challenged to explain exactly what actions lie outside the scope of FTC's powers given their authorization to act "as a court of equity" guided by the "spirit" of the Federal Trade Commission Act.

FEDERAL TRADE COMMISSION REGULATION OF WARRANTIES

Warranties, as is advertising, are subject to regulation by the Federal Trade Commission. The Magnuson-Moss Warranty Act of 1975 provides specific authorization for current regulation. However, as early as 1960 the FTC had adopted guides to protect consumers against deception in the advertising of guarantees and warranties.

The Magnuson-Moss Act provides, as the text of the Act contained in the Appendix indicates, specific federal minimum standards for written warranties. Implied warranties are also covered by the Act. However, warranties on consumer goods are not required but if warranties are made, the Act requires that they be explicitly designated as either "full" or "limited." The designation must be "clearly and conspicuously" captioned and clearly separated from the text of the warranty. For the purposes of the coverage of consumer products subject to the Act, a warranty is defined as:

[A]ny written affirmation of fact or written promise made in connection with the sale of a consumer product by a supplier to a buyer which relates to the nature of the material or workmanship or promises that such material or workmanship is defect free or will meet a specified level of performance over a specified period of time, or

[A]ny undertaking in writing in connection with the sale by a supplier of a consumer product to refund, repair, replace, or take other remedial action with respect to such product in the event that such product fails to meet the specifications set forth in the undertaking.

Details required in the warranty are specified in detail. They include identification of the warrantor, coverage of the warranty, remedies offered, exceptions, implementation methods, details for the settlement of disputes, available legal remedies, and time limits governing effectuation of the warranty. In addition, the Act requires clarity in presentation of the warranty by specifying: "The elements of the warranty [are to be presented] in words or phrases which would not mislead a reasonable, average consumer as to the nature or scope of the warranty." To implement these details, the Act specifically authorizes the Federal Trade Commission to "by rule define in detail the duties set forth in Section 104(a) of this Act and the applicability of such duties to warrantors of different categories of consumer products with 'full (statement of duration)' warranties."

Under this authorization to implement the warranty provisions of the Act, the Federal Trade Commission issued a number of rules and policy statements. Interpretations of the Act were issued and finalized in July, 1977.[48] Additional interpretive rules and guides covering enforcement,[49] disclosure of warranty terms and conditions,[50] presale availability of terms,[51] and informal dispute settlement mechanisms.[52]

Extensive regulations make it mandatory that marketers about to fashion a warranty covering a consumer product study the FTC guides carefully and, thereafter, consult a legal specialist. Violations are subject to the same remedies and penalties applicable to other trade regulation rules and to consent orders arising under the Federal Trade Commission Act. In addition, consumer class actions suits to enforce warranty provisions are authorized under the Act.

Marketers must be aware of the Act, but they must also recognize that the Magnuson-Moss Warranty Act was effectively incorporated into the broad grant of power conferred by Section 5 of the FTC Act. The Warranty Act provides that any person who fails to comply either with the terms of the Act "or rule thereunder," violates Section 5 of the FTC Act. Broader reach of the warranty regulations would be difficult to conceive.

REGULATION OF PRODUCT LABELING AND PACKAGING

Concern for consumer protection calls logically not only for protection against marketing abuses and warranty regulation but also suggests regulation of the labeling of products. The proliferation of packaging designations as "giant" or "extra large" and the slack-filling, whether inherent in the product or as a deceptive technique, led to extensive packaging and labeling regulations.

The Fair Packaging and Labeling Act: Generic Regulation

Specific labeling laws, as the Appendix reveals, existed prior to the adoption of the generic law regulating packaging and labeling. Although legislative concern for consumer protection seemed an important consideration, the major reason for the law may have been the protection of reputable marketers from competitive injury arising from deception in packaging and labeling.[53] However, the 1966 Fair Packaging and Labeling Act emphasized consumer information as a prerequisite for the "fair and efficient functioning of a free market economy" as its only rationale.[54] As with the warranty regulations, violations of the specific provisions of this general regulation of all consumer products are specifically designated to be violations of Section 5 of the Federal Trade Commission Act.[55] Except for foods, drugs, cosmetics, or "devices" regulated under the Federal Food, Drug, and Cosmetic Act by the Secretary of Health, Education, and Welfare, authority for the development and enforcement of implementing regulations is vested in the FTC.[56]

Specific Requirements of the Act of 1966   Although implementing regulations may be developed by the FTC, the Truth-in-Packaging Act (the popular title for the Fair Packaging and Labeling Act) contains specific requirements. First, the identity of the product and the name and place of business of the "manufacturer, packer, or distributor" must be provided. Second, an accurate designation of the "net quantity of contents" must be provided in a specifically required location. Third, the unit measurement requirements (fluid ounces, linear measures in foot, yard, or inches, among others) are mandated. Fourth, if contents are designated in "servings," the Act specifically requires that the appropriately denominated content of a "serving" be specified.

As marketers would expect, the FTC has seen fit to issue a number of implementing regulations. Coverage of rules extends from the requirement that in listing ingredients of consumer products, the ingredients be listed in order of descending quantitative importance to regulation of tire grades.[57] Adherence to regulations requires the marketer of any consumer product to procure and apply current rules. As in the case of warranty regulations, violations include the usual complaints, cease-and-desist orders, consent decrees and the penalties, and consumer redress threat for violation.

Specific Labeling Laws   In addition to the specific requirements embodied in the 1966 statute, earlier enactments in the wool products, fur, and textile fiber industries had been to assure protection, if not for the consumer, at least for the responsible marketers in those industries. (Relevant excerpts from the basic laws in those industries are included in the Appendix.)

The Wool Products Labeling Act required a label on wool products (specifically defined) and, as amended in 1980, the acts that constitute illegal "misbranding" are specified.[58] The percentage of wool, recycled wool, and other fibers contained (if constituting 5 percent or more of the fiber content by weight) must be clearly specified. Identification of the manufacturer must be provided although provisions for some alternative labeling is provided. Importation of misbranded woolen products is prohibited. Conviction carries penalties; enforcement is given to the Federal Trade Commission as the Act is considered to be incorporated into the FTC Act.

In a similar fashion the Fur Products Labeling Act provides that misbranding, false advertising, and false invoicing of fur products as defined by the Act constitutes misdemeanors with fines and possible imprisonment as penalties.[59] In addition to specific requirements for labeling and detailed explanations of what constitutes misbranding, the Act requires the FTC to develop a Fur Products Name Guide of "the true English names for the animals" (or appropriate foreign name for a non-English named fur) which guide must be utilized in labeling.

The Textile Fiber Products Identification Act is an act similar to the wool and to the fur products acts but is broader in reach.[60] Except for wool products excluded because of coverage under the 1940 Act, any yarn, fabric, or fiber, finished or unfinished, "used or intended for use in household textile articles," is covered by the Act. Misbranding and false advertising are prohibited and constituent fibers must be identified by generic name if by percentage weight the fibers total 5 percent or more of a given product. Product tags must include the required information. Reused fibers must be identified, removal of required labels or tags is prohibited, and, as is usual, enforcement is delegated to the Federal Trade Commission.

Promulgation of implementing rules and regulations is also authorized for the FTC. Penalties found in comparable acts are contained in this Act. Noteworthy, however, is the explicit addition of the power of the FTC to secure injunctions as enforcement techniques and by the specific exclusion of a number of products that might otherwise come under the jurisdiction of the Act.

Although the regulations contained in these labeling and packaging acts are industry-specific, marketers should be cognizant of them if they are involved directly or peripherally in them. Recognition, too, of the broad reach of the general movement toward requiring "truth" in packaging and labeling is essential. Few fields of production are free from the regulatory impact of the FTC with, it must be constantly emphasized, its virtually unlimited power under the "spirit" guide of the Supreme Court.

Early Regulations of General Product Characteristics

As early as 1906, the federal government undertook regulation of product characteristics with the enactment of the Pure Food Act[61] and subsequently with the more detailed and specific Federal Food, Drug and Cosmetic Act of 1938.[62] These acts, designed to exclude misbranded and adulterated foods and drugs in interstate commerce, include definitions of covered products and provide relatively minor penalties. They represent, however, the recognition that consumer protection can be a significant motivating force in the development of general marketing regulations with significant enforcement provisions.[63]

The Flammable Fabrics Act and Marketing Regulation

The expanding scope of regulatory control of marketing is manifest in an act to protect consumers from dangerously flammable "articles of wearing apparel and fabrics." The 1953 enactment provides that the "manufacture for sale, the sale, or the offering for sale" of wearing apparel or any "interior furnishing" (very broadly defined) violates Section 5 of the FTC Act.[64] The Secretary of Commerce is given specific power to establish tests for and findings of injurious flammability, and the FTC is empowered to enforce with appropriate legal techniques, including injunctions, the prohibitions emanating from the secretary's findings. Continuing studies of losses through injury and property destruction resulting from product flammability are to be conducted jointly by the Secretary of Commerce and the Secretary of Health, Education, and Welfare. Industry and consumer participation is assured by the creation of a National Advisory Committee for the Flammable Fabrics Act. Implementing rules and regulations are to be prescribed by the FTC. If a scintilla of a doubt exists, marketers must contact the FTC to secure any regulations, direct or peripheral, that might impinge on their product. The intellectual inference of the increasing power of the regulatory process on the marketing environment can also be made, but social responsibility, as society currently perceives it, forces adherence to an increasing battery of controls.

Other Regulations on Product Characteristics and Conditions of Sale

Not all the regulations that impinge on marketing operations can be examined here. Two areas of importance should be noted. The marketing of credit services encounters, as has been previously noted, a variety of regulations contained in the Truth in Lending Act, the Fair Credit Reporting Act, the Fair Credit Billing Act, the Equal Credit Opportunity

Act, and the Fair Debt Collection Practices Act. Since many marketers not only distribute products but also finance them, these constraints are requisite subjects for study and adherence.

In a similar way, the Consumer Products Safety Act calls for the marketer's cognizance and adherence.[65] The creation of an implementing Consumer Product Safety Commission with an elaborate divisional structure and extensive regulations as, however, peripheral to this examination of the regulations bearing directly on marketing promotion and conditions of sale.[66] Yet, the marketer must, through adequate research be constantly apprised of developments in these two fields.

PROMOTIONAL PROTECTION THROUGH TRADEMARKS

Marketers do have at least one device to protect their ability to market their product under some regulatory protection. The use of the trademark, a legal "name, term, or device" accords legal protection to the producer under the provisions of the Lanham Act.[67] The trademark name, symbol, or design must be registered and appropriateness verified with the United States Patent and Trademark Office. An approved trademark (channels of appeal are embodied in the rejection of an application for approval) is valid for twenty years with renewal possible.

International protection of a trademark, frequently a valuable marketing tool for protecting the consumer acceptance of the product and the product image and resulting goodwill, can be secured in countries signatory to the international trademark convention. Prerequisites exist for the approval of a trademark and requisites for its exclusive retention exist.

Two important problems are of special importance. The first problem is the avoidance of a generic term and the use of the term in such a way that it loses its individuality. Classic cases are "aspirin," which though once a trademark became a generic term, and "thermos" and "formica," which were challenged as generic terms no longer deserving of trademark protection. The FTC is specifically empowered to challenge trademarks as having become generic terms although Congress has, in recent years, restricted the use of appropriations for that purpose. The second problem is constant surveillance of trademark infringement. Unless a trademark holder diligently and continuously monitors its trademark, it may be lost from lack of adequate marketing policing. Yet, as a technique for protecting the consumer perception of a product's uniqueness, trademark protection affords regulatory protection of marketing operations rather than their restriction.

SUMMARY: REGULATION OF PRODUCT CHARACTERISTICS AND PROMOTION

Regulation of marketing operations in the areas of product characteristics and promotional methods are no less extensive than the regulation of pricing. A metamorphosis has occurred as the enforcing agency, the Federal Trade Commission, expanded its power. The expansion, supported by myriad legislative enactments and buttressed by favorable judicial decision granting the FTC extensive powers not explicit in the enabling Act, restrict marketing significantly. Some contemporary trends may indicate a softening of the positions taken by the members of the FTC, but the expansion of regulations, in part reflecting the need to protect consumers of unspecified nature, continues. The usual enforcement techniques of the FTC have been expanded by the codification of FTC practices in the form of trade regulations having no less binding effect on the marketer than a specific legislative enactment or court decree.

Only one caution need be appended. Proliferation of regulatory restraints invites inadvertent violation and resulting burdensome penalties. Marketers' protection from these difficulties inheres in the acceptance of the implicit premise of contemporary concepts of social responsibility that industry self-policing provides the maximum, albeit far from total protection against unforeseen attack. The days of caveat emptor are gone forever and laments for lost autonomy are rhetorical futility. Marketing operations now must accept caveat venditor as the guiding principle.

NOTES

1. *Wheeler-Lea Act*, 52 Stat. 111 (1938).

2. *Magnuson-Moss Warranty-Federal Trade Commission Improvements Act*, 88 Stat. 2193 (1975).

3. The use of agencies combining the power to develop regulations having the force of law, enforced by the agencies, and with adjudication of cases and controversies arising therefrom by the agencies, is so extensive as to have given rise to the name and analysis of "the Fourth Branch of Government."

4. Evidence is found in the compilation of regulatory statutes found in *Topical Law Reports*, vol. 4 (Chicago: Commerce Clearing House, 1984), pp. 30,001–30,667.

5. The four statutes regulating credit practices are the Consumer Credit Reporting Act (also cited as the Truth in Lending Act), 82 Stat. 146 (1968); the Fair Credit Reporting Act, 84 Stat. 1128 (1970); the Fair Credit Billing Act, 88 Stat. 1511 (1975); the Equal Credit Opportunity Act Amendments of 1976, 90 Stat. 251 (1976); and the Fair Debt Collection Practices Act, 91 Stat. 874 (1977). These credit statutes are not included in the Appendix but may be found in *United States Code Service*, Lawyer's Edition, title 15, chapter 41 (Rochester,

N.Y.:Lawyers Cooperative Publishing Co., 1982), pp. 422–865. Extensive explanations, court citations and bibliographical references are included.

6. See "Statement of the American Advertising Federation" in *Unfairness: Views on Unfair Acts and Practices in Violation of the Federal Trade Commission Act,* Committee on Commerce, Science, and Transportation, United States Senate, 96th Congress, 2d Sess. (Washington, D.C.: United States Government Printing Office, 1980), p. 3.

7. William J. Stanton, *Fundamentals of Marketing,* 7th ed., (New York: McGraw-Hill, 1984), p. 465.

8. For an extensive examination of the literature of advertising, the social utility it may create, and the problems it exacerbates, see William S. Comanor and Thomas A. Wilson, "Advertising and Competition: A Survey," *Journal of Economic Literature* (June 1979): 453–76. See also the papers on advertising in *Industrial Concentration: The New Learning,* Harvey Goldschmid and others, eds., (Boston: Little, Brown, 1974).

9. William J. Stanton, *Fundamentals of Marketing,* p. 467. Stanton's estimates may be too low because of the exclusion of direct-mail advertising (which he notes) and of expenditures made for nongroup activities.

10. *Federal Trade Commission v. Gratz,* 253 U.S. 421 (1920).

11. *Federal Trade Commission v. Raladam Co.,* 283 U.S. 643 (1931).

12. *Federal Trade Commission v. Winsted Hosiery Co.,* 258 U.S. 438 (1922).

13. *Federal Trade Commission v. Keppel & Bro.,* 291 U.S. 304, (1934).

14. Citations of material from the House Report No. 1613, 75th Congress, 1st Sess. (August 19, 1937), reprinted in *Unfairness: Views on Unfair Acts and Practices in Violation of the Federal Trade Commission Act,* pp. 7–8.

15. *Federal Trade Commission v. Sperry & Hutchinson Co.,* 405 U.S. 233 (1972).

16. This characterization of the ability of the FTC to reach offenses violating the "spirit" but not the letter of the law seems to have been developed in *Grand Union v. Federal Trade Commission,* 300 F 2d 92 (2d Cir. 1962).

17. *National Petroleum Refiners Association v. Federal Trade Commission,* 482 F 2d 672 (1974), certiorari denied, 415 U.S. 951 (1974).

18. *Petroleum Marketing Practices Act,* 92 Stat. 322 (1978).

19. A current list of Federal Trade Commission Trade Regulation rules can be found in *Topical Law Reports,* vol. 4 (Chicago: Commerce Clearing House, 1984), pp. 41,001–41,241.

20. Indicative of Congressional concern was the restriction embodied in the Federal Trade Commission Improvement Act of 1980, which blocked FTC enactment of a trade regulation regulating television advertising to children.

21. Reviews through 1989 have been scheduled and will cover such trade regulation rules as those governing advertising and labeling of home insulation and gasoline octane posting rules among twelve scheduled for 1985 or later.

22. See Federal Trade Commission announcement, 41 *Federal Register* 3322 (January 22, 1976).

23. The Federal Trade Commission Act provides that not more than three commissioners may be members of the same political party. Differing political orientations toward business regulation manifest themselves not only in the extent to which regulation of business by rule-making is undertaken but also in the scope and nature of the rules themselves.

24. It is noteworthy that since the *Sperry & Hutchinson* case was decided by the Supreme Court in 1972, only one other case involving the power of the Federal Trade Commission's decisions has reached the Supreme Court. That case, *(Federal Trade Commission) United States v. ITT Continental Baking Co.*, 429 U.S. 223 (1975), was procedural and supported the FTC's position that the penalty for defying a consent order was the prescribed fine with each day of defiance a new penalty rather than a continuing transaction representing a "violation." Since the first Supreme Court case involving the FTC in 1920, Michael A. Duggan cites sixty-three cases in which the FTC was a party but only three cases since 1967. See *Antitrust and the U.S. Supreme Court, 1829–1980; Supplement, 1980–1982*, 2d ed., (New York: Federal Legal Publications, 1980, 1983).

25. The current guides can be found in *Topical Law Reports*, vol. 4 (Chicago: Commerce Clearing House, 1984), pp. 41,601–41,916.

26. The interested reader might follow a line of articles by a foremost authority, Dorothy Cohen. See "The Federal Trade Commission and the Regulation of Advertising in the Consumer Interest," *Journal of Marketing* (January 1969): 40–44; "The Concept of Unfairness as It Relates to Advertising Legislation," *Journal of Marketing* (July 1974); 8–13; "Advertising and the First Amendment," *Journal of Marketing* (July 1978); "The FTC's Advertising Substantiation Program," *Journal of Marketing* (Winter 1980), pp. 26–35; "Unfairness in Advertising Revisited," *Journal of Marketing* (Winter 1982): 73–80. See also Earl W. Kintner, *An Antitrust Primer*, 2d ed. (New York: MacMillian, 1973) and extensive bibliographical references cited in Benjamin J. Katz, ed., *Advertising and Government Regulation: A Special Panel Report from the American Academy of Advertising* (Cambridge, Mass.: Marketing Science Institute, 1979).

27. *Federal Trade Commission Improvements Act of 1980*, 88 Stat. 2183 (1980).

28. "FTC's Policy Statement on Deception," Bureau of National Affairs, *Antitrust & Trade Regulation Report*, (October 27, 1983), 689–99.

29. Details of the controversy is found in "Dingell, Miller Tangle over New Enforcement Policy on Deception," Bureau of National Affairs, *Antitrust & Trade Regulation Report* (October 27, 1983): 664–66.

30. See hearings before the Subcommittee for Consumers of the Committee on Commerce, Science, and Transportation, United States Senate, 97th Cong., 2d. Sess., *FTC's Authority over Deceptive Advertising*, Serial No. 97–134, (July 22, 1982), p. 9.

31. Quotations embodying the interpretation of deception are all excerpted from the majority summary unless otherwise noted.

32. In re ITT Continental Baking Co., Inc., 83 FTC 865 (1976).

33. Illustrative is the FTC's enforcement actions under its Trade Regulation Rule prescribing a method of testing the insulation ability of insulation material and disclosing the insulating capacity in advertisements.

34. *Federal Trade Commission v. Algoma Lumber Co.*, 291 U.S. 67 (1934).

35. Patricia P. Bailey and Michael Pertschuk, *Analysis of the FTC Law of Deception*, Trade Regulation Reports no. 641, part II (March 27, 1984). As in the majority analysis, extensive judicial citations not only to Supreme Court decisions but to decisions of circuit courts of appeals and district courts are included.

36. *Beneficial Corporation v. Federal Trade Commission*, 542 F 2d 611 (3d Cir.,

1976), certiorari denied, 430 U.S. 983 (1977); *Resort Car Rental System, Inc. v. Federal Trade Commission*, 518 F 2d 962 (9th Cir., 1974), certiorari denied under name, *Mackenzie v. United States*, 423 U.S. 827 (1975).

37. Supreme Court acceptance of this standard of inference is found in *Federal Trade Commission v. Colgate-Palmolive Co.*, 380 U.S. 374 (1965).

38. The "need for federal intervention" criterion reflects that fact that every one of the fifty states has a version of a trade practices act. Adequate action under state law may occur.

39. In *Simeon Management Corp. v. Federal Trade Commission*, 579 2d 1137 (9th Cir., 1978), this position was emphasized: In reviewing findings of the FTC, courts will not "set aside the Commission's action unless it is apparent that it is unsupported by substantial evidence . . . or is arbitrary, capricious, an abuse of discretion or otherwise not in accordance with law."

40. *Jacob Siegel Co. v. Federal Trade Commission*, 327 U.S. 608 (1946).

41. *Posados de Puerto Rico Associates dba Condado Holiday Inn v. Tourism Company of Puerto Rico*, 92 L ed 2d 266 (1986) S. Ct. (July 1986). The standards governing such state action are outlined in *Central Hudson Gas & Electric Corp. v. Public Service Commission of New York*, 447 U.S. 557 (1980).

42. Although the classic attack on restrictions on dissemination of honest advertising, the Supreme Court has made clear that keeping the public ignorant of prices is not tolerable under the First and Fourteenth Amendments to the United States Constitution. See *Virginia State Board of Pharmacy v. Virginia Citizens Consumers Council, Inc.*, 425 U.S. 748 (1976).

43. *United States v. Reader's Digest Association*, 662 F 2d 955 (CA–3); certiorari denied 425 U.S. 748 (1976).

44. Details of the operation of the advertising substantiation program are found in Dorothy Cohen, "The FTC's Advertising Substantiation Program," *Journal of Marketing* (Winter 1980): 26–35.

45. In re ITT Continental Baking Co., Inc., 79 FTC 248 (1971).

46. *Warner-Lambert Co. v. Federal Trade Commission*, 562 F 2d 749 (D.C. Cir., 1977), certiorari denied, 435 U.S. 950 (1978).

47. See William L. Wilkie, Dennis L. McNeill, and Michael B. Mazis, "Marketing's 'Scarlet Letter': The Theory and Practice of Corrective Advertising," *Journal of Marketing* (Spring 1984): 11–31, for a detailed study of corrective advertising. An extensive bibliography is appended. All three authors have been in-house consultants to the FTC on this issue. A related but earlier assessment of the effectiveness of the corrective advertising program is Jacob Jacoby, Margaret C. Nelson, and Wayne D. Hoyer, "Corrective Advertising and Affirmative Disclosure Statements: Their Potential for Confusing and Misleading the Consumer," *Journal of Marketing* (Winter 1982): 61–72.

48. "Final Interpretations," 42 *Federal Register* 36112 (July 13, 1977); 42 *Federal Register* 38341 (July 28, 1977). All FTC warranty rules and policy statements may be found in *Topical Law Reports*, vol. 4 (Chicago: Commerce Clearing House, 1984), pp. 41,901–41,961.

49. "Magnuson-Moss Warranty Act: Implementation and Enforcement Policy," 40 *Federal Register* 257221 (June 18, 1975).

50. "Disclosure of Warranty Terms and Conditions," 40 *Federal Register* 60188 (December 31, 1976).

51. "Presale Availability of Terms," 40 *Federal Register* 60189 (December 31, 1975).

52. "Informal Dispute Settlement Mechanism," 40 *Federal Register* 60215 (December 31, 1975).

53. Marshall C. Howard, "Textile and Fur Labeling Legislation: Names, Competition, and the Consumer," *California Management Review*, (Winter 1971), 69–80, has argued persuasively that producer protection motivated forerunners to the 1966 Act.

54. Fair Packaging and Labeling Act, 80 Stat. 1296 (1966).

55. Specific exclusions are meat and meat products, poultry or poultry products, tobacco and tobacco products; and products covered by a very few limited coverage acts such as the Virus-Serum-Toxin Act and the Federal Seed Act.

56. Federal Food, Drug, and Cosmetic Act, 52 Stat. 1040 (1938).

57. For current applicable regulations, the marketer can secure rules, regulations, and general interpretations (including exemptions) from the Federal Trade Commission.

58. Wool Products Labeling Act, 54 Stat. 1128 (1940).

59. Fur Products Labeling Act, 65 Stat. 175 (1951).

60. Textile Fiber Products Identification Act, 72 Stat. 1717 (1958).

61. Pure Food Act, 34 Stat. 768 (1906).

62. Federal Food, Drug, and Cosmetic Act, 52 Stat. 1040 (1938).

63. Although extensive elaboration of the industry-specific restrictions of the food and drug acts are not undertaken, excerpts from the two basic laws are included in the Appendix.

64. Flammable Fabrics Act, 67 Stat. 11 (1953).

65. Consumer Product Safety Act, 86 Stat. 1207 (1972); Consumer Product Safety Act Amendment of 1981, 95 Stat. 703 (1981).

66. See Paul Busch, "A Review and Critical Evaluation of the Consumer Product Safety Commission: Marketing Management Implications," *Journal of Marketing* (October 1976): 41–49, for an analysis of the Commission (CPSC). The implementation and enforcement of the Flammable Fabrics Act was transferred to the CPSC and additionally, the CPSC administers the Federal Hazardous Substances Act, the Poison Packaging Act, and the Refrigerator Safety Act. In 1976, the Consumer Product Safety Commission Act, 90 Stat. 503, provided for consumer suits against the CPSC for specified failures to protect against the marketing of unsafe products.

67. Lanham Trademark Act, 60 Stat. 433 (1946).

7

The Legal Regulation of Procedures Affecting Marketing

Substantive regulations of marketing often seem to be the guidelines that determine the nature and scope of the marketer's functions. These regulations are of major importance. Yet changes in the regulatory techniques, both in meaning and in application, have also been vital in the ability and the way in which the marketing institution responds to its perception of revealed consumer preferences. Moreover, the diversity in the nature of regulatory procedures and the way in which they impinge on marketing constitutes a continuing source of annoyance, if not frustration, of marketers.

TORT LAW AND PRODUCT LIABILITY

Even before marketers were required to assume responsibility for their operations and organization because of the application of regulatory constraints explicitly fashioned to that end, the application of tort law exerted some measure of control over them. Tort law, the law of "wrongs" not embedded in a contractual relationship but which the judicial system will enforce, was the initial legal device to be utilized to attempt to require marketers to assume responsibility for their products and other marketing conduct. From its inception, however, tort law was hampered by the legal concept of "privity" in controlling marketing conduct and performance.[1]

The erosion of the doctrine of privity occurred gradually. The exact case that marked the watershed in either liability for negligence of a producer or for breach of warranty is probably not possible. Nor, is it contemporaneously important.[2] The significance is that as privity eroded, marketers were forced to accept increasing legal responsibility for their products and the surrounding conditions of sale. Strict tort liability emerged—and absolute liability seems to be evolving—so that marketers of defective, dangerous, or negligently produced goods may be assessed heavy penalties in civil actions.[3] Now the law of strict liability seems established and, as William L. Prosser has indicated, the incremental expansion has been spectacular.[4]

Strict liability requires the marketer of a good to assume heavy burdens to avoid potential damages. Care in production to utilize techniques of production unlikely to result in injury to careless consumers must be exercised. Certainly, given current interpretations, this requires utilization of techniques that are the least injurious given the current state of the productive art. The expansion of liability suggests, however, that even more may be required, although the extent to which the courts will go in imposing liability for injury resulting from products that are not safe as subsequent knowledge indicates they might have been is ambiguous.[5]

Significance inheres in this development of the application of tort law to marketing. Adherence to explicit regulations, even under broad grants of legislative and judicial power, does not involve the regulatory uncertainties—particularly in the area of product warranties and negligence—that arise under civil law. Jury decisions, seldom overturned on appeal and not often modified, may be costly.

Class Actions and Marketing Regulation

A procedural technique for attacking marketing operations and organizations currently growing in importance is the class action suit. The class action suit is a legal device by which several persons with a common legal issue of law or fact present the issue in a joint proceeding. The Federal Rules of Civil Procedure explicate the requirements of a class action. The participants in a class action suit may join only parties who are similarly situated. The participants must have received adequate notice of the proceedings and the resulting class must not be so large as to be "unmanageable." The intent of the class action proceeding was probably best outlined by Justice Douglas in the minority opinion in the *Eisen v. Carlisle & Jacquelin* case.[6]

I think in our society that is growing in complexity there are bound to be innumerable people in common disasters, calamities, or ventures who would go begging for justice without the class action but who could with all regard to due process be protected. Some of these are consumers whose claims may seem *de minimis* but who alone have no practical recourse for either remuneration or injunctive relief. . . . The class action is one of the few legal remedies the small claimant has against those who command the *status quo*. I would strengthen his hand with the view of creating a system of law that dispenses justice to the lowly as to those liberally endowed with wealth and power.

Although the *Eisen* case limited the class in its use of the technique, its introduction to marketing, with an increasingly sympathetic judiciary represented in the Douglas dissent, clearly foreshadowed its growing use.

In 1979, the Supreme Court gave its stamp of approval to a broadening use of the class action. That suit, instituted not under tort law but under Sections 4 and 16 of the Clayton Act providing for treble damages resulting from violations of the antitrust laws, raised the question of whether consumers were injured in their "business or property" as the prerequisite for the application of the Act. In the *Reiter* case, the Supreme Court examined the concept of property at length and concluded that monetary loss to a consumer, either individually or as a member of a class, was "property."[7] Consequently, class actions to enforce consumer rights, buttressed by contingent fee arrangements of class members with other class members, were sanctioned by the Court.[8]

Broadening of the class action device occurred in *Walsh v. Ford Motor Co.*[9] That case, arising under the Magnuson-Moss Warranty Act, necessitated one hundred or more members of a class to be joined to maintain an action. The Walsh class consolidated persons with diverse claims arising under different legal concepts (e.g., implied warranties and written warranties) to reach the required minimum of one hundred participants. The consolidation of diverse claims was accepted by the Court. The result was the broadening of the class action technique as a means of attacking alleged marketing transgressions.

Since the damages claimed by each member of a class in a class action suit may be small, unwise marketers might conclude that the loss of such a suit is trivial. Trends, however, as indicated in the *Greenshaw* case, in which 6,734 class members yielded a class with total damages of only $5,827 (trebled to $17,482), indicate a new and costly consequence of class action suits.[10] The court assessed attorney fees of $246,517, rendering the class action suit a very expensive financial burden on the firm convicted of price-fixing.

The gradual expansion of the class action procedure coupled with increasingly lenient legal interpretations render this procedural method a regulatory constraint of major importance. Shifts in judicial concern for consumer protection, supported by public interest organizations and emphasizing both the techniques and the legal grounds for action, signal to marketers the narrowing scope and the increasing penalties for autonomous actions that are not safely within the confines of modern conceptions of responsible marketing behavior.

Class Action Suits and Market Share Liability

Class actions presented a new and forbidding face in the *Sindell* case.[11] In that case, arising from a class action against five of nearly two hundred producers of DES, an animal food supplement that was also prescribed as a miscarriage preventative from 1941 to 1974, vaginal and cervical cancer and malformations were found in women whose mothers used DES during pregnancy. Charging negligence, Judith Sindell, whose mother used DES during her pregnancy with Judith, won a verdict against the five named producers for the full damages even though the specific producer of the injurious product purchased by her mother could not be identified. With the *Sindell* case, which the Supreme Court refused to consider and hence did not overturn, thirty years became a period within which class actions may be undertaken. Moreover, the actions may proceed against selected producers in the industry who then became liable, in the event of an unfavorable decision, for the full share of the liability assessed against the defendant producers.[12]

Right of Contribution and Class Action Costs

The potential burden of the expansive class action doctrine and the new concepts of liability are not allayed by the ability of producers to secure contributory payments from producers equally at fault. Damages assessed, either by the government or in private treble damage actions, against one firm when several firms participated in the action, cannot be recovered from firms not joined in the legal action. The right of contribution is definitively denied to a defendant convicted of violations of the antitrust laws. A guilty defendant cannot secure contributions from other participants for civil damages, costs, and attorney fees. In *Texas Industries v. Radcliff Materials,* the Supreme Court emphasized that since the purpose of treble damages was to punish past illegal conduct and to prevent it in the future, the antitrust laws were not concerned with reducing the liability of joint wrongdoers.[13] The Court also noted that if contribution of joint wrongdoers not a party to the case were intended, Congress would have to act to legislate that intention. Although Congress has, since the *Texas Industries* decision, continued to consider legislation to authorize actions to secure contributions, currently being singled out for action and losing can be lonesome and burdensome for a marketer.[14]

Synthesis of Liability, Class Actions, and Damage Awards

Each of the developments to which reference has been made may be annoying to the marketer. Together they constitute an onerous synthesis of legal constraints. The extension of strict liability enforced by class actions and treble damages on the basis of choosing limited but un- identifiable defendants who, if damages are imposed, cannot now secure indemnification from joint offenders, presents a somber picture to mar- keters. Each of the constraints may be difficult but manageable and any single marketer may not find them all combined in the way suggested here. Yet the fact remains that with the extant regulatory doctrines, the autonomous action that marketers may undertake grows increasingly unclear and the cost of a mistake increasingly great.

Avoidance of Liability for Actions Undertaken with State Approval

Earlier the state-action doctrine that emerged from the *Parker v. Brown* decision was noted.[15] If clearly articulated and supervised state policy is adopted that might otherwise run afoul of the antitrust laws, those persons effectuating the state policies may be exempt from antitrust prosecution. However, in the *Town of Hallie* and in the *Southern Motor Carriers Rate Conference* cases,[16] both decided in 1985, the Supreme Court applied the *Parker v. Brown* guidelines and effectively extended the re- quirements that must be met before the state action doctrine comes into force to immunize marketers acting under it. Marketers, as well as public officials, are cautioned to remember that the requirements for the pro- tection afforded by the state action doctrine are clear and specific and their application is rigorous.

Intraenterprise Conspiracy and the Avoidance of Legal Action

Marketers discovered in the *Copperweld* case of 1984 that coordination of marketing plans, policies, and operations of a company and its wholly owned subsidiary did not constitute an illegal conspiracy in restraint of trade.[17] Lower courts had followed a long standing intraenterprise con- spiracy doctrine that held that a conspiracy in violation of the antitrust laws could occur between a parent company and a wholly owned sub- sidiary. The Supreme Court reversed this traditional doctrine grounded in the 1947 *Yellow Cab* decision[18] and reinforced in the 1951 *Kiefer-Stewart* case.[19]

In explaining its *Copperweld* decision, the Supreme Court noted that the parent and it subsidiary have a legitimate unity of interest and com- mon objectives that call for the subsidiary to act in the parent company's interest. Nor, added the Court, is there a sudden joining of interest of the parent and the subsidiary that might render joint action suspect. Looking beyond form to the substance of a parent-subsidiary relationship, the Court immunized normal and expected intraenterprise joint action from antitrust attack.

CRIMINAL SANCTIONS AS AN UNRESOLVED THREAT

The length to which legal action may be stretched to reach business practices became increasingly unclear when the State of Illinois filed murder charges against officers of a Chicago company that recovered silver from used photographic film. Charges of manslaughter were also filed against the corporation. Convictions of individuals might have led to sentences of as much as forty years. While the charges of murder were grounded in the firm's and individuals' knowing toleration of unsafe workplace conditions, the implication of "knowingly and intentionally" causing death portends a major shift in legal liability not only in workplace safety but, by inference, in production and marketing of goods found to be defective. The ultimate outcome and its extension remains debatable, but the marketer is cautioned that the accretion of regulatory restraints from situations such as the Chicago murder indictments is the path by which marketing restraints have grown, especially in recent years.

RETROACTIVE LAWS AND THE REGULATION OF MARKETING

Marketers may have felt secure in the knowledge that although the course of judicial decisions may have been difficult to see and although legislative actions are subject to interpretative modification, they were at least safe from the retroactive application of new legislation. This security became somewhat illusory in the 1984 term of the Supreme Court.

The common belief that the United States Constitution assures protection against retroactive laws by virtue of the denial to both the federal government and the states of the right to adopt ex post facto laws is not as accurate and protective as persons generally think. First, as held in *Calder v. Bull*, the prohibition of retroactive legislation "relates only to penal and criminal legislation and not to civil laws which affect private rights adversely."[20] Second, a longstanding belief that retroactive legislation is inherently unfair and hence is to be avoided restrained legislators from adopting retroactive legislation.

Late in its 1984 term, the Supreme Court, in *Pension Benefit Guaranty Corporation v. R. A. Gray & Co.*, gave its support to a congressional act with significant retroactive provisions.[21] While the Act's subject was not marketing operations or organization, the grant of power and the rationale for it certainly extend to the marketing field. The Court declared, quoting its analysis in *Usery v. Turner Elkhorn Mining Company*,

It is now well established that legislative Acts adjusting the burdens and benefits of economic life come to the Court with a presumption of constitutionality, and that the burden is on one complaining of a due process violation to establish that the legislature has acted in an arbitrary and irrational way.

We further explained that the strong deference accorded legislation in the field of national economic policy is no less applicable when that legislation is applied retroactively. Provided that the retroactive application of a statute is supported by a legitimate legislative purpose furthered by rational means, judgments about the wisdom of such legislation remain within the exclusive province of the legislative and executive branches.

This is true even though the effect of the legislation is to impose a new duty or liability based on past acts.[22]

Thus, even the threat of expanding legislation with retroactive provisions now seems to constitute a threat to marketers. Restraint must come, of course, from the sense of justice of the legislators for it is no longer considered by the judicial system to be within its purview.

LEGISLATIVE CONTROL OF ADMINISTRATIVE AGENCIES

Deep beneath all the expansion of restraints on business generally and upon marketing specifically has been the recognition of the growing complexity of a technological society. Associated problems of the consumer for whom the implementing economy exists have grown more complex. An economy producing an incomprehensible gross national product in excess of three trillion dollars yearly can no longer be controlled by simple laws and a relaxed judicial system capable of understanding all the intricacies with which it is confronted.

Congress, in an attempt to exert a modicum of control over the administrative agencies it has created to meet the growing complexity of modern life, adopted a "legislative veto" as a controlling device. It embodied that veto procedure, in a variety of forms, in over two hundred specific legislative acts. In its general form, the legislative veto provides that administrative agencies such as the Federal Trade Commission utilizing its broad grant of power must submit rules they adopt to Congress. Congress, then, within a legislated period of time, may consider the administrative regulation and, either by action of one designated house or jointly by both houses, nullify the regulation. This procedure, Congress once believed, would assure it at least of the ability to reach actions of its created agencies that it found to be unintended or undesirable.

In an area far removed from marketing, the right of Congress to utilize the legislative veto was held by the Supreme Court to be unconstitutional. In the *Chada* case, involving the legislative veto embodied in the Immigration and Naturalization Act, the Court held that the veto violated the separation of powers provision of the Constitution.[23] This resulted, the Court held, because once the administrative agency such as the FTC was created, it became an agency of the executive branch of government. Since this was the case, the legislative veto abridged the powers of the executive branch. Moreover, the Court declared, if the legislature wishes to alter its delegation of power to the executive branch, it must act by specific legislation submitted for presidential veto and subsequent overriding by the required two-thirds Congressional vote. Justice White's dissent may have been perceptive that the decision destroys "the central means by which Congress secures the accountability of executive and independent agencies," but that control has, nevertheless, been lost.

The remaining congressional controls are by the specific restriction of appropriations to administrative agencies and by specific legislation on specific subjects. This is an improbable means of control given the myriad subjects of marketing such as slack-filling or the substantiation of advertisements, not to mention the vast array of other nonmarketing endeavors subject to administrative regulation. The legal basis upon which the Supreme Court acted in the *Chada* case may have been indisputable, but the economic consequences both in marketing and other functional areas are legion.[24]

SUMMARY

The legal profession, much as other professions, has always used the mysticism of its methods as a means for complicating the operations and the organizations of enterprises. Marketers, confronted not simply with the procedural development outlined here, which have so changed their operations and organizations, must recognize that the evolution of regulation will continue. Perhaps, as in recent years, the trend will accelerate. Neither its existence nor its importance can be denied.

NOTES

1. Privity is the legal principle that "strangers to a contract cannot sue on it." Thus, a consumer who purchased from a retailer who in no way was negligent in a good's production could not secure damages for injuries resulting from a dangerous or deficiently made good from either the manufacturer or the wholesaler. The recourse would have been against the retailer from whom the purchaser contracted to buy the product since the retailer had not been the negligent producer. The complexity of the concept of privity and how it historically allowed producers freedom from legal accountability is discussed in Friedrich Kessler, "Product Liability," *Yale Law Journal* (April 1967): 887–938. Not only

does Kessler discuss the American development of regulation through case law in the United States, he also develops the foreign roots of the doctrine of privity and product liability.

2. Frequently cited is *Greenman v. Yuba Power Products, Inc.*, 59 Cal. 2d 57, 377 P. 2d 897 (1963). Kessler, in developing the long line of cases, notes that "[t]he frequent 'confusion' of warranty and negligence concepts is, therefore, not surprising." Kessler, *Yale Law Journal*, fn. 57, p. 898.

3. William L. Prosser's "The Assault upon the Citadel (Strict Liability to the Consumer)," *Yale Law Journal* (May 1960): 1,099–1,148 is a revealing analysis of the development of the doctrine of strict liability and the erosion of the privity doctrine.

4. See Prosser, "The Assault upon the Citadel," 1112; Roland N. McKean, "Products Liability: Implications of Some Changing Property Rights," *Quarterly Journal of Economics* (November 1970): 611–626.

5. The economics of the ultimate real cost of the concept of strict product liability is analyzed extensively in Harold Demsetz in "Information and Efficiency: Another Viewpoint," *Journal of Law and Economics* (April 1969): 1–22 and in "The Exchange of Property Rights," *Journal of Law and Economics* (October, 1964): 11–26. See also Walter Y. Oi, "The Economics of Product Safety," *The Bell Journal of Economics and Management Science* (Spring 1973): 3–28. The economics of product liability may prove to be relatively unimportant especially as juries make awards in specific cases in which arcane economic theories may be difficult for lawyers to explain and more difficult for the unsophisticated to understand and accept.

6. *Eisen v. Carlisle & Jacquelin*, 417 U.S. 156 (1964).

7. *Kathleen R. Reiter v. Sonotone Corp. et al.*, 442 U.S. 330 (1979).

8. See Ray O. Werner, "Marketing and the United States Supreme Court, 1975–1981," *Journal of Marketing* (Spring 1982): 73–81.

9. *John F. "Jack" Walsh, et al. v. Ford Motor Co.* (DC-DC, March 1984), reported in the Bureau of National Affairs, *Antitrust and Trade Regulation Reports* (April 12, 1984): 736; certiorari denied, 96 L Ed 2d 677 (1987). Although this case was appealed, the judicial propensity to broaden class action usage appears to emerge from the case.

10. *David Greenshaw on behalf of himself and all others similarly situated v. Lubbock County Beverage Assn. et al.*, (CA–6, 721 F 2d 1019 (1983).

11. *Sindell et al. v. Abbott Laboratories et al.*, 26 Cal. 3d 588 (1980); certiorari denied, 499 U.S. 912 (1980).

12. The definitive marketing analysis of the *Sindell* case, its background, and its implications are found in Mary Jane Sheffet, "Market Share Liability: A New Doctrine of Causation in Product Liability," *Journal of Marketing* (Winter 1983): 35–43.

13. *Texas Industries v. Radcliff Materials*, 451 U.S. 630 (1981).

14. Proposals for the authorization of contributions by joint wrongdoers not a party to a suit is found in the Antitrust Equal Enforcement Act, Report of the Committee on the Judiciary, United States Senate, 97th Cong., 2d Sess., Report No. 97 359, (U.S. Government Printing Office, 1982), pp. 1–57. The entire issue of the treble damage remedy seems to be constantly under Congressional consideration. Illustrative is George Garvey, "Study of Antitrust Treble Damage

Remedy: Report to the Committee on the Judiciary, U.S. House of Representatives," in Bureau of National Affairs, *Antitrust and Trade Regulation Reporter*, (March 1, 1984): 356–71.

15. *Parker v. Brown*, 338 U.S. 341 (1943).

16. *Town of Hallie et al. v. City of Eau Claire*, 471 U.S. 34 (1985); *Southern Motor Carriers Rate Conference, Inc. et al. v. United States*, 471 U.S. 48 (1985).

17. *Copperweld Corp. et al. v. Independence Tube Corp.*, 469 U.S. 927 (1984).

18. *United States v. Yellow Cab Co.*, 332 U.S. 218 (1947).

19. *Kiefer-Stewart Co. v. Seagram & Sons, Inc. et al.*, 340 U.S. 211 (1951).

20. *Calder v. Bull*, 3 Dall. 386 (1798) and a succession of amplifying decisions are cited in *Constitution of the United States of America: Revised and Annotated* (Washington, D.C.: United States Government Printing Office, 1964), p. 376.

21. *Pension Benefit Guaranty Corporation v. R. A. Gray & Co.*, 467 U.S. 717 (1984).

22. *Usery v. Turner Elkhorn Mining Co.*, 428 U.S. 1 (1976).

23. *Immigration & Naturalization Service v. Chada; U.S. House of Representatives v. Immigration & Naturalization Service; U.S. Senate v. Immigration & Naturalization Service*, 462 U.S. 919 (1983).

24. The Federal Trade Commission's control by legislative veto was before the Supreme Court when the *Chada* decision was announced. In brief retort, the Supreme Court applied its decision of unconstitutionality of the legislative veto to the FTC legislative veto in *United States Senate v. Federal Trade Commission et al.; United States House of Representatives v. Federal Trade Commission et al.*, 463 U.S. 1211 (1983).

The Future of Marketing Regulation: Summary and Conclusions

Extensive examination of the regulation of marketing organization, operations, and the governing procedures provide convincing evidence that regulation is pervasive. The same examination demonstrates that regulation has expanded from elemental roots in common law and civil law to a melange of statutory enactments, judicial clarifications and interpretations, and administrative rules and decrees. No less clear but of dominating future concern are the forces that support strongly the inference that the past is, indeed, prologue.

THE RATIONALE OF THE REGULATORY MOVEMENT

In its inception, regulation was motivated by the concern that any economic system with marketing as an integral function existed to maximize consumer welfare. While the consumer was a mystical figure in the haze of theoretical formulations, the agencies of government nevertheless recognized the consumer's presence. Consumer sovereignty held sway but it did so in an economic world primarily informed and rational in its behavior. Given this perception, embodiment of regulation in extensive marketing controls did not develop quickly. Only the most egregious of business practices was brought under expanding regulatory control. Underlying faith in a competitive milieu cautioned that interference by law was seldom required.

Increasing complexity of the economic world—the full range of change from steam engines to microcomputers, to the contemporary information revolution—needs no documentation. Only necessary is the recognition that with the increasing complexity of a technological world came challenges to the fundamental assumptions of a highly competitive world dominated by rational actors. Forces at work suggested that the economy was not the simple competitive system it had once been believed to be.

As the number of businesses grew and their individual size increased, questions about the applicability of a simple competitive model followed. Threats to the viability of competition in satisfying the consumer's wants and needs seemed to appear. Acting on perception, its truth irrelevant in the action of legislators and judges, regulation burgeoned.

Not chronologically coincident with the specific legislative acts and the judicial holdings was an economic theory not of a simple competition in which rivalry of many producers protected the consumer's well-being but of "workable" competition. The departures from the simple model of competition both called for and rationalized increasing regulatory controls. The public—acting or reacting—in the growing complex economy supported and perhaps even welcomed controls designed to protect it. Rapacity of some firms and related marketing abuses led to a catalog of controls.

Currently the trend continues. Both in marketing and in the underlying theoretical base, change evolves. The theory of "workable" competition is under attack from the concept of "contestable" competition. Business size is now subjected to searching study to ascertain what kind of regulation is consistent with the goal of consumer sovereignty. Inroads of producer sovereignty occur, most frequently as recession-induced aberrations, but dominating the expansion of regulatory controls has been an ambiguous acceptance of consumer sovereignty in an increasingly less competitive world.

SHIFTING CONCEPTIONS OF REGULATORY GUIDELINES

Ambivalence has characterized the regulators' choice of guiding criterion of regulation. While early attitudes, perceiving monopolistic departures from simple competition, emphasized structure as the dominant criterion, a metamorphosis occurred. Conduct came to the fore as a criterion of regulatory action, and, as the evolution of regulatory control shows so well, conduct led to regulations on a variety of practices. Typical was the control of advertising by the unfairness doctrine and the control of pricing through price discrimination laws. Lip service was given to performance as a regulatory criterion, but the clear inference in the majority of the marketing constraints was that acceptable performance could be assured only by regulating structure and—sometimes—conduct.

American society in the mid–1980s does not yet seem willing to entrust the consumer's welfare to regulation guided by the criterion of performance. The distrust of American business is well documented.[1] Single-issue special interest groups exacerbate distrust by focusing on perceived abuses. The result, illuminated by control of labeling and advertising not only of specific products but by all product labeling and warranties, is the continued expansion of regulation of business behavior. The judicial system, supporting the expertise accorded administrative agencies designed to implement controls over marketing conduct, has rarely indicated a major reversal of the continuing evolution of control.

Yet none of the expansion of marketing regulation should be surprising. The growing affluence of the American consumer—cries of impoverishment neither surprising in a relativistic world nor accurate—supports the growing "intellectual elite" so feared by Joseph Schumpeter in his analytical declaration that capitalism could not survive.[2] Dissatisfaction with the existing system's shortcomings prompts calls for remedial and controlling actions. Technological imperatives, complicating but also creating this affluence, exacerbate the evolutionary development of regulatory growth.

Specific directions of the expansion of marketing regulation in the future are not as clear as the very high probability of their development. Discerning the fields into which consumer protection will be pushed may depend upon the direction of technological change. In an era of exploding computer technology and the joining of robotics to it, the problems that will be perceived in the future seem shadowy and even not comprehended.

A growing affluent society will, however, believe itself able to afford the growing inefficiencies and restrictions on autonomy of business that will follow.

THE NATURE OF REGULATORY CONTROLS

Proliferation of controls suggests that the certainty that flows from per se rules and specific prohibitions may give way to the flexibility of rules of reason in regulatory administration. Difficulties arise for marketers when the certainty of per se rules is replaced by the flexibility that rules of reason introduce into a judicial system that has embraced the class action suit, expanded concepts of property, absolute liability, and heavy penalties for unspecified transgressions. The rule of reason concept contains all the seeds of conflict and potential liability for unintended business errors that can be imagined in the definition of reason itself.

THE MARKETER'S RESPONSE TO REGULATORY EVOLUTION

Faced with growing regulatory restraint, marketers—and indeed the whole private business sector—must adjust as efficiently as recognition of future trends allows. The advice that follows is both unoriginal and prosaic. Marketers must make every effort to remain abreast of the changing regulatory environment within which they function. Acceleration of change suggests the growing problems with this suggestion. Moreover, it implies the development of a kind of paralegal marketing specialist to winnow the proliferating laws and regulations. Such a technological imperative also requires access to legal specialists skilled not only in general marketing controls—growing now into the field of criminal law—but the specific regulations of the industry within which the marketer functions.

AND IN THE END . . .

Too often rapid and extensive change becomes the cause for lamentations. Yet, no one laments the decline of the Empire that was neither "Holy," "Roman," nor "Empire." Marketers—as both women and men have demonstrated over the long sweep of history—can adapt to changing, though trying, times. Gradualness of evolution makes adaptation less traumatic than analysis of the nature of evolutionary changes suggests. When the trauma fades, the marketers will have demonstrated that a clear vision of the legal environment in which they operate has enabled them, too, to have contributed to a future for the public they exist to serve.

NOTES

1. Illustrative are numerous polls showing public distrust of business. Between 1970 and 1979, the percentage of poll respondents who believed "business tries to strike a fair balance between profits and the interests of the public" fell from a low 33 percent to a dismal 19 percent. In response to what business would do if it failed to "make high enough profits," 64 percent answered that "the quality and amounts of goods and services I will be able to choose from in our economy will decline" and 52 percent (only 32 percent disagreed) replied that "my standard of living will fall." The percentage of poll respondents expressing "a great deal of confidence" in the leaders of major companies fell from 55 percent in 1966 to 18 percent in 1979. See "Opinion Roundup: The Balance Sheet on Business," *Public Opinion* (April-May 1980): 21–29.

2. Joseph Schumpter, *Can Capitalism Survive?*, Colophon edition, (New York: Harper & Row, 1978).

Appendix: Selected Excerpts from Statutes Affecting Marketing

This appendix presents the most significant sections of the major federal laws regulating marketing organization, operations, and procedure. There are extensive omissions from the citations that will be apparent to the reader by the interruptions in the numbering of the sections.

At the end of the excerpts from each law, the official citation to the *United States Statutes at Large*, the official source of the federal laws, is noted parenthetically. The reader interested in examining the omitted sections can find them in the source cited. Thus, the Sherman Act is cited as 26 Stat. 209 (1890). The full citation is found in volume 26 of the *Statutes at Large* beginning on page 209. The date of the enactment is 1890. These statutes are also reprinted in *Topical Law Reports*, volume 4 (Chicago: Commerce Clearing House) and are kept current by including the citation and the reprinted text of any federal statutes which have amended the basic act since its adoption. The *United States Statutes at Large* is available in most college and university libraries and in most public libraries of significant size. The Commerce Clearing House publications are found in the business school libraries of most universities and in most law libraries.

SHERMAN ANTITRUST ACT

Sec. 1. Every contract, combination in the form of trust or otherwise, or conspiracy in restraint of trade or commerce among the several States, or with foreign nations, is hereby declared to be illegal. Every person who shall make any contract or engage in any combination or conspiracy hereby declared to be illegal shall be deemed guilty of a felony, and, on conviction thereof, shall be punished by a fine not exceeding one million dollars if a corporation, or, if any other person, one hundred thousand dollars, or by imprisonment not exceeding three years, or both said punishments, in the discretion of the court.

Sec. 2. Every person who shall monopolize, or attempt to monopolize, or combine or conspire with any other person or persons, to monopolize any part of the trade or commerce among the several States, or with foreign nations, shall be deemed guilty of a felony, and, on conviction thereof, shall be punished by a fine not exceeding one million dollars if a corporation, or if any other person, one hundred thousand dollars, or by imprisonment not exceeding three years, or by both said punishments, in the discretion of the court.

Sec. 3. Every contract, combination in the form of trust or otherwise, or conspiracy, in restraint of trade or commerce in any Territory of the United States or of the District of Columbia, or in restraint of trade or commerce between any such Territory or Territories and any State or States or the District of Columbia, or with foreign nations is hereby declared illegal. Every person who shall make any such contract or engage in such combination, or conspiracy, shall be deemed guilty of a felony, and on conviction thereof, shall be punished by fine not exceeding one million dollars if a corporation, or, if any other person, one hundred thousand dollars, or by imprisonment not exceeding three years, or by both said punishments, in the discretion of the court.

Sec. 4. The several district courts of the United States are hereby invested with jurisdiction to prevent and restrain violations of this act; and it shall be the duty of the several district attorneys of the United States, in their respective districts, under the direction of the Attorney General, to institute proceedings in equity to prevent and restrain such violations. Such proceedings may be by way of petition setting forth the case and praying that such violation shall be enjoined or otherwise prohibited. When the parties complained of shall have been duly notified of such petition the court shall proceed, as soon as may be, to the hearing and determination of the case; and pending such petition and before the final decree, the court may at any time make such temporary restraining order or prohibition as shall be deemed just in the premises.

Sec. 5. Whenever it shall appear to the court before which any proceeding under section four of this act may be pending, that the ends of justice require that other parties should be brought before the court, the court may cause them to be summoned, whether they reside in the district in which the court is held or not; and subpoenas to that end may be served in any district by the marshall thereof.

Sec. 8. That the word "person," or "persons," whenever used in this act shall be deemed to include corporations and associations existing under or authorized by the laws of either the United States, the laws of any of the Territories, the laws of any State, or the laws of any foreign countries. (26 Stat. 209 [1890]).

CLAYTON ACT

Sec. 2. (a) That it shall be unlawful for any person engaged in commerce, in the course of such commerce, either directly or indirectly, to discriminate in price between different purchasers of commodities of like grade and quality, where either or any of the purchases involved in such discrimination are in commerce, where such commodities are sold for use, consumption, or resale within the United States or any Territory thereof or the District of Columbia or any insular possession or other place under the jurisdiction of the United States, and where the effect of such discrimination may be substantially to lessen competition or tend to create a monopoly in any line of commerce, or to injure, destroy, or prevent competition with any person who either grants or knowingly receives the benefit of such discrimination, or with customers of either of them: *Provided:* That nothing herein contained shall prevent differentials which make only due allowance for differences in the cost of manufacture, sale, or delivery resulting from the differing methods or quantities in which such commodities are to such purchasers sold or delivered: *Provided however,* That the Federal Trade Commission may, after due investigation and hearing to all interested parties, fix and establish quantity limits, and revise the same as it finds necessary, as to particular commodities or classes of commodities, where it finds that available purchasers in greater quantities are so few as to render differentials on account thereof unjustly discriminatory or promotive of monopoly in any line of commerce; and the foregoing shall then not be construed to permit differentials based on differences in quantities greater than those so fixed and established. *And provided further,* That nothing herein contained shall prevent persons engaged in selling goods, wares, or merchandise in commerce from selecting their own customers in bona fide transactions and not in restraint of trade: *And, provided further,* That nothing herein contained shall prevent price changes from time to time where in response to changing conditions affecting the market for or the marketability of the goods concerned, such as but not limited to actual or imminent deterioration of perishable goods, obsolescence of seasonal goods, distress sales under court process, or sales in good faith in discontinuance of business in the goods concerned.

(b) Upon proof being made, at any hearing or complaint under this section, that there has been discrimination in price or service or facilities furnished, the burden of rebutting the prima facie case thus made by showing justification shall be upon the person charged with a violation of this section, and unless justification shall be affirmatively shown, the Commission is authorized to issue an order terminating the discrimination: *Provided, however,* That nothing herein contained shall prevent a seller rebutting the prima facie case thus made by showing that his lower price or the furnishing of services or facilities to any purchaser or purchasers was made in good faith to meet an equally low price of a competitor, or the services or facilities furnished by a competitor.

(c) That it shall be unlawful for any person engaged in commerce, in the course of such commerce, to pay or grant, or to receive or accept, anything of value as a commission, brokerage, or other compensation, or any allowance or discount in lieu thereof, except for services rendered in connection with the sale or purchase of goods, wares, or merchandise, either to the other party in such transaction or to an agent, representative, or other intermediary therein where such intermediary is acting in fact for or in behalf, or subject to the direct or indirect control, of any party to such transaction other than the person by whom such compensation is so granted or paid.

(d) That it shall be unlawful for any person engaged in commerce to pay or contract for the payment of anything of value to or for the benefit of a customer or such person in the course of such commerce as compensation or in consideration for any services or facilities furnished by or through such customer in connection with the processing, handling, sale, or offering for sale of any products or commodities manufactured, sold, or offered for sale by such person, unless such payment or consideration is available on proportionally equal terms to all other customers competing in the distribution of such products or commodities.

(e) That it shall be unlawful for any person to discriminate in favor of one purchaser against another purchaser or purchasers of a commodity bought for resale, with or without processing, by contracting to furnish or furnishing, or by contributing to the furnishing of, any services or facilities connected with the processing, handling, sale, or offering for sale of such commodity so purchased upon terms not accorded to all purchasers on proportionally equal terms.

(f) That it shall be unlawful for any person engaged in commerce, or in the course of such commerce, knowingly to induce or receive a discrimination in price which is prohibited by this section.

Sec. 3. That it shall be unlawful for any person engaged in commerce, in the course of such commerce, to lease or make a sale or contract for sale of goods, wares, merchandise, machinery, supplies or other commodities, whether patented or unpatented, for use, consumption or resale within the United States or any Territory thereof or the District of Columbia or any insular possession or other place under the jurisdiction of the United States, or fix a price charged therefor, or discount from or rebate upon, such price, on the condition, agreement or understanding that the lessee or purchaser thereof shall not use or deal in the goods, wares, merchandise, machinery, supplies, or other commodities of a competitor or competitors of the lessor or seller, where the effect of such lease, sale, or contract for sale or such condition, agreement or understanding may be to substantially lessen competition or tend to create a monopoly in any line of commerce.

Sec. 4. That any person who shall be injured in his business or property by reason of anything forbidden in the antitrust laws may sue therefor in any district court of the United States in the district in which the defendant resides, or is found, or has an agent, without respect to the amount in controversy, and shall recover threefold the damages by him sustained, and the cost of suit, including a reasonable attorney's fee.

Sec. 4 C (a) (1) Any attorney general of a State may bring a civil action in the name of such State, as parens patriae on behalf of natural persons residing in such State, in any district court of the United States having jurisdiction of the defendant, to secure monetary relief as provided in this section for injury sustained by such natural persons to their property by reason of any violation of the Sherman Act. The court shall exclude from the amount of monetary relief awarded in such action any amount of monetary relief awarded in such action (A) which duplicates amounts which have been awarded for the same injury, or (B) which is properly allocable to (i) natural persons who have excluded their claims pursuant to subsection (b) (2) of this section, and (ii) any business entity.

(2) The court shall award the State as monetary relief threefold the total damage sustained as described in paragraph (1) of this subsection, and the cost of suit, including a reasonable attorney's fee.

Sec. 4 D. In any action under Section 4C(a)(1), in which there has been a determination that a defendant agreed to fix prices in violation of the Sherman Act, damages may be proved and assessed in the aggregate by statistical or sampling methods, by the computation of illegal overcharges, or by such other reasonable system for estimating aggregate damages as the court in its discretion may permit without the necessity of separately proving the individual claim of, or amount of damage to, persons on whose behalf the suit was brought.

Sec. 4 E. Monetary relief recovered in an action under Section 4C(a)(1) shall—

(1) be distributed in such manner as the district court in its discretion may authorize; or

(2) be deemed a civil penalty by the court and deposited with the State as general revenue; subject in either case to the requirement that any distribution procedure adopted afford each person a reasonable opportunity to secure his appropriate portion of the net monetary relief.

Sec. 5. (a) A final judgment or decree heretofore or hereafter rendered in any civil or criminal proceeding brought by or on behalf of the United States under the antitrust laws to the effect that a defendant has violated said laws shall be prima facie evidence against such defendant in any action or proceeding brought by any other party against such defendant under said laws or by the United States under section 4A, as to all matters respecting which said judgment or decree would be an estoppel as between the parties thereto: *Provided,* that this section shall not apply to consent judgments or decrees entered before any testimony has been taken or to judgments or decrees entered in actions under Section 4A.

(e) Before entering any consent judgment proposed by the United States under this section, the court shall determine that the entry of such judgment is in the public interest. For the purpose of such determination, the court may consider—

(1) the competitive impact of such judgment, including termination of alleged violations, provisions for enforcement and modification, duration or relief sought, anticipated effects of alternative remedies actually considered, and any other considerations bearing upon the adequacy of such judgment;

(2) the impact of entry of such judgment upon the public generally and individuals alleging specific injury from the violations set forth in the complaint including consideration of the public benefit, if any, to be derived from a determination of the issues at trial.

Sec. 6. That the labor of a human being is not a commodity or article of commerce. Nothing contained in the antitrust laws shall be construed to forbid the existence and operation of labor, agricultural, or horticultural organizations, instituted for the purposes of mutual help, and not having capital stock or conducted for profit, or to forbid or restrain individual members of such organizations from lawfully carrying out the legitimate objects thereof; nor shall such organizations, or the members thereof, be held or construed to be illegal combinations or conspiracies in restraint of trade, under the antitrust laws.

Sec.7. That no corporation engaged in commerce shall acquire, directly or indirectly, the whole or any part of the stock or other share capital and no corporation subject to the jurisdiction of the Federal Trade Commission shall acquire the whole or any part of the assets of another corporation engaged also in commerce, where in any line of commerce in any section of the country, the effect of such acquisition may be substantially to lessen competition, or tend to create a monopoly.

No corporation shall acquire, directly or indirectly, the whole or any part of the stock or other share capital and no corporation subject to the jurisdiction of the Federal Trade Commission shall acquire the whole or any part of the assets of another corporation engaged also in commerce, where in any line of commerce in any section of the country, the effect of such acquisition, may be substantially to lessen competition, or to tend to create a monopoly.

No corporation shall acquire, directly or indirectly, the whole or any part of the stock or other share capital and no corporation subject to the jurisdiction of the Federal Trade Commission shall acquire the whole or any part of the assets of one or more corporations engaged in commerce, where in any line of commerce in any section of the country, the effect of such acquisition, of such stocks or assets, or the use of such stock by the voting or granting of proxies or otherwise, may be substantially to lessen competition, or to tend to create a monopoly.

Sec. 14. That whenever a corporation shall violate any of the penal provisions of the antitrust laws, such violation shall be deemed to be also that of the individual directors, officers, or agents of such corporation who shall have authorized, ordered, or done any of the acts constituting in whole or in part such violation shall be deemed a misdemeanor, and upon conviction thereof of any director, officer, or agent he shall be punished by a fine of not exceeding $5,000 or by imprisonment for not exceeding one year, or by both, in the discretion of the court. (38 Stat. 730, as amended, [1914]).

FEDERAL TRADE COMMISSION ACT

An act to create a Federal Trade Commission, to define its powers and duties, and for other purposes.

Sec. 1. *Be it enacted by the Senate and House of Representatives of the United States of America in Congress assembled,* That a commission is hereby created and established, to be known as the Federal Trade Commission (hereinafter referred to as the commission), which shall be composed of five commissioners, who shall be appointed by the President, by and with the advice and consent of the Senate. Not more than three of the commissioners shall be members of the same political party. The first commissioners appointed shall continue in office for terms of three, four, five, six, and seven years, respectively, from the date of the taking effect of this Act, the term of each to be designated by the President, but their successors shall be appointed for terms of seven years, except that any person chosen to fill a vacancy shall be appointed only for the unexpired term of the commissioner whom he shall succeed: *Provided, however,* That upon the expiration of his term of office a Commissioner shall continue to serve until his successor shall have been appointed and shall have qualified. The commission shall choose a chairman from its own membership. No commissioner shall engage in any other business, vocation, or employment. Any commissioner may be removed by the President for inefficiency, neglect of duty or malfeasance in office. A vacancy in the commission shall not impair the right of the remaining commissioners to exercise all the powers of the commission.

The commission shall have an official seal, which shall be judicially noticed.

Sec. 5. (a) (1) Unfair methods of competition in or affecting commerce, and unfair or deceptive acts of practices in or affecting commerce, are hereby declared unlawful.

(2) Nothing contained in this Act or in any of the Antitrust Acts shall render unlawful any contracts or agreements prescribing minimum or stipulated prices, or requiring a vendee to enter into contracts or agreements prescribing minimum or stipulated prices, for the resale of a commodity which bears, or the label or container of which bears, the trademark, brand or name of the producer or distributor of such commodity and which is in free and open competition with commodities of the same general class produced or distributed by others, when contracts or agreements of that description are lawful as applied to intrastate transactions under any statute, law, or public policy now or hereafter in effect in any State, Territory, or the District of Columbia in which such resale is to be made, or to which the commodity is to be transported for such resale.

(4) Neither the making of contracts or agreements described in paragraph (2) of this subsection, nor the exercise or enforcement of any right or right of action as described in paragraph (3) of this subsection shall constitute an unlawful burden or restraint upon, or interference with, commerce.

(5) Nothing contained in paragraph (2) of this subsection shall make lawful contracts or agreements providing for the establishment or maintenance of minimum or stipulated resale prices on any commodity referred to in paragraph (2) of this subsection, between manufacturers, or between producers, or between wholesalers, or between brokers, or between factors, or between retailers, or between persons, firms, or corporations in competition with each other.

(6) The Commission is hereby empowered and directed to prevent persons, partnerships, or corporations, except banks, common carriers subject to the Acts to regulate commerce, air carriers, and foreign air carriers subject to the Federal Aviation Act of 1958, and persons, partnerships, or corporations insofar as they are subject to the Packers and Stockyards Act, 1921, as amended, except as provided in section 406(b) of said Act, from using unfair methods of competition in commerce and unfair or deceptive acts or practices in commerce.

(b) Whenever the Commission shall have reason to believe that any such person, partnership, or corporation has been or is using any unfair method of competition or unfair or deceptive act of practice in commerce, and if it shall appear to the Commission that a proceeding by it in respect thereof would be in the interests of the public, it shall issue and serve upon such person, partnership, or corporation a complaint stating its charges in that respect and containing a notice of a hearing upon a day and at a place therein fixed at least thirty days after the service of said complaint. The person, partnership, or corporation so complained of shall have the right to appear at the place and time so fixed and show cause why an order should not be entered by the Commission requiring such person, partnership, or corporation to cease and desist from the violation of the law so charged in said complaint. Any person, partnership, or corporation may make application, and upon good cause shown may be allowed by the Commission to intervene and appear in said proceeding by counsel or in person. The testimony in any such proceeding shall be reduced to writing and filed in the office of the Commission. If upon such hearing the

Commission shall be of the opinion that the method of competition or the act or practice in question is prohibited by this Act, it shall make a report in writing in which it shall state its findings as to the facts and shall issue and cause to be served on such person, partnership, or corporation an order requiring such person, partnership, or corporation to cease and desist from using such method of competition or such act or practice. Until the expiration of the time allowed for filing a petition for review, if no such petition has been duly filed within such time, or, if a petition for review has been filed within such time then until the record in the proceeding has been filed in a court of appeals of the United States, as hereinafter provided, the Commission may at any time, upon such notice and in such manner as it shall deem proper, modify or set aside, in whole or in part, any report or any order made or issued by it under this section. After the expiration of the time allowed for filing a petition for review, if no such petition has been duly filed within such time, the Commission may at any time, after notice and opportunity for hearing, reopen and later, modify, or set aside, in whole or in part, any report or order made or issued by it under this section, whenever in the opinion of the Commission conditions of the fact or of law have so changed as to require such action or if the public interest shall so require: *Provided, however*, that the said person, partnership, or corporation, may, within sixty days after service upon him or it of said report or order entered after service upon him or it of said report or order entered after such a reopening, obtain a review thereof in the appropriate court of appeals of the United States in the manner provided in subsection (c) of this section.

(c) Any person, partnership, or corporation required by an order of the Commission to cease and desist from using any method of competition or act or practice may obtain a review of such order in the court of appeals of the United States, within any circuit where the method of competition or the act or practice in question was used or where such person, partnership, or corporation resides or carries on business, by filing in the court within sixty days from the date of the service of such order, a written petition praying that the order of the Commission be set aside. A copy of such petition shall be forthwith transmitted by clerk of the court to the Commission, and thereupon the Commission shall file in the court the record in the proceeding, as provided in section 2111 of title 28, United States Code. Upon such filing of the petition the court shall have jurisdiction of the proceeding and of the question determined therein concurrently with the Commission until the filing of the record and shall have power to make and enter a decree affirming, modifying, or setting aside the order of the Commission, and enforcing the same to the extent that such order is affirmed and to issue such writs as are ancillary to its jurisdiction or are necessary in its judgment to prevent injury to the public or to competitors pendente lite. The findings of the Commission as to the facts, if supported by evidence, shall be conclusive. To the extent that the order of the Commission is affirmed, the court shall thereupon issue its own order commanding obedience to the terms of such order of the Commission. If either party shall apply to the court for leave to adduce additional evidence, and shall show to the satisfaction of the court that such additional evidence is material and that there were reasonable grounds for the failure to adduce such evidence in the proceeding before the Commission, the court may order such additional evidence to be taken before the Commission and to be adduced upon the hearing in such manner and upon such terms and conditions as to the court may seem proper. The Commission may modify its findings as to the facts, or make new findings, by reason of the additional evidence so taken, and it shall file such modified or new findings, which, if supported by evidence, shall be conclusive, and its recommendations, if any, for the modification or setting aside of its original order, with the return of such additional evidence. The judgment and decree of the court shall be final, except that the same shall be subject to review by the Supreme Court upon certiorari, as provided in section 240 of the judicial code.

(d) Upon the filing of the record with it, the jurisdiction of the court of appeals of the United States to affirm, enforce, modify, or set aside orders of the Commission shall be exclusive.

(e) Such proceedings in the court of appeals shall be given precedence over other cases pending therein, and shall be in every way expedited. No order of the Commission or judgment of the court to enforce the same shall in anywise relieve or absolve any person, partnership, or corporation from any liability under the Antitrust Acts.

(f) Complaints, orders, and other processes of the Commission under this section may be served by anyone duly authorized by the Commission, either (a) by delivering a copy thereof to the person to be served, or to a member of the partnership to be served, or the president, secretary, or other executive officer or a director of the corporation to be served; or (b) by leaving a copy thereof at the residence or the principal office or place of business of such person, partnership, or corporation; or (c) by mailing a copy thereof by registered mail or by certified mail addressed to such person, partnership, or corporation at his or its residence or principal office or place of business. The verified return by the person so serving said complaint, order, or other process setting forth the manner of said service shall be proof of the same, and the return post office receipt for said complaint, order, or other process mailed by registered mail or certified mail as aforesaid shall be proof of the service of the same.

(g) An order of the Commission to cease and desist shall become final—

(1) Upon the expiration of the time allowed for filing a petition for review, of no such petition has been duly filed within such time; but the Commission may thereafter modify or set aside its order to the extent provided in the last sentence of subsection (b); or

(2) Upon the expiration of the time allowed for filing a petition for certiorari, if the order of the Commission has been affirmed, or the petition for review dismissed by the court of appeals, and no petition for certiorari has been duly filed; or

(3) Upon denial of a petition for certiorari, if the order of the Commission has been affirmed or the petition for review dismissed by the court of appeals; or

(4) Upon the expiration of thirty days from the date of issuance of the mandate of the Supreme Court, if such Court directs that the order of the Commission be affirmed or the petition for review dismissed.

(h) If the Supreme Court directs that the order of the Commission be modified or set aside, the order of the Commission rendered in accordance with the mandate of the Supreme Court shall become final upon the expiration of thirty days from the time it was rendered, unless within such thirty days either party has instituted proceedings to have such order corrected to accord with the mandate, in which event the order of the Commission shall become final when so corrected.

(i) If the order of the Commission is modified or set aside by the court of appeals, and if (1) the time allowed for filing a petition for certiorari has expired and no such petition has been duly filed, or (2) the petition for certiorari has been denied, or (3) the decision of the court has been affirmed by the Supreme Court, then the order of the Commission rendered in accordance with the mandate of the court of appeals shall become final on the expiration of thirty days from the time such order of the Commission was rendered, unless within such thirty days either party has instituted proceedings to have such order corrected so that it will accord with the mandate, in which event the order of the Commission shall become final when so corrected.

(j) If the Supreme Court orders a rehearing or if the case is remanded by the court of appeals to the Commission for a rehearing, and if (1) the time allowed for filing a petition for certiorari has expired, and no such petition has been duly filed, or (2) the petition for certiorari has been denied, or (3) the decision of the court has been affirmed by the Supreme Court, then the order of the Commission rendered upon such rehearing shall become final in the same manner as though no prior order of the Commission had been rendered.

(k) As used in this section, the term "mandate," in case a mandate has been recalled prior to the expiration of thirty days from the date of issuance thereof, means the final mandate.

(l) Any person, partnership, or corporation who violates any order of the Commission to cease and desist after it has become final, and while such order is in effect, shall forfeit and pay to the United States a civil penalty of not more than $10,000 for each violation, which shall accrue to the United States and may be recovered in a civil action brought by the Attorney General of the United States. Each separate violation of such an order shall be a separate offense, except that in the case of a violation through continuing failure or neglect to obey a final order of the Commission each day of continuance of such failure or neglect shall be deemed a separate offense. In such actions, the United States District Courts are empowered to grant mandatory injunctions and seek such other and further equitable relief as they deem appropriate in the enforcement of such final orders of the Commission. (938 Stat. 717, as amended, [1914]).

MAGNUSON-MOSS WARRANTY—FEDERAL TRADE COMMISSION IMPROVEMENT ACT

Sec. 104. (a) In order for a warrantor warranting a consumer product by means of a written warranty to meet the Federal minimum standards for warranty—

(1) such warrantor must as a minimum remedy such consumer product within a reasonable time and without charge, in the case of a defect, malfunction, or failure to conform with such written warranty;

(2) notwithstanding section 108(b), such warrantor may not impose any limitation on the duration of any implied warranty on the product;

(3) such warrantor may not exclude or limit consequential damages for breach of any written or implied warranty on such product, unless such exclusion or limitation conspicuously appears on the face of the warranty; and

(4) if the product (or a component part thereof) contains a defect or malfunction after a reasonable number of attempts by the warrantor to remedy defects of malfunctions in such product, such warrantor must permit the consumer to elect either a refund for or replacement without charge of such product or part (as the case may be). The Commission may by rule specify for purposes of this paragraph, what constitutes a reasonable number of attempts to remedy particular kinds of defects or malfunctions under different circumstances. If the warrantor replaces a component part of a consumer product, such replacement shall include installing the part in the product without charge.

(b)(1) In fulfilling the duties under subsection (a) respecting a written warranty, the warrantor shall not impose any duty other than notification upon any consumer as a condition of securing remedy of any consumer product which malfunctions, is defective, or does not conform to the written warranty, unless the warrantor has demonstrated in a rulemaking proceeding, or can demonstrate in an administrative or judicial enforcement proceeding (including private enforcement), or in an informal dispute settlement proceeding, that such a duty is reasonable.

(2) Notwithstanding paragraph (1), a warrantor may require, as a condition to replacement of, or refund for, any consumer product under subsection (a), that such consumer product shall be made available to the warrantor free and clear of liens and other encumbrances, except as otherwise provided by rule or order of the Commission in cases in which such a requirement would not be practicable.

(3) The Commission may, by rule define in detail the duties set forth in section 104(a) of the Act and the applicability of such duties to warrantors of different categories of consumer products with "full (statement of duration)" warranties.

(4) The duties under subsection (a) extend from the warrantor to each person who is a consumer with respect to the consumer product.

(c) The performance of the duties under subsection (a) of this section shall not be required of the warrantor if he can show that the defect, malfunction, or failure of any warranted consumer product to conform with a written warranty, was caused by damage (not resulting from defect or malfunction) while in the possession of the consumer, or unreasonable use (including failure to provide reasonable and necessary maintenance.)

(d) For purposes of this section and of section 102(c), the term "without charge" means that the warrantor may not assess the consumer for any costs the warrantor or his representatives incur in connection with the required remedy of a warranted consumer product. An obligation under subsection (a)(1)(A) to remedy without charge does not necessarily require the warrantor to compensate the consumer for incidental expenses; however, if any incidental expenses are incurred because the remedy is not made within a reasonable time or because the warrantor imposed an unreasonable duty upon the consumer as a condition of securing remedy, then the consumer shall be entitled to recover reasonable incidental expenses which are so incurred in any action against the warrantor.

(e) If a supplier designates a warranty applicable to a consumer product as a "full (statement of duration)" warranty, then the warranty on such product shall, for purposes of any action under section 110(d) or under any State law, be deemed to incorporate at least the minimum requirements of this section and rules prescribed under this section.

Full and Limited Warranting of a Consumer Product

Sec. 105. Nothing in this title shall prohibit the selling of a consumer product which has both full and limited warranties if such warranties are clearly and conspicuously differentiated. (88 Stat. 2183 [1975].

PURE FOOD ACT

Be it enacted by the Senate and House of Representatives of the United States of America in Congress assembled, That it shall be unlawful for any person to manufacture within any Territory or the District of Columbia any article of food or drug which is adulterated or misbranded, within the meaning of this Act; and any person who shall violate any of the provisions of this section shall be guilty of a misdemeanor, and for each offense shall, upon conviction thereof, be fined not to exceed five hundred dollars or shall be sentenced to one year's imprisonment, or both such fine and imprisonment, in the discretion of the court, and for each subsequent offense and conviction thereof shall be fined not less than one thousand dollars or sentenced to one year's imprisonment, or both such fine and imprisonment in the discretion of the court.

Sec. 2. That the introduction into any State or Territory or the District of Columbia from any other State or Territory or the District of Columbia, or from any foreign country, or shipment to any foreign country of any article of food or drugs which is adulterated or misbranded, within the meaning of this Act, is hereby prohibited; and any person who shall ship or deliver for shipment from any State or Territory or the District of Columbia, to any other State or Territory or the District of Columbia, or to a foreign country, or who shall receive in any State or Territory or the District of Columbia from any other State or Territory or the District of Columbia, or foreign country, and having so received, shall deliver in original unbroken packages, for pay or otherwise, or offer to deliver to any other person, any such article so adulterated or misbranded within the meaning of this Act, or any person who shall sell or offer for sale in the District of Columbia or the Territories of the United States any such adulterated or misbranded foods or drugs, or export or offer to export the same to any foreign country, shall be guilty of a misdemeanor, and for such offense be fined not exceeding two hundred dollars for the first offense, and upon conviction for each subsequent offense not exceeding three hundred dollars or be imprisoned not exceeding one year, or both, in the discretion of the court: *Provided,* That no article shall be deemed misbranded or adulterated within the provisions of this Act when intended for export to any foreign country and prepared or packed according to the specifications or directions of the foreign purchaser when no substance is used in the preparation or packing thereof in conflict with the laws of the foreign country to which said article is intended to be shipped; but if said article shall be in fact sold or offered for sale for domestic use or consumption, then this proviso shall not exempt said article from the operation of any of the other provisions of this Act.

Sec. 6. That the term "drug," as used in this Act, shall include all medicines and preparations recognized in the United States Pharmacopoeia or National Formulary for internal or external use, and any substance or mixture of substances intended to be used for the cure, mitigation, or prevention of disease of either man or other animals. The term "food," as used herein, shall include all articles used for food, drink, confectionery, or condiment by man or other animals, whether simple, mixed, or compound.

Sec. 7. That for the purposes of this Act an article shall be deemed to be adulterated:

In the case of drugs:

First, If, when a drug is sold under or by a name recognized in the United States Pharmacopoeia or National Formulary, it differs from the standards of strength, quality, or purity, as determined by the test laid down in the United States Pharmacopoeia or National Formulary official at the time of investigation: *Provided*, That no drug defined in the United States Pharmacopoeia or National Formulary shall be deemed to be adulterated under this provision if the standard of strength, quality, or purity be plainly stated upon the bottle, box, or other container thereof although the standard may differ from that determined by the test laid down in the United States Pharmacopoeia or National Formulary.

Second, If its strength or purity fall below the professed standard or quality under which it is sold.

In the case of the confectionery:

If it contain terra alba, barytes, talc, chrome yellow, or other mineral substance or poisonous color or flavor, or other ingredient deleterious or detrimental to health, or a vinous, malt or spirituous liquor or compound or narcotic drug.

In the case of food:

First. If any substance has been mixed and packed with it so as to reduce or lower or injuriously affect its quality or strength.

Second. If any substance has been substituted wholly or in part for the article.

Third. If any valuable constituent of the article has been wholly or in part abstracted.

Fourth. If it be mixed, colored, powdered, coated, or stained in a manner whereby damage of inferiority is concealed.

Fifth. If it contain any added poisonous or other added deleterious ingredient which may render such article injurious to health: *Provided*, That when in the preparation of food products for shipment they are preserved by an external application applied in such manner that the preservative is necessarily removed mechanically, or by maceration in water, or otherwise, and directions for the removal of said preservative shall be printed on the covering or the package, the provisions of this Act shall be construed as applying only when said products are ready for consumption.

Sixth. If it consists in whole or in part of a filthy, decomposed, or putrid animal or vegetable substance, or any portion of an animal unfit for food, whether manufactured or not, or if it is the product of a diseased animal, or one that has died otherwise than by slaughter.

Sec. 8. That the term "misbranded," as used herein, shall apply to all drugs, or articles of food, or articles which enter into the composition of food, the package or label of which shall bear any statement, design, or device regarding such article, or the ingredients, or substances contained therein which shall be false or misleading in any particular, and to any food or drug product which is falsely branded as to the State, Territory, or country in which it is manufactured or produced.

That for the purposes of this Act an article shall also be deemed to be misbranded:

In the case of drugs:

First. If it be an imitation of or offered for sale under the name of another article.

Second. If the contents of the package as originally put up shall have been removed, in whole or in part, and other contents shall have been placed in such package, or if the package fail to bear a statement on the label of the quantity or proportion of any alcohol, morphine, opium, cocaine, heroin, alpha or beta eucane, chloroform, cannabis indica, chloral hydrate, or acetanilide, or any derivative or preparation of any such substances contained therein.

In the case of food:

First. If it be an imitation of or offered for sale under the distinctive name of another article.

Second. If it be labeled or branded so as to deceive or mislead the purchaser, or purport to be a foreign product when not so, or if the contents of the package as originally put up shall have been removed in whole or in part and other contents shall have been placed in such package, or if it fail to bear a statement on the label of the quantity or proportion of any morphine, opium, cocaine, heroin, alpha or beta eucane, chloroform, cannabis indica, chloral hydrate, or acetanilide, or any derivative or preparation of any such substances contained therein.

Third, If in package form, and the contents are stated in terms of weight or measure, they are not plainly and correctly stated on the outside of the package.

Fourth. If the package containing it or its label shall bear any statement, design, or device regarding the ingredients for the substances contained therein, which statement, design or device shall be false or misleading in any particular: *Provided*, That an article of food which does not contain any added poisonous or deleterious ingredients shall not be deemed to be adulterated or misbranded in the following cases:

First. In the case of mixtures or compounds which may be now or from time to time hereafter known as articles of food, under their own distinctive names, and not an imitation of or offered for sale under the distinctive name of another article, if the name be accompanied on the same label or brand with a statement of the place where said article has been manufactured or produced.

Second. In the case of articles labeled, branded, or tagged so as to plainly indicate that they are compounds, imitations, or blends, and the word "compound," "imitation," or "blend," as the case may be is plainly stated on the package in which it is offered for sale: *Provided*, That the term blend as used herein shall be construed to mean a mixture of like substances, not excluding harmless coloring or flavoring ingredients used for the purpose of coloring and flavoring only: *And provided further,* That nothing in this Act shall be construed as requiring or compelling proprietors or manufacturers of proprietary foods which contain no unwholesome added ingredient to disclose their trade formulas, except in so far as the provisions of this Act may require to secure freedom from adulteration or misbranding.

Sec. 9. That no dealer shall be prosecuted under the provisions of this Act when he can establish a guaranty signed by the wholesaler, jobber, manufacturer, or other party residing in the United States, from whom he purchases such articles, to the effect that the same is not adulterated or misbranded within the meaning of this Act, designating it. Said guaranty, to afford protection, shall contain the name and address of the party or parties making the sale of such articles to such dealers, and in such case said party or parties shall be amenable to the prosecution, fines, and other penalties which would attach, in due course, to the dealer under the provisions of this Act. (34 Stat. 768 [1906]).

FEDERAL FOOD, DRUG AND COSMETIC ACT

An act to prohibit the movement in interstate commerce of adulterated and misbranded food, drugs, devices, and cosmetics, and for other purposes.
Definitions

Sec. 201. For the purposes of this Act—

(f) The term "food" means (1) articles used for food or drink for man or other animals, (2) chewing gum, and (3) articles used for components of any such article.

(g)(1) The term "drug" means (A) articles recognized in the official United States Pharmacopoeia, official Homeopathic Pharmacopoeia of the United States, or official National Formulary, or any supplement to any of them; and (B) articles intended for use in the diagnosis, cure, mitigation, treatment or prevention of disease in man or other animals; and (C) articles (other than food) intended to affect the structure or any function of the body of man or other animals; and (D) articles intended for use as a component of any article specified in clause (A), (B), or (C); but does not include devices or their components, parts, or accessories.

(h) The term "device" (except when used in paragraph (n) of this section and in sections 301(i), 403(f), 502(c), and 602(c)) means instruments, apparatus, and contrivances, including their components, parts, and accessories, intended (1) for use in the diagnosis, cure, mitigation, treatment, or prevention of disease in man or other animals; or (2) to affect the structure or any function of the body of man or other animals.

(i) The term "cosmetic" means (1) articles intended to be rubbed, poured, sprinkled, or sprayed on, introduced into, or otherwise applied to the human body or any part thereof for cleansing, beautifying, promoting attractiveness, or altering the appearance, and (2) articles intended for use as a component of any such articles; except that such term shall not include soap.

Sec. 701. (a) The authority to promulgate regulations for the efficient enforcement of this Act, except as otherwise provided in this section, is hereby vested in the Secretary. (52 Stat. 1040, as amended, [1938]).

FAIR PACKAGING AND LABELING ACT

Sec. 3. (a) It shall be unlawful for any person engaged in the packaging or labeling of any consumer commodity (as defined in this Act) for the distribution in commerce, or for any person (other than a common carrier for hire, a contract carrier for hire, or a freight forwarder for hire) to engage in the distribution in commerce of any packaged or labeled consumer commodity, to distribute or to cause to be distributed in commerce and such commodity if such commodity is contained in a package, or if there is affixed to that commodity a label, which does not conform to the provisions of this Act and of regulations promulgated under the authority of this Act.

(b) The prohibition contained in subsection (a) shall not apply to persons engaged in business as wholesale or retail distributors of consumer commodities except to the extent that such persons (1) are engaged in the packaging or labeling of such commodities, or (2) prescribe or specify by any means the manner in which such commodities are packaged or labeled.

Sec. 4. (a) No person subject to the prohibition contained in section 3 shall distribute or cause to be distributed in commerce any packaged consumer commodity unless in conformity with regulations which shall be established by the promulgating authority pursuant to section 6 of this Act which shall provide that—

(1) The commodity shall bear a label specifying the identity of the commodity and the name and place of business of the manufacturer, packer, or distributor;

(2) The net quantity of contents (in terms of weight, measure, or numerical count) shall be separately and accurately stated in a uniform location upon the principal display panel of that label;

(3) The separate label statement of net quantity of contents appearing upon or affixed to any package—

(A)(i) if on a package containing less than four pounds or one gallon and labeled in terms of weight or fluid measure, shall, unless subparagraph (ii) applies and such statement is set forth in accordance with such subparagraph, be expressed both in ounces (with identification as to avoirdupois or fluid ounces) and, if applicable, in pounds for weight units, with any remainder in terms of ounces or common or decimal fractions of the pound; or in the case of liquid measure, in the largest whole unit quarts, quarts and pints, or pints, as appropriate) with any remainder in terms of fluid ounces or common or decimal fractions of the pint or quart;

(ii) if on a random package, may be expressed in terms of pounds and decimal fractions of the pound carried out to not more than two decimal places;

(iii) if on a package labeled in terms of linear measure, shall be expressed both in terms of inches and the largest whole unit (yards, yards and feet, or feet, as appropriate) with any remainder in terms of inches or common or decimal fractions of the foot or yard;

(iv) if on a package labeled in terms of measure of area, shall be expressed both in terms of square inches and the largest whole square unit (square yards, square yards and square feet, or square feet, as appropriate) with any remainder in terms of square inches or common or decimal fractions of the square foot or square yard;

(B) shall appear in conspicuous and easily legible type in distinct contrast (by typography, layout, color, embossing, or molding) with other matter on the package;

(C) shall contain letters or numerals in a type size which shall be (i) established in relationship to the area of the principal display panel of the package, and (ii) uniform for all packages of substantially the same size; and

(D) shall be so placed that the lines of printed matter included in that statement are generally parallel to the base on which the package rests as it is designed to be displayed; and

(4) The label of any package of a consumer commodity which bears a representation as to number of servings of such commodity contained in such package shall bear a statement of the net quantity (in terms of weight, measure, or numerical count) of each such serving.

(5) For purposes of paragraph (3)(A)(ii) of this subsection the term "random package" means a package which is one of a lot, shipment or delivery of packages of the same consumer commodity with varying weights, that is, packages, with no fixed weight pattern.

(b) No person subject to the prohibition contained in section 3 shall distribute or cause to be distributed in commerce any packaged consumer commodity if any qualifying words or phrases appear in conjunction with the separate statement of the net quantity of contents required by subsection (a), but nothing in this subsection or in paragraph (2) of subsection (a) shall prohibit supplemental statements, at other places on the package, describing in nondeceptive terms the net quantity of contents: *Provided,* That such supplemental statements of net quantity contents shall not include any term qualifying a unit of weight, measure, or count that tends to exaggerate the amount of the commodity contained in the package. (80 Stat. 1296, as amended, [1966]).

WOOL PRODUCTS LABELING ACT

Sec. 3. The introduction, or manufacture for introduction, into commerce, or the sale, transportation, or distribution, in commerce, of any wool product which is misbranded within the meaning of this Act or the rules and regulations hereunder, is unlawful and shall be an unfair method of competition, and an unfair and deceptive act or practice, in commerce under the Federal Trade Commission Act; and any person who shall manufacture or deliver for shipment or ship or sell or offer for sale in commerce, any such wool product which is misbranded within the meaning of this Act and the rules and regulations hereunder is guilty of an unfair method of competition, and an unfair and deceptive act or practice, in commerce within the meaning of the Federal Trade Commission Act. (54 Stat. 1128 [1940]).

FUR PRODUCTS LABELING ACT

Sec. 3. (a) The introduction, or manufacture for introduction, into commerce, or the sale, advertising or offering for sale in commerce, or the transportation or distribution in commerce, of any fur product which is misbranded or falsely or deceptively advertised or invoiced, within the meaning of this Act or the rules and regulations prescribed under section 8 (b), is unlawful and shall be an unfair and deceptive act or practice, in commerce under the Federal Trade Commission Act.

(b) The manufacture for sale, advertising, offering for sale, transportation or distribution, of any fur product which is made in whole or in part of fur which has been shipped and received in commerce, and which is misbranded or falsely or deceptively advertised or invoiced, within the meaning of this Act or the rules and regulations prescribed under section 8 (b), is unlawful and shall be an unfair method of competition, and an unfair and deceptive act or practice, in commerce under the Federal Trade Commission Act.

(c) The introduction into commerce, or the sale, advertising or offering for sale in commerce, or the transportation or distribution in commerce, of any fur which is falsely or deceptively advertised or falsely or deceptively invoiced, within the meaning of this Act or the rules and regulations prescribed under Section 8(b), is unlawful and shall be an unfair method of competition, and an unfair and deceptive act or practice, in commerce under the Federal Trade Commission Act. (65 Stat. 175 [1951]).

FLAMMABLE FABRICS ACT

Sec. 3. (a) The manufacture for sale, the sale or the offering for sale, in commerce, or the importation into the United States, or the introduction, delivery for introduction, transportation or causing to be transported, in commerce, or the sale or delivery after a sale or shipment in commerce, of any product, fabric, or related material which fails to conform to an applicable standard or regulation issued or amended under the provisions of section 4 of this Act, shall be unlawful and shall be an unfair method of competition and an unfair and deceptive act or practice in commerce under the Federal Trade Commission Act.

(b) The manufacture for sale, the sale, or the offering for sale, of any product made of fabric or related material which fails to conform to an applicable standard or regulation issued or amended under section 4 of this Act, and which has been shipped or received in commerce shall be unlawful and shall be an unfair method of competition and an unfair and deceptive act or practice in commerce under the Federal Trade Commission Act. (67 Stat. 111, as amended, [1953]).

TEXTILE FIBER PRODUCTS IDENTIFICATION ACT

Sec. 3. (a) The introduction, delivery for introduction, manufacture for introduction, sale, advertising, or offering for sale, in commerce, or the transportation or causing to be transported in commerce, or the importation into the United States, of any textile fiber product which is misbranded or falsely or deceptively advertised within the meaning of this Act or the rules and regulations promulgated thereunder, is unlawful, and shall be an unfair method of competition and an unfair and deceptive act or practice in commerce under the Federal Trade Commission Act.

(b) The sale, offering for sale, advertising, delivery, transportation, or causing to be transported, of any textile fiber product which has been advertised or offered for sale in commerce, and which is misbranded or falsely or deceptively advertised, within the meaning of this Act or the rules and regulations promulgated thereunder, is unlawful, and shall be an unfair method of competition and an unfair and deceptive act or practice in commerce under the Federal Trade Commission Act.

(c) The sale, offering for sale, advertising, delivery, transportation, or causing to be transported, after shipment in commerce, of any textile fiber product, whether in its original state or contained in other textile fiber products, which is misbranded or falsely or deceptively advertised within the meaning of this Act or the rules and regulations promulgated thereunder, is unlawful, and shall be an unfair method of competition and an unfair and deceptive act or practice in commerce under the Federal Trade Commission Act.

Sec. 4. (a) Except as otherwise provided in this Act, a textile fiber product shall be misbranded if it is falsely or deceptively stamped, tagged, labeled, invoiced, advertised or otherwise identified as to the name or amount of constituent fibers contained therein.

(c) For the purpose of this Act, a textile fiber product shall be considered to be falsely or deceptively advertised if any disclosure or implication of the fiber content is made in any written advertisement which is used to aid, promote, or assist directly or indirectly in the sale or offering for sale of such textile fiber product, unless the same information as that required to be shown on the stamp, tag, label, or other identification under section 4(b)(1) and (2) is contained in the heading, body, or other part of such written advertisement, except that the percentages of the fiber present in the textile fiber product need not be stated. (72 Stat. 1717 [1958]).

LANHAM TRADE-MARK ACT

An act to provide for the registration and protection of trademarks used in commerce, to carry out the provisions of certain international conventions, and for other purposes.

Sec. 14. A verified petition to cancel a registration of a mark, stating the grounds relied upon, may, upon payment of the prescribed fee, be filed by any person who believes that he is or will be damaged by the registration of a mark on the principal register established by this Act, or under the Act of March 3, 1881, or the Act of February 20, 1905—

(a) within five years from the date of the registration of the mark under this Act; or

(b) within five years from the date of publication under section 12(c) hereof of a mark registered under the Act of March 3, 1881, or the Act of February 20, 1905; or

(c) at any time if the registered mark becomes the common descriptive name of an article or substance, or has been abandoned, or its registration was obtained fraudulently or contrary to the provisions of section 4 of subsections (a), (b), or (c) of section 2 of this Act for a registration hereunder, or contrary to similar prohibitory provisions of said prior Acts for a registration thereunder, or if the registered mark is being used by, or with the permission of, the registrant so as to misrepresent the source of the goods or services in connection with which the mark is used; or

(d) at any time if the mark is registered under the Act of March 3, 1881, or the Act of February 20, 1905, and has not been published under the provisions of subsection (c) of section 12 of this Act; or

(e) at anytime in the case of a certification mark on the ground that the registrant (1) does not control, or is not able legitimately to exercise control over, the use of such mark, or (2) engages in the production or marketing of any goods or services to which the certification mark is applied, or (3) permits the use of the certification mark for purposes other than to certify, or (4) discriminately refuses to certify or to continue to certify the goods or services of any person who maintains the standard or conditions which such mark certifies; *Provided,* That the Federal Trade Commission may apply to cancel on the ground specified in subsections (c) and (e) of this section any mark registered on the principal register established by this Act, and the prescribed fee shall not be required.

Sec. 33. (a) Any registration issued under the act of March 3, 1881, or the Act of February 20, 1905, or of a mark registered on the principal register provided by this Act and owned by a party to an action shall be admissible in evidence and shall be prima facie evidence of registrants's exclusive right to use the registered mark in commerce on the goods or services specified in the registration subject to any conditions or limitations stated therein, but shall not preclude an opposing party from proving any legal or equitable defense or defect which might have been asserted if such mark had not been registered.

(b) If the right to use the registered mark has become incontestable under section 15 hereof, the registration shall be conclusive evidence of the registrant's exclusive right to use the registered mark in commerce on or in connection with the goods or services specified in the affidavit filed under the provisions of said section 15 subject to any conditions or limitation stated therein except when one of the following defenses or defects is established:

(1) That the registration or the incontestable right to use the mark was obtained fraudulently; or

(2) That the mark has been abandoned by the registrant; or

(3) That the registered mark is being used, by or with the permission of the registrant or a person in privity with the registrant, so as to misrepresent the source of the goods or services in connection with which the mark is used; or

(4) That the use of the name, term, or device charged to be an infringement is a use, otherwise than as a trade or service mark, of the party's individual name in his own business, or of the individual name of anyone in privity with such party, or of a term or device which is descriptive of any use fairly and in good faith only to describe to users of goods or services of such party, or their geographic origin; or

(5) That the mark whose use by a party is charged as an infringement was adopted without knowledge of the registrant's prior use and has been continuously used by such party or those in privity with him from a date prior to registration of the mark under this Act or publication of the registered mark under subsection (c) of section 12 of this Act: *Provided, however,* That this defense

or defect shall apply only for the area in which such continuous prior use is proved, or

(6) That the mark whose use is charged as an infringement was registered and used prior to the registration under this Act or publication under subsection (c) of section 12 of this Act of the registered mark of the registrant, and not abandoned: *Provided, however,* That this defense or defect shall apply only for the area in which the mark was used prior to such registration or such publication of the registrant's mark; or

(7) That the mark has been or is being used to violate the antitrust laws of the United States. (60 Stat. 433, as amended, [1946]).

WEBB-POMERENE ACT

Sec. 2. That nothing contained in the act entitled "An Act to protect trade and commerce against unlawful restraints and monopolies," approved July second, eighteen hundred and ninety, shall be construed as declaring to be illegal an association entered into for the sole purpose of engaging in export trade and actually engaged solely in such export trade, or an agreement made or act done in the course of export trade by such association, agreement, or act is not in restraint of trade within the United States, and is not in restraint of the export trade of any domestic competitor of such association: *And provided further,* That such association does not, either in the United States or elsewhere, enter into any agreement, understanding, or conspiracy, or do any act which artificially or intentionally enhances or depresses prices within the United States of commodities of the class exported by such association or which substantially lessens competition within the United States or otherwise restrains trade therein. (40 Stat. 516, as amended, [1918]).

Selected Bibliography

Areeda, Phillip, and Donald F. Turner. "Predatory Pricing and Related Practices under Section Two of the Sherman Act." *Harvard Law Review* 88 (1975): 697–733.

Armentano, Dominick. *Antitrust and Monopoly: Anatomy of Policy Failure.* New York: John Wiley & Sons, 1982.

Bailey, Elizabeth E., and William J. Baumol. "Deregulation and the Theory of Contestable Markets." *Yale Journal on Deregulation* 1 (1984): 111–37.

Bork, Robert. *The Antitrust Paradox.* New York: Basic Books, 1978.

Bowman, Ward S. "Restraint of Trade by the Supreme Court: The Utah Pie Case." *Yale Law Journal* (November 1967): 70–85.

——— ."Tying Arrangements and the Leverage Problem." *Yale Law Journal* (November 1957): 19–36.

Boyle, Stanley E. "An Estimate of the Number and Size Distribution of Domestic Joint Subsidiaries." *Antitrust Law and Economics Review* (Spring 1968): 81–92.

Burstein, M. L. "A Theory of Full-Line Forcing." *Northwestern University Law Review* (March–April 1960): 62–95.

Busch, Paul. "A Review and Critical Evaluation of the Consumer Product Safety Commission: Marketing Management Implications." *Journal of Marketing* (October 1976): 41–49.

"Business Review Procedures and Business Review Letters." *Antitrust and Trade Regulation Reports. Special Supplement* 45, 1124 (July 21, 1983). Washington, D.C.: Bureau of National Affairs, 1983.

Caves, Richard. *American Industry: Structure, Conduct, Performance* 5th ed. Englewood Cliffs, NJ: Prentice-Hall, 1982.

Cohen, Dorothy. "Advertising and the First Amendment." *Journal of Marketing* (July 1978): 59–68.

————."The Concept of Unfairness as It Relates to Advertising Legislation." *Journal of Marketing* (July 1974): 8–13.

————."The Federal Trade Commission and the Regulation of Advertising in the Consumer Interest." *Journal of Marketing* (January 1969): 40–44.

————."The FTC's Advertising Substantiation Program." *Journal of Marketing* (Winter 1980): 26–35.

————."Unfairness in Advertising Revisited." *Journal of Marketing* (Winter 1982): 73–80.

"Collusive Practices" in "Legal Developments in Marketing," *Journal of Marketing* 51 (January 1987): 110.

Commanor, William S., and Thomas A. Wilson. "Advertising and Competition: A Survey." *Journal of Economic Literature* (June 1979): 453–76.

Constitution of the United States of America: Revised and Annotated. Washington, D.C.: Government Printing Office, 1964.

Cournot, Augustin. *Researches into the Mathematical Principles of the Theory of Wealth.* Translated by N. T. Bacon. Homewood, IL: Irwin, 1957.

Demsetz, Harold. "The Exchange of Property Rights." *The Journal of Law and Economics* (October 1964): 11–26.

————."Information and Efficiency: Another Viewpoint." *The Journal of Law and Economics* (April 1969): 1–22.

"Department of Justice Business Review Procedures." *Code of Federal Regulations* 28, sec. 50.6: 413. Washington, D.C.: Government Printing Office, 1968.

"Department of Justice Business Review Procedures Amendments." *Federal Regulations* 42: 11,831. Washington, D.C.: Government Printing Office, 1977.

Dewey, Donald. *Monopoly in Economics and Law.* Chicago: Rand McNally, 1959.

Dirlam, Joel B. "Marginal Cost Pricing Tests for Predation: Naive Welfare Economics and Public Policy." *The Antitrust Bulletin* (Winter 1981): 769–813.

"Disclosure Requirements and Prohibitions Concerning Franchising and Business Ventures." *Federal Register* 44 (May 31, 1979), 31170.

Dixon, William D. "Rules and Guides of Federal Trade Commission's Bureau of Consumer Protection." In *Franchising and Antitrust,* International Franchise Association's Sixth Annual Legal and Governmental Affairs Symposium. Washington, D.C.: International Franchising Association, 1973.

Duggan, Michael A. *Antitrust and the U.S. Supreme Court. 1829–1980,* 2d ed. New York: Federal Legal Publications, 1981.

————."Creative Probations Are Beneficial in Punishing Corporate Wrongdoers." *The Marketing News* (March 30, 1984): 6.

————.*Supplement to Antitrust and the U.S. Supreme Court, 1829–1980 Including 1980–1981 and 1981–1982 Terms.* New York: Federal Legal Publications, 1982.

————."United States v. Wm. Anderson Co., Inc." In "Legal Developments in Marketing." *Journal of Marketing* (Spring 1983): 121.

Edwards, Corwin. *The Price Discrimination Law.* Washington, D.C.: Brookings Institution, 1959.

Einhorn, Henry Adler, and William P. Smith., eds. *Economic Aspects of Antitrust.* New York: Random House, 1968.

Elzinga, Kenneth. "Predatory Pricing: The Case of the Gunpowder Trust." *The Journal of Law and Economics.* (April 1970): 233–40.

Elzinga, Kenneth G., and Thomas F. Hogarty. "Utah Pie and the Consequences of Robinson-Patman." *The Journal of Law and Economics* (October 1978): 427–34.

Erickson, Walter B. "Economics of Price Fixing." *Antitrust Law & Economics Review* (Spring 1969): 83–122.

Fox, Eleanor. "The New Merger Guidelines—A Blueprint for Microeconomic Analysis." *The Antitrust Bulletin* (Fall 1982): 519–92.

"Federal Trade Commission Advisory Opinions." *Trade Regulation Reports* 1: 17, 515–17. Chicago: Commerce Clearing House, 1984.

"Federal Trade Commission Premerger Notification Rules and Interpretations." *Trade Regulations Reports* 4: 42, 203–296. Chicago: Commerce Clearing House, 1982.

Garvey, George. "Study of Antitrust Treble Damage Remedy." Report to the Committee on the Judiciary, U.S. House of Representatives in Bureau of National Affairs *Antitrust and Trade Regulation Reports*. (March 1, 1984): 356–71.

Goldschmid, Harvey, et al., editors. *Industrial Concentration: The New Learning*. Boston: Little, Brown, 1974.

Green, Mark J., with Beverly C. Moore, Jr., and Bruce Wasserstein. *The Closed Enterprise System*. New York: Grossman Publishers, 1972.

Hirschman, Albert O. *National Power and the Structure of Foreign Trade*. Berkeley: University of California Press, 1945.

Howard, Marshall C. *Antitrust and Trade Regulation: Selected Issues and Case Studies*. Englewood Cliffs, NJ: Prentice-Hall, 1983.

———."Textile and Fur Labeling Legislation: Names, Competition, and the Consumer." *California Management Review* (Winter 1971): 69–80.

Hunt, Shelby D. "Franchising: Promises, Problems, Prospects." *Journal of Retailing* (Fall 1977): 71–84.

"Informal Dispute Settlement Mechanism." *Federal Register* (December 31, 1975): 60215.

Jacoby, Jacob, Margaret C. Nelson, and Wayne D. Hoyer. "Corrective Advertising and Affirmative Disclosure Statements: Their Potential for Confusing and Misleading the Consumer." *Journal of Marketing* (Winter 1982): 61–72.

Josephson, Matthew. *The Robber Barons*. New York: Harcourt Brace Jovanovich, 1962.

Joskow, Paul, and Alvin K. Klevorick. "A Framework for Analyzing Predatory Pricing Policy." *Yale Law Journal* (December 1979): 213–70.

Katz, Benjamin, *Advertising and Government Regulation: A Special Report from the American Academy of Advertising*. Cambridge, MA: Marketing Science Institute, 1979.

Kessler, Friedrich. "Product Liability." *Yale Law Journal* (April 1967): 887–938.

Kintner, Earl W. *A Robinson-Patman Act Primer*. New York: Macmillan 1970.

Koller, Roland. "The Myth of Predatory Pricing: An Empirical Study." *Antitrust Law and Economics Review* (Summer 1971): 105–23.

Larson, David A. "An Economic Analysis of the Webb–Pomerene Act." *The Journal of Law and Economics* (October 1970): 461–500.

Letwin, William. *Law and Economic Policy in America: The Evolution of the Sherman Antitrust Act*. New York: Random House, 1965.

Machlup, Fritz. *The Basing-point System*. Philadelphia: The Blaikston Company, 1949.

McGee, John S. "Predatory Price Cutting: The Standard Oil (N.J.) Case." *The Journal of Law and Economics* (October 1958): 137–69.

McGee, John S. "Predatory Pricing Revisited." *The Journal of Law and Economics* (October 1980), 289–330.

Miller, Richard A. "The Herfindahl-Hirschman Index as a Market Structure Variable: An Exposition for Antitrust Practitioners." *The Antitrust Bulletin* (Fall 1982), 593–618.

Oi, Walter Y. "The Economics of Product Safety." *Bell Journal of Economics and Management Science* (Spring 1973): 3–28.

Predatory Pricing: The Journal of Reprints for Antitrust Law and Economics. New York: Federal Legal Publications, 1980.

"Presale Availability of Terms." *Federal Register* 40 (December 31, 1975): 60189.

Prosser, William L. "The Assault upon the Citadel (Strict Liability to the Consumer)." *Yale Law Journal* (May 1960): 1099–1148.

Ranlett, John G., and Robert L. Curry. "Economic Principles: The 'Monopoly,' 'Oligopoly,' and 'Competition' Models." In Duggan, Michael A., *Antitrust and the United States Supreme Court, 1829–1980*, 2d ed. New York: Federal Legal Publications, 1981, 353–78.

Reynolds, Lloyd G. *Economics*, 3d ed. Homewood, IL: Irwin, 1969.

"Robinson-Patman: Dodo or Golden Rule?" *Business Week* (November 12, 1966): 72.

Rowe, Frederick M. *Price Discrimination under the Robinson–Patman Act*. Boston: Little Brown, 1962.

Scherer, F. M. *Industrial Market Structure and Economic Performance*, 2d. ed. Chicago: Rand McNally. College Publishing Co., 1980.

Schumpeter, Joseph. *Can Capitalism Survive?* Colophon edition. New York: Harper & Row, 1978.

Sheffet, Mary Jane. "Market Share Liability: A New Doctrine of Causation in Product Liability." *Journal of Marketing* (Winter 1983): 35–43.

Sheffet, Mary Jane, and Debra L. Scammon. "Resale Price Maintenance: Is It Safe to Suggest Retail Prices?" *Journal of Marketing* 49 (Fall 1985), 82–91.

Shepherd, William. "Causes of Increased Competition in the U.S. Economy, 1939–1980." *The Review of Economics and Statistics* (November 1982): 613–26.

———. *Public Policies toward Business*, 7th ed. Homewood, IL: Irwin, 1985.

Smith, Adam. *An Inquiry into the Nature and Causes of the Wealth of Nations*. New York: Modern Library, 1937.

Stanton, William J. *Fundamentals of Marketing*, 7th ed. New York: McGraw-Hill, 1984.

"Statement of American Advertising Federation." In *Unfairness: Views on Unfair Acts and Practices in Violation of the Federal Trade Commission Act*. Committee on Commerce, Science, and Transportation, United States Senate, 96th Cong., 2d Sess. Washington, D.C.: Government Printing Office, 1980.

Stigler, George. "Imperfections in the Capital Market." *Journal of Political Economy* (June, 1967): 287–92.

———.*The Theory of Price.* New York: MacMillan, 1946.

Stocking, George W., and Willard F. Mueller. "The Cellophane Case and the New Competition." *American Economic Review* (March 1955): 31–63.

Swartzfager, Polly. *Economic and Administrative Evaluation of the Areeda-Turner Predatory Pricing Rule.* Unpublished thesis. Colorado Springs: The Colorado College, 1984.

Thompson, George C., and Gerald P. Brady. *Antitrust Fundamentals: Text, Cases and Materials,* 3d ed. St Paul, MN: West Publishing, 1979.

United States Code Service, Lawyer's edition, title 15, chapter 41. Rochester, NY: Lawyers Cooperative Publishing Co., 1982, 422–865.

U.S. Department of Justice. *The Investigation of White-Collar Crime.* Washington, D.C.: Government Printing Office, 1977.

U.S. Department of Justice and Federal Trade Commission. *Merger Guidelines— 1982.* Chicago: Commerce Clearing House, 1982.

U.S. Senate, Hearings before the Subcommittee for Consumers of the Committee on Commerce, Science, and Transportation, 97th Cong., 2d sess, *FTC's Authority over Deceptive Advertising* (July 22, 1982): 9.

Waldman, Don E. "The duPont Cellophane Case Revisited." *The Antitrust Bulletin* (Winter 1980), 805–30.

Werner, Ray O. "The Economics of the Joint Antitrust Dissents of Justices Harlan and Stewart." *Washington Law Review* 48 (1973): 577–79.

———."The Knowing Inducement of Discriminatory Prices." *Journal of Purchasing* (May 1968), 5–16.

———."Marketing and the United States Supreme Court, 1975–1981." *Journal of Marketing* (Spring 1982), 73–81.

———. "A New Look at the Inducement of Discriminatory Prices." *Journal of Purchasing* (August 1971): 5–10.

Wilkie, William L., Dennis L. McNeill, and Michael B. Mazis. "The Theory and Practice of Corrective Advertising." *Journal of Marketing* (Spring 1984): 11–31.

Zerbe, Richard. "The American Sugar Refining Co " *The Journal of Law and Economics* (October 1969): 351–75.

Index of Cases Cited

Index

About the Author

RAY O. WERNER, Professor of Economics at The Colorado College in Colorado Springs, is the Editor of the "Legal Developments in Marketing" section of the *Journal of Marketing*. He has served as expert witness in court cases relating to marketing law and regulations.